ARCHERY

USA Archery
Editor

Human Kinetics

Library of Congress Cataloging-in-Publication Data

Archery / USA Archery, editor.
   p. cm.
 Includes bibliographical references and index.
 1. Archery--Training. I. USA Archery.
 GV1185.A73 2012
 799.3'2--dc23

                        2012042421

ISBN-10: 1-4504-2020-6 (print)
ISBN-13: 978-1-4504-2020-4 (print)

The web addresses cited in this text were current as of October 2012, unless otherwise noted.

Acquisitions Editor: Tom Heine; **Project Coordinator:** Teresa Iaconi; **Developmental Editor:** Laura Floch; **Assistant Editor:** Elizabeth Evans; **Copyeditor:** Erin Cler; **Indexers:** Robert and Cynthia Swanson; **Permissions Manager:** Martha Gullo; **Graphic Designer:** Joe Buck; **Graphic Artist:** Tara Welsch; **Cover Designer:** Keith Blomberg; **Photograph (cover):** © Teresa Iaconi; **Photographs (interior):** Figures 2.1-2.13, 7.1-7.18 © Mel Nichols; figures 3.2-3.13, 4.1-4.13, 4.15-4.19, 5.1-5.12, 5.14-5.17, 6.3, 6.6, 6.8, 8.7-8.16, 9.2-9.19 © Geovanna Soler; figure 4.14 © Teresa Iaconi; figures 5.13, 5.18, 6.1, 6.2, 6.4, 6.5, 6.7 © Guy Krueger; **Photo Production Manager:** Jason Allen; **Art Manager:** Kelly Hendren; **Associate Art Manager:** Alan L. Wilborn; **Illustrations:** © Human Kinetics, unless otherwise noted; **Printer:** United Graphics

Human Kinetics books are available at special discounts for bulk purchase. Special editions or book excerpts can also be created to specification. For details, contact the Special Sales Manager at Human Kinetics.

Printed in the United States of America   10   9   8   7   6   5   4   3   2   1

The paper in this book is certified under a sustainable forestry program.

Human Kinetics
Website: www.HumanKinetics.com

United States: Human Kinetics
P.O. Box 5076
Champaign, IL 61825-5076
800-747-4457
e-mail: humank@hkusa.com

Canada: Human Kinetics
475 Devonshire Road Unit 100
Windsor, ON N8Y 2L5
800-465-7301 (in Canada only)
e-mail: info@hkcanada.com

Europe: Human Kinetics
107 Bradford Road
Stanningley
Leeds LS28 6AT, United Kingdom
+44 (0) 113 255 5665
e-mail: hk@hkeurope.com

Australia: Human Kinetics
57A Price Avenue
Lower Mitcham, South Australia 5062
08 8372 0999
e-mail: info@hkaustralia.com

New Zealand: Human Kinetics
P.O. Box 80
Torrens Park, South Australia 5062
0800 222 062
e-mail: info@hknewzealand.com

E5591

ARCHERY

Contents

Foreword vii | Preface ix | Acknowledgments xi

Chapter 1   **Becoming a Competitive Archer**............1
Butch Johnson

Chapter 2   **Equipment and Tuning Tips**.............11
Mel Nichols

Chapter 3   **Developing Your Shot Sequence** 29
Guy Krueger

Chapter 4   **Recurve Shooting: Setting Up** 45
KiSik Lee

Chapter 5   **Recurve Shooting: Drawing the Shot**......63
KiSik Lee

Chapter 6   **Recurve Shooting: Completing the Shot** ...81
KiSik Lee

Chapter 7   **Compound Shooting:
Setting Up and Completing the Shot** 93
Mel Nichols

Chapter 8   **Making Practice More Effective**.........111
KiSik Lee

Chapter 9 **Nutrition and Physical Training for Archers** **133**
Guy Krueger

Chapter 10 **Mental Training for Archers** **155**
KiSik Lee

Chapter 11 **Planning to Win** **165**
Butch Johnson

Chapter 12 **Preparing and Peaking for Competition** . . **173**
Sheri Rhodes

Chapter 13 **Developing Young Archers** **183**
Diane Watson

Chapter 14 **Building Your Support Team** **193**
Robby K. Beyer

Appendix: Working With Para-Archers   201

References   207 ┃ Index   209

About USA Archery   215 ┃ About the Contributors   217

Foreword

In my years of competitive shooting, I have been fortunate to have several great mentors and coaches to guide me to two Olympic teams and an Olympic silver medal. However, there was never a comprehensive book that brought together several experts in the field of competitive shooting—including some of my own coaches and mentors—until now.

Whether you are a beginning, intermediate, or even advanced archer, *Archery* will give you something that's almost impossible to find elsewhere: a complete picture of the steps you must take to pursue excellence in the sport, presented by some of the most knowledgeable people in competitive archery. The topics covered in *Archery*—technical form, equipment choices and tuning, mental training, physical training, planning to compete, processing thoughts about winning, putting together a support team, and working with young archers—are critical to the athletes as well as the coaches and family members who support them.

If you are a parent, instructor, or coach, this book will help you to better understand the archer you are working with and learn how to be the best support system possible for the archer. This book is the most comprehensive archery resource I have seen yet, by people who have coached me and whose knowledge and experience I have a deep respect for. I encourage you to read this book, use it as a reference, and take all that you can from it.

—Brady Ellison
Two-time Olympian, Olympic silver medalist, World Cup gold medalist,
Pan Am Games champion, top-ranked archer worldwide since 2011,
USA Archery resident athlete

Preface

Archery—a modern sport with ancient roots—has experienced a massive surge in popularity. Thanks to films such as *The Hunger Games, Brave,* and *The Avengers* and television shows such as *Respect the Game,* as well as the excitement surrounding the sport at the Olympic and Paralympic Games, USA Archery has seen a significant increase in membership, social media reach, and website visitors.

Archery was the most-watched sport during the first week of NBC's coverage of the 2012 Olympic Games. At one point in the first week of the Olympics, archery had more tweets—30,000-plus—than any other sport. With sequels to *The Hunger Games* expected in 2013, 2014, and 2015 and the Rio 2016 Olympic and Paralympic Games not far behind, it's our hope that interest in archery will continue to grow, new instructors and club leaders will continue to help develop this wonderful sport, and new archers will find programs, events, and training opportunities fun and exciting.

This book addresses the needs of many kinds of archers. Every athlete's journey is different, and the path that each archer takes in finding fulfillment will be full of rich and diverse experiences. In this book, we talk a lot about learning to become competitive at many levels in the sport, though we also teach great fundamentals for recreational archers who just want to improve in the game.

The goal in becoming an archer is not just to win, though that is certainly something most competitive athletes hope for. Rather, the goal is to experience the thrill of archery found in so many places along the journey—from the moment of drawing the bow for the first time to the moment of releasing the arrow. It's in the first shot at 70 meters, when there's a heartbeat or two before the arrow hits the target. It's in the camaraderie at an archery tournament. It's found when an archer achieves her very first 9-meter award pin in Junior Olympic Archery Development and when a disabled archer has success with a bow and arrow on the international stage. For instructors and coaches, the excitement is in seeing an archer find success and confidence in shooting. For club leaders, it's helping to develop the sport in their communities. For parents, it's the simple joy of seeing their children gain the great life skills that archery teaches—patience, discipline, and focus—or watching children make lifelong friends at tournaments. Whatever your role in archery, this book has something great for you.

Veteran archers and coaches from various paths in the sport have collaborated on this book. Each author offers a personal perspective, so there may be some overlapping of subject matter or even differences in perspective among authors. We hope this contributes to a rich archery experience for you. KiSik Lee and Guy Krueger discuss recurve technique and mental and physical training, Mel Nichols advises on equipment tuning and compound shooting technique, and Butch Johnson advises on deciding to compete and the athlete's perspective on competition. You'll appreciate Sheri Rhodes' advice on preparing for competition, Robby Beyer's advice on building support teams, Diane Watson's instruction on developing youth archers, and Randi Smith's tips on working with para-archers.

We hope that you benefit from the information in *Archery* and that you share our excitement as you begin or continue your journey in this safe, fun, and exciting lifetime sport!

Acknowledgments

USA Archery offers its deep gratitude to each of the authors who have taken the time to share their expertise and personal experiences in this publication.

We would also like to acknowledge the contributions of Human Kinetics and its staff, including acquisitions editor Tom Heine and developmental editor Laura Floch, who played key roles in developing this publication.

The sport of archery is in a wonderful period of growth and transition. We are extremely thankful to all the people who, as the result of seeing archery in books, movies, and the Olympic and Paralympic Games, have turned that interest into a new hobby or competitive passion.

USA Archery instructors and coaches, and those who help facilitate Junior Olympic Archery Development and Adult Archery Achievement programs across the country, are responsible for encouraging much of that interest and helping people to make that transition from a passing curiosity into love of a lifelong sport. So many other people give back to the sport by hosting tournaments or serving as tournament officials, and each is giving archery a place to grow in our communities.

Organizations and companies like the U.S. Olympic Committee, Easton Foundations, Hoyt, Easton Technical Products, Nike, United Airlines, Axcel Sights and Scopes, Arizona Archery Enterprises, B-Stinger, Flexor Archery, Mental Management Systems, and the Archery Trade Association have been outstanding sponsors and partners in helping USA Archery to fulfill its mission of providing the resources to foster strong athlete participation, competition, and training.

Perhaps most important, USA Archery thanks all of its members, especially the athletes who have gone a step further by representing the United States in international competition. Each of those dedicated archers has inspired this book, which we hope will serve as a road map for new archers beginning on that path. Thank you for providing an outstanding example of excellence to others.

Becoming a Competitive Archer

Butch Johnson

Once you decide to become a competitive archer, you need to focus on finding a coach, developing proper shooting technique, developing a solid mental program, and finding and tuning the right equipment. You must also determine your level of seriousness about archery, because a recreational archer will not necessarily have the same goals as an aspiring Olympian.

Many top athletes and coaches would say that the ability to take direction and apply it, combined with a strong sense of determination and self-discipline, predispose a person to succeed in the sport. Natural talent may be a determining factor; some of the best archers became good because they started winning from a very early age, often against adults. But there are really only three traits of top competitors: passion for the sport, a strong work ethic, and a determination to succeed.

Perhaps the greatest moment you can have as a competitive archer is the joy of knowing that you accomplished something you are great at. That knowledge comes from winning a tournament, or losing but setting a new personal best, or learning an important lesson. And it comes from amazing competitive moments, such as receiving your first national team shirt with your name and country on the back, hearing the roar of the crowd at an elite-level event, and knowing that you are representing your country as you shoot your bow. All of these moments are reasons to compete, and all of these moments are reasons that people continue to strive for excellence in this sport, even in the face of losses and challenges.

In this book, we talk about athlete development, shooting techniques, selection and tuning of equipment, and mental and physical training. But the very first step is always determining what you want to do with your shooting. This is a decision that you alone, the athlete, must make. Although you require a support team (especially if you are a minor), the initial decision to compete must be yours. The process is unique for each athlete. Many archers are introduced to the sport in a camp, school, or club setting. Through trying an initial tournament, they find that competing is a fun and friendly way to enjoy the sport. For other archers, who are introduced to the sport later in life by a friend or through bowhunting, competing is the next logical step after practicing archery at the local range or at home. Some archers are also motivated by the opportunity to compete in the Olympics and are focused on attaining placement on an Olympic or Paralympic team. Whatever the motivation, the important thing is that the dream belongs to you, and you must be focused on the dream for the right reasons. One of the key elements must be a true passion for the sport.

MOMENT OF DECISION

My first defining moment was when I shot at the National Indoor Championships in Pennsylvania at the age of 16. Though I was young enough to compete in the youth divisions, I won the tournament as an adult. As a former recreational archer, I was shooting at an unfamiliar target face—which is actually the multicolored target shot at events today—that I didn't even know how to keep score on. My championship-winning finish was a new national record—the highest score overall for the men's adult class—and made me realize that perhaps there was a future for me in the sport. The journey for many competitive archers starts with a moment like that. It may take the form of a high score, or, more likely, it may just be the recognition that competing feels fun and natural. Whatever the moment, the idea is to seize it and decide on a plan of action.

Once that moment of decision occurs, questions are often raised about where to go from there. After winning the National Indoor Championships, I continued attending local tournaments and practicing consistently, hoping to improve my technique and ability to compete. Often, that next step is defined not only by the goals of the archer, but by external factors too, such as budget, the need for new equipment, and the ability to train consistently and obtain coaching. The only answer is that if you want to become successful, you have no choice but to try. Having the right attitude in meeting those challenges is an absolute must. If you look at challenges as insurmountable obstacles, questions of doubt are raised that will be difficult to silence. Rather, the focus should always be on getting the most out of every experience, learning a lesson each time you are on the range, and striving to improve.

People who succeed in athletics and in business often share the traits of passion and determination. The desire to have the best technique can mask the stress of events and help you become more focused with a consistent mental program. To continue to be competitive, you will need that sense of tenacity at each level on which you compete, whether local, state, national, or international. The focus must be on achieving something rather than not losing something, and the most important factors that will affect this are the way you train, the coaching you obtain, and your willingness to work as hard as required in order to achieve your goals.

FINDING A PROGRAM

Imagine that a young person has heard about archery and is interested in getting started. The first step is to find a local archery program that has a certified instructor or coach who is trained to teach proper safety and technique in the archery range. The first program you might encounter is the After School Archery Program (ASAP), which is a joint program of USA Archery, the National Field Archery Association, and the Archery Shooters Association. ASAP is a four- to six-week program that teaches archers safety on the range and basic shooting technique. It is meant as an introduction to archery; frequently, young archers become quickly engaged in the sport and want to learn more and continue to progress in skill and technique.

The other more prevalent program is Junior Olympic Archery Development (JOAD), which is run through archery ranges, sport clubs, pro shops, park and recreation departments, 4-H, YMCAs, and Boys and Girls Clubs. JOAD is a longer-term program that is run year-round, usually in 12-week or longer sessions. The goal of JOAD is to offer beginning, intermediate, or advanced shooters the opportunity to enjoy the sport either recreationally or through competition. Many of the best young archers in the United States are currently members of JOAD clubs, but they join many other students who wish to just enjoy archery during a classroom setting each week. Like many facets of archery, the question of initial age of learning and competing is based on the individual. Some archers may start shooting in a classroom setting as young as eight years of age; some may start even younger with direct assistance from an adult in a backyard. USA Archery recommends that archers begin shooting no earlier than the age of eight, when they can understand and obey safety commands at ranges as well as have enough manual dexterity to shoot with correct technique. For more detailed information on developing young archers, see chapter 13.

Young archers in the United States who have begun competing and are having success can apply to become part of the Junior Dream Team, or JDT. This is a national development program that offers training camps to archers who are using national training system form and wish to enjoy the benefit of an intensive training environment with specialized coaching. Some competitive archers, especially those shooting with a compound bow, choose instead to continue competing alongside their JOAD teammates. In either case, archers can choose to compete in local, state, or national events as soon as they and their support team decide that they are ready. For older recurve archers who are close to or at college age, there is also the opportunity to apply to the Resident Athlete Program at the Olympic Training Center in Colorado Springs, which is a full-time training position geared toward archers seeking placement on the Olympic team.

All archers in the United States, depending on their national ranking and competitive progress, may have the opportunity to qualify for the U.S. archery team—there are cadet, junior, senior, and para teams—or qualify for some of the international teams that USA Archery sends to World Cups and other events. Check www.usarchery.org for details on team selection procedures. For some events, such as the World Archery Championships, there are team trials events; placement on other teams can be based on national ranking or other factors. The beauty of archery is that whether you are 8 or 88, lots of competition opportunities are available for you in this sport. See table 1.1 for a breakdown of the USA Archery age divisions.

Table 1.1 USA Archery Age Divisions

Division	Ages of competitors
Bowmen	Through calendar year of 12th birthday
Cub	Through calendar year of 14th birthday
Cadet	Through calendar year of 17th birthday
Junior	Through calendar year of 20th birthday
Senior	Technically defined as archers competing during or after the calendar year of their 21st birthday; however, some top younger archers choose to shoot in this division
Masters	Often separated in 10-year increments: masters 50-plus, 60-plus, 70-plus

DETERMINING EQUIPMENT STYLE

In becoming a competitive archer, you need to decide about whether to shoot the recurve bow or compound bow (see table 1.2 for the characteristics of these bows). In many cases, this decision is made based on the equipment or coaching that is available to you at the time you begin shooting. However, if you have a particular area of focus that you want to pursue, the beginning of the competitive journey is a good time to make that determination. In beginning my own competitive career, I pursued recurve and then compound. When I became successful with the compound bow and won several national titles, I decided to pursue Olympic competition, which made the recurve bow the clear choice at the time.

Table 1.2 Characteristics of Compound and Recurve Bows

	Compound	Recurve
Uses	Allowed in all competitive events except for Pan Am, Parapan Am and Olympic and Paralympic Games	Allowed in all competitive events, including Olympic and Paralympic and Pan Am and Parapan Am Games
Length	Shorter axle-to-axle (end-to-end) length; uses wheels and cams to conduct energy of bow	Much longer length from limb tip to limb tip; energy of bow is stored in limbs
Limbs	Bow has a more compact appearance, with limbs that are constantly flexed; limbs may be parallel to one another	Bow has an elongated appearance, with limbs that curve out from riser and then curve again out to limb tip
Weight	Has let-off (i.e., the archer pulls back the full weight of the bow but holds only 15 to 35 percent of bow weight while aiming)	Archer pulls and holds the full weight of the bow when aiming
Release	Mechanical release is used to release the string, though a limited number of archers use a finger tab with a compound bow	Archers always use their fingers to release the string, most often protected by a finger tab (a piece of leather that covers the fingers) or, less often, a shooting glove

CHOOSING A COACH AND COACHING STYLE

If you have decided that you want to become a competitive athlete and are willing to put in the time and effort to train properly and are keeping an open mind about getting the most out of tournament experiences, win or lose, then the next step is to get the best possible technical coaching as early as possible. Finding the right coach for you is a personal process that is unique for each athlete. Generally, the first step is to look for a coach with a solid track record of experience in the area in which you are focused. Beginning archers may work with a certified level 1 or level 2 instructor. They receive training in range safety and shooting technique; more experienced and highly certified coaches have more specialized training in athlete development and shooting technique, including mental management, periodization, fitness for archery, and in-depth technical expertise. Generally, the requirements for completion of a given level of certification become more comprehensive as the level increases. To become a level 4 coach, a person must complete an intensive four-day course with the national head coach, including skills training with other certified coaches; must pass a comprehensive written exam; and then must pass a strict practical exam with the national head coach in order to demonstrate their ability to teach National Training System technique. Certified level 2 instructors, and coaches of all levels, have completed a background check, and are insured by USA Archery's insurance partner. For more information on certified instructors and coaches, including what is required for each level and help finding an instructor or coach near you, visit www.usarchery.org.

You'll also want to think about the experience you're seeking in a coach. For example, if you are a compound archer, you'll want to find a coach with solid experience in compound bows and technical know-how. The same applies if you're a recurve archer seeking a coach. This process can have positive and negative aspects and will require some balance as an archer, since input from lots of people, no matter how well intentioned, can give you conflicting opinions and cause you to lose focus on what is most important: finding the best fit with a technically strong coach you can believe in. However, once you have made a choice about a coach and think you can have faith in the coach's direction and decisions, it is best to commit to that coach and listen to that person's direction exclusively.

The most important thing is that you have a strong comfort level with the coach and his or her level of experience and coaching style. If you have doubts about your coach's ability to coach you, it will be a difficult road to travel together. One of the first steps in finding a coach is to talk to many people and try to get a sense of which coach or coaching style suits you best. Some archers will respond better to a command-style coach, while other archers will do well with a coach whose style is more cooperative. Whatever the best fit is for you, have conversations with a few people until you have found a coach whose level of experience and personality are in line with what you want to do. Here are other key points to consider:

- How often can I see this coach?
- Does the coach's communication style make sense to me? Do we understand one another?
- What does this coach think of the goals I have set for myself?
- Do I feel inspired and supported by this coach? Or do I feel a sense of expectation?
- Do I want support from this coach during tournaments? If so, is this coach willing to coach at competitions?

SETTING GOALS AND MANAGING YOUR TIME

Once you have found your coach, you should have an open and honest conversation about your goals in the sport. If you haven't done so already, now is the time to set and write down the goals you have set for yourself. Goals should be categorized as short term (attainable in 0 to 6 months), midrange (6 to 18 months) and long term (18 months to 3 years). The goals should be process based, performance based, and outcome based, as described here:

- *Process-based goals* include benchmarks that deal with your training, your shooting technique, and mental focus. An example of a process-based goal is to perfect hook and grip or increase arrow count to 120 high-quality shots five days per week.

Importance of the Support Team

On a related note, archery is very much a mental sport. As such, you must take care in surrounding yourself with people who will be part of a supportive, cohesive team. For example, a younger archer may have his or her parents, coach, archery club teammates, siblings, and friends on a support team. An adult archer may count a spouse, coach, parents, archery friends, and other encouraging people as support team members. More details on building your support team are covered in chapter 14. Also, whether looking at the external environment, members of a support team, or your own technique for self-talk, you need to determine whether the messages you receive are positive ones. Are you expecting yourself to do well and focusing too heavily on who you are competing against or what your scores are? Or are you passionate about being the best archer on the field regardless of the performances of others? Do the people around you tell you that they want you to reach specific scores? Or do they support you in pushing yourself harder to be the best archer *you* can be? The best athletes take a role in creating an environment in which they push forward because they want to get there rather than because someone else expects them to reach a goal. If you are reading this book as the parent, coach, spouse, or friend of a competitive archer, remember that if you help the athlete by using positive encouragement to set and meet healthy goals, the archer will be more empowered to reach those goals. However, if members of the support team—especially a parent or coach—are focused too heavily on the athlete's outcomes, such as score or event placement, it can impede the athlete's progress and damage the athlete's self-image and your relationship with the athlete.

One top archer who competed on several teams with me noted that a good way to remember this concept is to ask whether your mood changes based on the athlete's performance. If it does, you as a member of a support team have crossed a line that shouldn't be crossed. If you become angry or upset based on how the athlete does competitively, you are too invested to be an objective source of support, and you need to gain a better perspective on the situation. Remember that athletes across the board respond better to positive rewards than negative ones. If you are the athlete, your thought process and affirmations must be positive, and your focus must be on your own process and technique rather than your score or the outcome of the athlete you're competing against. When your focus changes from shooting one good arrow at a time to how your competitors are shooting or where you are in the standings, you have turned your attention to something you can't help or control and have lost a valuable learning opportunity. Always, always keep a positive attitude about what you want to achieve that is within your control: your shot process and your mental game.

- *Performance-based goals* deal with achievements concerning your shooting performance. A good example is to reach a new personal best score of ___ in an outdoor tournament.

- *Outcome-based goals* are goals for which the result is, to some extent, outside of your control. An example of an outcome-based goal is to earn placement on next year's national archery team. Though you may shoot very high scores in that season, whether you attain this goal will also be affected by the performance of the archers with whom you compete.

Think of your goals as a road map for success. Though we cover the logistics of competing, remember that having reasonable short-term goals of each kind and attaining them will help you to build confidence and assist you in reaching your midrange goals. In turn, those will help you to achieve your long-term goals. Here are a few key points about goal setting: Keep your goals measurable and attainable. Though making the Olympic team might be a great long-term outcome-based goal when you are just starting out, include several midrange and long-term goals of each kind that will help you reach that major long-term goal you have set for yourself. Remember that your goals will help to keep you inspired. So rather than set goals that feel difficult or impossible to achieve, set goals that you can achieve within a reasonable time so that you can set new goals, complete those, and thus make your way toward achieving those long-term objectives.

Once you have created this road map to success, make sure that you have an open dialogue with the people who will support you throughout your journey. Sit down and talk to the people in your life who may be in a position to help you along the road to success. For example, if your parents will be providing your transportation to practice and events, talk to them openly about the goals you have set and why you have set them. If your spouse might want to accompany you to tournaments, have a talk about your feelings on the subject and whether it will be beneficial or detrimental to have them watch you compete. If someone is with you when you practice, let him know if you feel that watching is helpful or not. If training is a priority that will cut into your other commitments, have a frank discussion with those affected about your decision to train instead. Whatever your circumstances, the important thing is to be as honest and open as possible with those who will be affected by your decision and to continue that open dialogue throughout your time as a competitive archer.

Finally, on a very practical level, focus on time management. Look at your schedule and determine what needs to happen in order for you to have the time you need to train. Talk to your coach about realistic goals for practice and what it will take to reach your goals. Then evaluate your schedule to see where you need to make the time you need. This is where the question of prioritization comes in: Perhaps, two nights per week, you play another sport, but you know that you need those two evenings to complete a five-day practice week. Now is the time to determine whether you are passionate enough about archery to move forward with the number of practice days necessary to meet the goal you've set. Remember that not everyone's goal is to make a world, Olympic, or Paralympic team, and that's okay. For some people, the first goal might be to compete in a local indoor tournament for the experience of trying a competition. In that case, an appropriate training regimen might be two or three days per week, and the arrow count (number of arrows shot) might depend on the format of the tournament. For example, the first goal is a 60-arrow indoor tournament. The competition will start with two ends of practice and then 20 ends of three arrows each. Therefore, you would need to train enough to be able to shoot consistently for approximately 70 arrows. If your goal is more focused on national or international outdoor competitions, which require more arrows and longer hours out in the elements, you should intensify your training regimen accordingly.

If you are still in school, you might need to sit down at the beginning of the week with your academic schedule and plan out homework in advance in order to accommodate your goal. Even if the goal focuses on local, state, or regional competition, remember that the goal still may require that you take more time on the weekends for academics in order to have the time during the week to meet with your coach for a lesson and accommodate two additional practices at the archery range.

If you are fortunate enough to have a place to shoot at home, time management may be slightly less challenging, since you will not need to travel as often to practice. However, if you need to practice at a local range or pro shop, remember to factor in the time necessary to travel to the range, unpack and repack your equipment, and still get in a good practice. When you are making the time to practice, whether at home or at the range, make an effort to set up an environment that is conducive to focusing on the task at hand. Try to make that environment mimic the competitive arena as closely as possible. For example, in a tournament, you wouldn't answer text messages or stop to take phone calls while shooting. Keep yourself honest in practice by doing the same when you are shooting on your own. Remember also that practice needs to be fun and challenging so that you stay with it. Keeping practice fun while still staying focused during that time is a balancing act that every archer must remember to do. For example, many World Cup tournaments play music throughout the competition, though the type of music may vary between cultures represented at the event. Therefore, if music keeps you motivated, you might try using a radio while you practice. But remember to change up the music so that you're not distracted when you hear a different soundtrack at a tournament.

While distraction training (intentionally creating distractions, such as noise, and then teaching yourself to stay focused despite them) can be very helpful, remember that the point of practice is to prepare you for competition. So you must be focused on your shooting technique and your mental routine. See chapter 10 for more on mental training. If the training environment does not allow you to do that, take an honest look at how you are practicing to determine whether you can take steps to make practice more productive. Here are good questions to ask yourself:

- Am I able to focus when I'm practicing?
- Do I find myself easily distracted?
- Is the environment consistent with what I would encounter at a tournament?
- Do I find myself doing things I wouldn't do in a tournament, such as texting?
- Am I practicing at a time of day when I have energy, or am I leaving training to the very end of my day?
- Am I able to create pressure when I practice, or do I find my mind wandering?
- Do I prepare for practice the way I prepare for tournaments, or do I take shortcuts?
- Is my attitude positive during training? Am I feeling inspired, or am I practicing because of expectation?

Asking these questions will help you to have an honest dialogue with yourself and with your coach about whether you are getting the most out of your training time and whether you are training appropriately to reach the goals you have set for yourself. Remember that shooting 300 arrows per day but being focused for only 100 of those shots does you no more good than shooting 100 high-quality arrows. If the goal is to shoot 150 high-quality shots, examine your training routine and environment and make the changes necessary in order to make those arrows count.

In the end, what are you working for? Are you shooting for the love of releasing the bowstring and the sound of an arrow hitting the target? Are you driven to be the very best in the sport and willing to train as hard as you must in order to get there? Or are you focused on whom you will compete against at tournaments and the scores that your competitors are shooting? Are your scores a by-product of your determination to have the best technique on the field? Or are your scores the only focus you have? You get an amazing sense of achievement when you win. It feels good to win, and there is tremendous satisfaction and pride in knowing that you stated the goal, put in the effort, kept the right attitude, and made it happen. This builds self-confidence, because now you have learned the trick of winning. You have a sense of accomplishment that you will never lose regardless of how long you compete or what else you accomplish. One of the great things about archery is the fact that it is a lifelong sport. I was a multi-time national champion with the compound bow before I switched to recurve, and I made the first of five Olympic teams at the age of 36. My first Olympic medal came at age 40. At the end of the 2012 season, I was ranked fourth in the United States, and the sport of archery is still a major part of my life.

At National Target Championships, you will witness archers well into their 70s and 80s enjoying the camaraderie and fun of a national tournament. But make no mistake: Those archers are competing as seriously in their retirement years as the teenage superstars who are focused on placement on the Olympic team. The feeling of success is one that will stay with you through your entire life, beyond archery, school, and work. You will always know that you worked hard enough and strived long enough to achieve something great on whatever level that you achieve that goal. Whether the goal is a local tournament, a state championship, a youth event, or a world event, the result is the same: a tremendous sense of pride in reaching the goal you set for yourself.

CREATING AN OPTIMAL TRAINING ENVIRONMENT

The secret to success in competitive archery is a multitude of factors. Perhaps one of the most important is how you practice. You have heard the expression "quality versus quantity," and it certainly applies to archery. In my own training, and in coaching others, I focus heavily on getting the most out of every single shot and making every arrow a thoughtful one. Just shooting arrows for the sake of hitting high numbers in practice is not only unproductive but will almost certainly lead to the development of bad habits. In some cases, it can cause injury. In an ideal world, you will have both high-quality shots and a quantity of shots sufficient for preparing for the rigors of competition, but quality should always come first.

As noted previously, both the physical technique and the mental routine must come into play when practicing. Multiple distractions will come into play at any given moment in a tournament: the pressure to succeed, the knowledge of parents or other loved ones nearby, and environmental issues such as wind, rain, and changing lighting. Think about the pressure you would face during your first arrow at an Olympic or Paralympic Games:

the crowd, the environment, the fans, the pressure of winning a medal. Hundreds of camera shutters clicking at once as you draw your bow for the first time. That sort of pressure is tough and can cause significant stress if you have not trained yourself to focus on technique rather than outside pressures. When you are under pressure, fine motor skills can leave you, causing a fight-or-flight response and making your thoughts speed up. During moments like this, pressure, if channeled appropriately, can help. Or, if you have not practiced mental control, the pressure can become your worst enemy, especially during circumstances such as heavy wind. The successful competitive archer practices as though he is shooting a tournament and competes as though he's at practice. In other words, the training routine and mental program are consistent from practice to tournament, and vice versa.

In terms of physical form, you must be biomechanically strong. When under pressure, you can depend less on muscles and soft tissue and must be able to use the skeletal structure in order to support the shot, which is more dependable in stressful situations. In focusing on mental technique, you will be prepared with a positive attitude and a passion for having the best technique on the field, knowing that stressful situations will happen to everyone and that pressure is an opportunity to grow as an athlete. By making the body the strongest it can be and staying focused on your technique and mental program, you create a consistent experience from shot to shot that will serve you well, whether you are competing in your first youth tournament or at the World Championships.

Many people will ask what it takes to become an Olympian. Often, the question is asked in terms of sacrifice: What do I have to give up to make five Olympic teams? The reality is that I never felt as though I was giving up something I wanted, because I enjoy shooting and want to train to be the best. To accomplish that goal, I knew what I had to do: give myself enough time to train between competitions, forgo some social activities when they conflict with practice or tournaments, and get enough rest at tournaments even if I'm invited to go out at night with friends I haven't seen in a while. Would I like to take a month off at the end of the season? Sure. But for me—and this is not the case for every archer—I know that a month off sets me back approximately two months in terms of training and muscle memory, so I limit my postseason break to a week at a time. In other words, the changes I have made to my lifestyle have helped me to reach my goals in the sport I love, but I don't consider them sacrifices. I consider them part of my commitment to striving for excellence in archery.

As you continue on your journey, you will have many experiences in training and competition. There will be great days and days when you wish you shot better. You will have moments of frustration and moments of success. All of these experiences are part of being a competitive archer, and they are necessary for teaching you what you need to learn in order to win. Start with a plan and set measurable, attainable goals that will become your road map to success. Be honest with yourself, your support team, and your coach. Don't be afraid to ask for help when you need it, because everyone needs help sometimes. But know when to trust your instincts about the best path for yourself. Train hard because you want to be better, and make the most of every moment of training. Embrace challenges as opportunities to be great. Perhaps most important, remember to keep your passion for archery at the forefront of all that you do as you pursue your goals. You will enjoy the satisfaction of achieving what you set out to do.

2

Equipment and Tuning Tips

Mel Nichols

Archery requires a lot of equipment, specifically fit to each archer. What is good for one archer might not be good for another. The two types of bows—compound bows and recurve bows—require specific tuning techniques, which we discuss in this chapter.

TYPES OF BOWS

You need to determine whether you prefer to shoot with a recurve bow or a compound bow. The recurve bow is just a riser, limbs, and string, whereas the compound bow is a riser, limbs, a string, and cams. Compound bows, which are used mostly for hunting and target archery, are easier to learn to shoot than recurve bows because the cams allow you to have a percentage of let-off so you are not holding the complete bow poundage at full draw.

Recurve Bows

Recurve bows are used in Olympic and other major archery competitions. This type of bow consists of a riser (handle), and upper and lower limbs are attached to the riser. The limbs of the recurve bow are elongated and curved, hence the name "recurve." These types of bows are very archer specific. Shooting a recurve bow takes much more practice and body control than shooting a compound bow. Because you will be releasing the string with your fingers, you should look for equipment that fits your ability level and feels good to you. Releasing the string with the fingers makes the bow much more "critical." In other words, this means that the actions of the archer have a profound effect on the outcome of the shot making it vital that the bow fits you in terms of size, weight and ability level, so that the best possible release can be achieved. Recurve bows are available in several configurations, with short, medium, and long limbs, and 23-, 25-, and 27-inch risers. A good place to start to determine what length bow you should shoot is to check your draw length. If your draw length is 26 inches or shorter, try a 66-inch bow; from 26- to 29-inch draw lengths, use a 68- or 70-inch bow; and for 29 inches and longer draw lengths, use a 70- or 72-inch bow. Some archers might get a little more finger pinch with the string from different draw lengths. The best bow length for you is a bow that feels good to you and has the least amount of finger pinch. Recurve bows are fun to shoot, and they teach you good body control.

Compound Bows

The three types of compound bows are solo cam, two cam, and cam and a half. Solo-cam bows are a little slower than the two-cam bows because they have only one cam, but these bows are fairly easy to shoot. Two-cam bows are the fastest of the three because they have a top and a bottom cam working in sync to propel the arrow. Cam-and-a-half bows are the best of both worlds. They have good speed and are easy to shoot. Each archer will have a preference about which style of compound bow to shoot.

Solo-Cam Compound Bows

These bows are easy to draw because they have only one cam and are fairly easy to shoot. The bow tuning is also easy; all you have to do is follow the manufacturer's specifications, and the bows should shoot well. Most single-cam bows will have marks on the cams to line up with a cable or limb to help keep them in timing. If any timing adjustments are needed, all you have to do is adjust the cable. By adding twist, you will increase the poundage and lengthen the draw. To shorten the draw or decrease the poundage, take twist out of the cable.

Two-Cam Compound Bows

Two-cam compound bows are usually the fastest of the three cam designs. Two-cam bows have the same type of cam on the top and on the bottom, so the cam timing is fairly easy to adjust. Make sure both cams are drawing at the same time or that the top cam is about one millimeter faster than the bottom cam. This is called cam timing. The top cam being just a little faster than the bottom cam will allow the arrow to be slightly lifted off the arrow rest and will help to create a good tune. Tuning on the two-cam bow is fairly easy. Simply adjust a cable to get the timing correct. You will need the help of a friend or a shooting machine to check the timing. I use a shooting machine because it allows me to tune bows by myself. On two-cam bows, I usually set the top cam a little faster than the bottom cam, which is the best position I have found for tuning. I like the feel of a two-cam bow because it has a good wall. The wall is when a bow hits its full draw length. A solid wall will not move, whereas a soft wall will feel like a sponge when you hit the wall. A soft wall could mean the timing is off a little.

Cam-and-a-Half Compound Bows

Cam-and-a-half bows are a combination of two-cam and single-cam bows. These bows usually draw smoothly. I shoot cam-and-a-half bows because I like the accuracy I get with them. Most cam-and-a-half bows are designed with a string and two different length cables. This combination works together to create a smooth-drawing bow with good speed.

Materials

Compound bows are made of three types of materials: cast aluminum, machine aluminum, and carbon fiber. Most lower-end to middle-end bows are made of cast aluminum. Casting is the process of adding aluminum to a mold, a fairly inexpensive way to make a riser, thus keeping the cost of the bow down. Many competitive archers prefer the machined aluminum riser, which is usually cut on a Computer Numerical Control (CNC) machine out of a single piece of aluminum. A carbon fiber bow is one of the strongest of the riser designs because it is made to reduce flex in the riser, which also reduces twisting, as happens with aluminum risers. I have seen trucks drive over carbon riser bows, and the bows still shot an arrow in a 1-inch (~2.5 cm) diameter dot at 20 yards (~18 m). A carbon bow is also lighter. For example, my carbon bow is about 1.5 pounds (~0.7 km) lighter than my aluminum riser bow.

OTHER EQUIPMENT

Though the bow is the largest, and perhaps seemingly the most significant piece of archery equipment, archers must have several other components, correctly fitted to them, in order to shoot successfully. These items include arrows, arrow rests, sights, stabilizers and other items, all designed to help your bow do the best possible job of getting your arrows to their intended target consistently. We'll explain each of these items in detail throughout this chapter.

Arrows

With so many arrows to choose from, make sure you know what you want out of your arrows before purchasing them. For example, arrows are available in different types of materials, at different price points, work with different components, and are designed differently, but all to achieve the best possible results.

If you are shooting indoors, there are two basic choices: large-diameter aluminum arrows and large-diameter carbon arrows. The large-diameter aluminum arrow is my choice for indoors because I like the heavier weight of aluminum arrows over carbon arrows. When shooting indoors, the arrow speed does not matter because you are shooting only 18 meters. A heavy arrow is easier to shoot and is more forgiving than a lighter arrow. For example, if I'm shooting 18 meters indoors, I want a heavy arrow so I can put a heavy point inside of the shaft. At 18 meters, the arrow flexes a great deal, so a lightweight arrow will get much wear on it. The arrow will also take a pounding from the target, and a light arrow could bend when hitting the target or pulling the arrow from the target. A heavy-walled aluminum arrow holds up better than a light-walled arrow. When using carbon arrows for indoor shooting, you can use lighter points because of the light weight of the carbon. Carbon arrows are a good fit for shorter draw-length archers and archers who are not drawing very much poundage. Check the carbon arrow after every shot to see whether the carbon is damaged or cracked.

For target archery, a small-diameter barreled arrow shaft with an aluminum core and carbon on the outside works well. These arrows are designed to be shot at long distances. The barreled design cuts through air like a javelin, and the small diameter helps reduce arrow drag.

Also available is a parallel arrow that is made of aluminum and carbon, which can be used for a variety of archery events, such as field shooting. This style is a good all-around arrow. It can be shot at long-distance events such as at full FITA events and international rounds. It can also be used at 3D events that have no speed limit. These arrow is very fast at high poundage, and when the archer has close sight marks, 3D shooting is a little easier.

Arrow Rests

The two most common arrow rests are fixed-blade arrow rests (see figure 2.1*a*) and fall-away arrow rests (see figure 2.1*b*). Most target archers use a fixed-blade type. The blade holds the arrow at a set position, and the bottom of the arrow has a little contact with the arrow rest blade. The blades are usually made in various thicknesses (.008, .010, and .012 inch), which allows you to tune a rest for a specific size and weight of arrow.

The fall-away arrow rest is a rest with zero arrow contact after the shot. The fall-away rest is designed to hold the arrow in place for about two to three inches before it falls out of the way and has zero arrow shaft and vane contact. This is a preferred arrow rest for many hunters; some target archers also like this because when it is set up correctly, it allows good arrow flight.

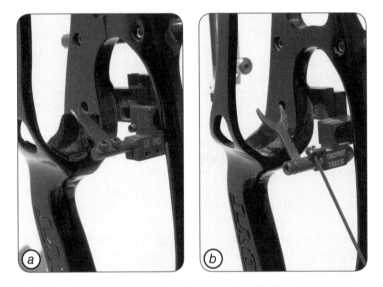

Figure 2.1   Arrow rests: (*a*) fixed-blade and (*b*) fall-away.

Sights

There are many styles of sights available on the market. Some are made of carbon; some are made of aluminum. The type of material you choose will be based on different factors, including reputation for quality, cost, and of course, personal preference. Choose a sight that will work for all styles of archery you will be shooting. The two most common styles are movable sights and pin sights.

Most target archers use a movable sight. Movable sights have elevation and windage adjustments and are good when shooting uphill and downhill shots. The adjustments allow your sight to be level at any angle. A good movable sight should have enough yardage adjustment so you can go from 10 to 100 yards (~9-91 m), thus allowing you to shoot any target from point blank up to long distances. The sight should also have at least a quarter inch of windage adjustment, which is the left and right adjustment of the sight. This will let you exactly dial in your left and right arrows. A good movable sight will also have a third axis adjustment to allow a sight's scope to be leveled with the sight when the bow is not aimed at a level target. A moveable sight should also allow a scope to be connected, which will allow minimal movement of the scope when locked on.

What I look for in a good target sight is that it has enough up-and-down travel. I want a sight that has enough vertical adjustment so I can shoot any type of archery event. The greatest yardage adjustment is needed for full FITA events, where adjustments range from 90 meters to 30 meters for adults and 90 meters to 20 meters for youth. This takes a lot of vertical adjustment. I also like a sight bar extension that gives me enough movement so I can adjust it in or out for a good sight picture. The sight bar is the bar that bolts to the riser. When shooting long-distance target events, you might need to bring the sight bar in close to the riser. Doing this will allow you to get the most distance out of your sight and will give you the most yardage adjustments. When shooting indoors, usually over an 18-meter distance, I put the bar as far away from the riser as the sight bar will allow, creating the best accuracy of a sight. You might need to try the sight bar in various positions to help clear up the scope picture. Everyone's eyesight is different, so the clearest sight picture you can have will make it easier to shoot. I also like a scope that locks into the sight bar, helping me to keep my scope level at all times. If your scope uses a threaded rod into a sleeve, make sure you use a locking washer to keep it from moving.

When choosing a scope for a movable sight, make sure you look through several scopes. When I look for a scope, I want to be sure it is made from aluminum or a strong housing. The scope diameter depends on the shooter's preference. A small-diameter scope works well when shooting target. The smaller diameter allows you to get a clear view of the target area, without looking at a lot of other things. You can move your sight bar in and out to help clear up the scope vision if needed. Make sure your peep sight matches the outside diameter of the scope housing. The correct size peep sight will make aiming easier.

I also make sure the lens is good quality and that I can see clearly. Only you can determine whether a scope will work for you. Just make sure the view through the scope is clear. Remember a higher magnification will bring the target size closer, but it will also make the bow more difficult to hold steady because the archer will perceive more sight movement with greater magnification. Most good archers I know shoot magnifications from a 4x to a 6x scope.

The other type of sight used is a pin sight. Pin sights usually have five or more pins coming out the side. How many pins are on a sight depends on the archer's preference. Pin sights are used primarily by hunters, but there are classes for pin shooters to compete in. Most pin sights are set in 10-yard increments, but you will need to learn how to gap your pins if you are shooting uneven distances (for example, if you have a target at 24 yards and 20- and 30-yard pins, you would have to learn how to split pins for shooting this distance). See figure 2.2 for an example of a moveable scope and pin sight.

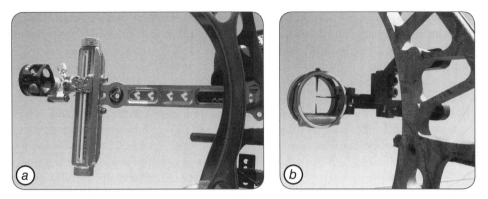

Figure 2.2 Sights: (*a*) moveable scope and (*b*) pin sight.

Stabilizers

A stabilizer is the front bar extending from the front of the riser and sometimes a side bar or V-bar (see figure 2.3). Stabilizers help with aiming during the shot. I look at two criteria of a stabilizer system to help me determine which type to purchase: I want a stabilizer that helps me aim and a system that takes out some of the bow shock. Almost all stabilizers have some way to remove bow shock. If you like the feel of shock in your hand, you should look for a stabilizer system that does not have any dampener system on it. I like a stabilizer that aims well and feels good during the shot. For me a good dampener on a stabilizer is a must (see figure 2.4).

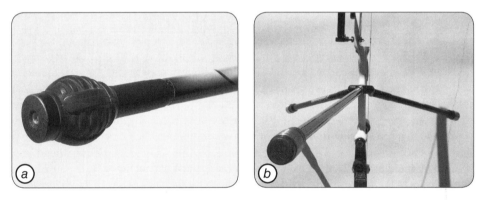

Figure 2.3 Stabilizers: (*a*) side bar and (*b*) V-bar.

Figure 2.4 Stabilizer with a dampener.

A stabilizer is an important piece of equipment. It is used to improve your aim at full draw. The balance of your bow in a static state does not matter; you should see how the stabilizer calms your bow when aiming. The amount of weight you have on your stabilizer will affect how your bow reacts. Try various weights to see which one calms your aim.

If you use V-bars or a single side bar, your stabilizer system should help reduce rotational torque. The back bars and front stabilizer should work as one. With proper weights on each end, your bow should become a well-balanced unit. You can adjust the V-bars in and out and up and down to get the proper balance. The more weight you can handle on your stabilizer and V-bars, the more they will help your aim. You will be able to tell when your setup is working well because your aim will improve and your groups will tighten up. A good starting point for how much weight you need on a stabilizer is to put as much weight on it as you can hold steady by just lifting your bow arm. You will need more weight on the back bar or V-bar than you do on the front stabilizer.

COMPOUND AND RECURVE BOW SETUP

Setting up recurve and compound bows is done differently. With recurve bows, you have to consider that you are setting up a bow that will be shot with fingers and that does not have cams. The arrow will react differently on a recurve bow than on a compound bow because the string goes around the fingers on release. When setting up recurve bows, also consider that you will be shooting with one finger above the arrow on the string and two fingers below the arrow. This means you will have to adjust the bow to get the correct nocking point. Compound bows are easier to set up than recurve bows. With compound bows, make sure the cam timing and the nocking point are correct. Most compound bows are shot with release aids, which makes tuning fairly quick. With releases, the arrow is released almost straight, thus allowing the string to travel in a true line quicker than when a string is released with fingers. Both types of bows have unique ways to set them up, and I will go over them in the following sections.

Compound Bow Setup

When setting up your compound bow, there are several steps you need to take to ensure that the bow fits you properly and that it performs correctly. Checking the draw length, draw weight and installing a nocking point are the first basic steps of compound bow setup that should always be done.

Check Draw Length

When choosing a bow, make sure you have the correct draw length. If you do not know your draw length, grab a friend and a tape measure, and extend your arms out to your sides as wide as you can. Measure the distance from fingertip to fingertip. Divide the number by 2.5 for your correct draw length. For example, if your length from fingertip to fingertip is 72.5 inches, your draw length is 29 inches (72.5 divided by 2.5). Also, make sure you can handle the draw weight you choose.

Another good way to check the draw length is to make sure the nock of the arrow is in line with your eye or close to the corner of your mouth. Have a friend look at you when you are at full draw to see whether the fit is correct. If the draw length is correct, your elbow will be slightly higher than and in line with the arrow. The arrow line should be even with the bottom of your hand. Your position should feel natural and not too extended or bound up. Consider what style of release you will be using. Every release is a little different in length, which will change the draw length; so keep this in mind if you plan to shoot different releases with the same setup.

Check Draw Weight

Make sure you can draw your bow in a controlled and smooth manner. Shooting good form is much easier when you are not struggling with draw weight. As you progress and get stronger, you can increase poundage. If you have to draw the bow over your head, you should decrease poundage. A good test is to draw the bow and aim at a spot about 20 meters away. See whether you can hold the dot or pin on the spot for 15 seconds. If you can, you have a good draw weight for you. If you start to shake after a few seconds, decrease poundage. Another good way to check whether the poundage is good for you is to sit in a chair and draw back the bow. You should be able to draw in a smooth and controlled manner, keeping the bow drawn fairly level to the ground.

Set Nocking Point

Before you set a nocking point, decide which type of nocking point you are going to use. You will also need to know whether you are going to use a string loop or a loop on a release. This is all personal preference. I like shooting with a string loop, so I tie two string nocks, one on the top side of the arrow nock and the other on the bottom side. I use center serving to tie on the nocks. Now I can install a string loop to the string. I like this type of nocking point because if I have any string loop problems or loop wear, I can change out the string loop without changing the nocking point, which means I will not have to retune. As a starting point, I make sure the arrow is 90 degrees to the string. Use a T-square and level the bottom of the square with the arrow rest. On the string, place a quarter-inch mark higher than the bottom of the square on the string. Use this mark as the bottom of your top nocking point. This should be very close to 90 degrees; it depends on arrow diameter. As I mentioned, this is just a starting point, as fine-tuning will get the nocking point in the proper position.

Note that the lower nock position will help keep a string loop in place while holding to the top of the arrow at full draw. If you are using a release loop, you will need only a top nocking point; the string loop will hold upward pressure on the nock, thus holding it in place (see figure 2.5).

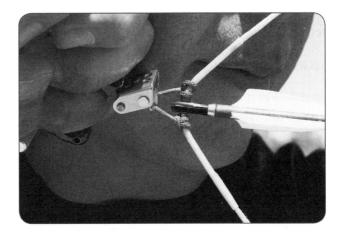

Figure 2.5 When using a release loop, the string loop will maintain upward pressure on the nock, thus holding the loop in place.

Adjust Tiller

Tiller adjustments on the bow are important because they can change the tune and the nocking point. Start by setting the tiller even for both top and bottom. Use a silver pen and mark a line on the limb bolts in the same location so you will know whether anything changes (see figure 2.6). Just make sure that every time you make an adjustment to your tiller, you reset your nocking point back to your original setting. Try a few different tiller settings to see what works best for you and take notes for each tiller position. To help set the tiller in the best position for you, I would try setting the tiller at one-quarter, one-half, and three-quarter turns and one full turn on the top limb bolt. At each setting, reset the nocking point to its original position. Keep good notes on the group size at each setting and how the bow holds. Do these tests on the bottom limb bolts as well. One of these positions will give you the best groups and will also hold the best. Tiller tuning takes a long time, so be patient; it will pay off in the long run.

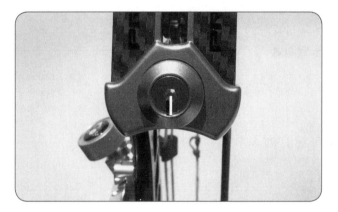

Figure 2.6 Mark the limb bolts when setting the tiller to ensure precision in turning the limb bolts correctly on each limb.

Set Center Shot

A good starting point for setting center shot is straight down the center of the arrow line. Some bow manufacturers will give you center shot measurements, but these are only starting points; you might have to move the center shot slightly when you start tuning. Your arrow spline can change how the center shot is on a specific bow. When you start tuning the arrow to the bow, your center shot could change to give you the correct tune.

Bow Poundage

Draw-weight poundage is critical to having a good consistent shot. I see many people try to pull more bow weight than they can handle. Make sure you are very comfortable with the weight you choose. It is much easier to start off at a lower poundage and work your way up. Good form is more important than speed. Too heavy a draw weight could result in injury because of improper form. With all the technologies bow companies have, they are making bows faster and faster at lower poundages. Just remember, if you can control the weight of the bow, you can make a good shot. Accuracy is all about controlling the draw poundage with confidence and ease.

Recurve Bow Setup

Setting up a recurve bow requires a few specialty tools. You will need a T-square, Allen wrenches, and Beiter blocks. The T-square will be used to check the brace height and tiller. The Allen wrenches can be used to make all limb, tiller, and brace height adjustments. The Beiter blocks will be used to align the string, arrow, riser, and stabilizer. A recurve bow takes a little more setting up because unlike with a compound bow, you will take it apart every time you shoot it to transport it from and to the range.

Determine Bow Length

A bow does not have a set length for a specific height, so you'll want to try several configurations. When choosing a bow length, choose a setup with the least amount of finger pinch. Finger pinch is the amount of pinch created on the fingers when you are at full draw. For example, a 64-inch bow would have more finger pinch than a 70-inch bow. With this in mind, don't be afraid to try a long bow length. Recurve bows look fairly long compared to compound bows.

Initial Setup Steps

First, use a bow stringer to string the bow. I have seen many limbs fly apart because people were stringing the bow by just pushing the bow away and sliding the string onto the limb tip. Check to make sure all bolts are tight and then install an arrow rest and plunger. There are many types of arrow rests on the market today. Some arrow rests stick on the riser with tape, and some will bolt to the riser. Both work well, so whichever arrow rest you choose, be sure the rest holds the arrow in the same position every time and that you are able to adjust the height easily.

Screw the plunger into the riser and tighten until snug. Every plunger has a spring in it, so set the spring to the medium setting, thus allowing you to stiffen or weaken the plunger, and helping you to fine-tune. Bolt the sight to the bow at this time; it will be adjusted at a later time. Now put a stabilizer on the riser. You need the stabilizer on the bow because you are going to use it to hold up the riser so you can check the limb alignment and center shot. You do not need the V-bars at this time.

Tie Nocking Point

Now tie a nocking point onto your string. The easiest way to tie nocking points is to tie eight over and under knots. Tie two nocking points, one on top of the arrow nock and one on the bottom. You will need a T-square and two pieces of serving about one foot long. Attach the T-square to the string and bring the bottom side of the T-square to the arrow rest. The T-square should just touch the arrow rest, just like an arrow would. A good starting point to tie the top nock is three-eighths of an inch above the bottom of the arrow rest. This measurement is only a starting point and is for small-diameter arrows. The tuning will help you set the nocking point. Now tie a bottom nock below the arrow nock.

Check Limb Alignment

Now it is time to check the limb alignment. Nock an arrow on the string and lean the bow against a chair. Find the center of the limbs either by putting a piece of tape on the limbs and then measuring to the center and marking or, as I prefer, using Beiter blocks, which have marks on them so you can see the center of the limb. These blocks are made to snap on and off your limbs with ease. Now look down the string and see whether the string lines up with the limb bolts. If the string is not in perfect alignment with the limb bolt holes, adjust the limbs. Depending on the brand of bow you have, either adjust the limb alignment with adjustment screws or with adjust shims. Both ways work well, so take your time to make sure you get a good alignment.

Align Stabilizer

The next step is to align the stabilizer with the bow. You want the bow in the same position as when you aligned the limbs. Look down the string and use the bolt holes or Beiter blocks as your center gauge to see whether the stabilizer is in line with the string and the riser (see figure 2.7). If it is in line, you can move to the next step. If your stabilizer does not line up, you can use the limb alignment adjustments to get the string in line. Just make sure you adjust the top limb the same distance as you do the bottom limb.

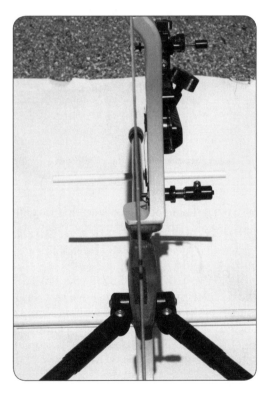

Figure 2.7 Stabilizers should be in line with the string and arrow to allow for good bow reaction to the target.

Set Center Shot

Once you have the stabilizer in line, you can now adjust the center shot. A good starting point is to have the tip of the arrow about two millimeters outside the string (see figure 2.8). I have found that if you can see half the arrow shaft outside of the string, that is too much. This will usually cause the arrow to kick from side to side. When you start the tuning process, you will be able to fine-tune the arrow rest.

Figure 2.8 The arrow's point should be just outside the string line. When looking from the back side, you should see only about half the arrow point.

Install Stabilizer Setup

Now you can install the complete stabilizer setup. For a recurve, it is best to shoot with some type of V-bar setup. A few people have shot without V-bars and shot well, but the V-bars give the bow stability. It is easy to get the right feeling with V-bars because you can adjust the balance of the bow. You can also adjust the amount of weight you have on the ends to get the bow to hold as you would like.

TUNING COMPOUND AND RECURVE BOWS

Tuning is the heart of the bow setup. It is good to take all equipment out of the outcome of the shot. What I mean by this is, if your bow is tuned properly, you will feel confident with your equipment. Having confidence in your equipment means you will shoot a stronger shot. Take your time to make sure you are fully satisfied with the tune of your bow.

Tuning Compound Bows

There are many ways to tune a compound bow, so here I explain ways that have helped me coach archers to World Championships. I believe the way I tune is a fairly easy way to get a bow performing at its peak ability. You will have all the confidence in your equipment if you follow these tuning steps.

Paper Tuning

Paper tuning is an easy and quick way to check your arrow flight. All you do is shoot an arrow through a piece of paper to see what the arrow tear looks like. You can make a paper tuning stand for under $10. I made a stand out of PVC and bought a roll of painter's paper and clamps at a local home improvement store (see figure 2.9). Paper tuning can be shot at about three meters. Make sure your target is placed directly behind

Figure 2.9 Homemade paper tuner.

the paper tuner. A well-tuned bow will shoot a good hole; it will not tear the paper. You should see only the arrow hole and vanes in the paper (see figure 2.10). If your nocking point is too high, your arrow hole will impact the point at the bottom of the tear, and the vanes will be much higher (see figure 2.11*a*). This could mean your arrow is a little weak. Move your arrow rest down and retest. Keep adjusting the arrow rest until you get a good paper tear. A low nocking point will produce the opposite results (see figure 2.11*b*). This could mean your arrow is a little stiff. Move your nocking point up and retest. If the center shot is off, you will get a left or right tear (see figure 2.12). Make the proper adjustments and shoot again. If the tear is to the right, move your rest to the left. You can also increase the poundage or go down one arrow size. If the tear is to the left, move your rest to the right. You can also decrease the bow poundage or go up one arrow size.

Figure 2.10 Good arrow hole through paper.

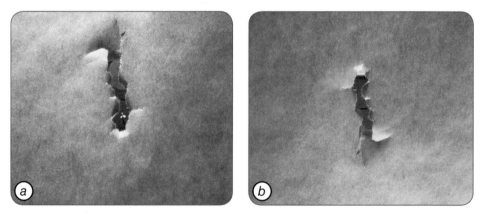

Figure 2.11 *(a)* Move the arrow rest down if the tear is high, and *(b)* move the arrow rest up if the tear is low.

Figure 2.12   A tear to the right means that the center shot is off.

Tiller Tuning

Tiller tuning means experimenting with tiller position, using a consistent method of adjusting the position, that helps you to achieve consistent groups. What I like to do is use nine pieces of paper each with a one-inch dot in the center at which to aim. At the bottom of each piece of paper, I write the different tiller settings I will be shooting (even tiller, one-quarter top, one-half top, three-quarters top, and one full top). Repeat the same on the bottom side. Adjust your bow to the tiller setting you have on the paper and shoot six arrows. Every time you make a new tiller adjustment, reset your nocking point to its original starting point. Check the size of your groups and write down how your bow felt while aiming. Different tiller settings will improve groups and help aiming. Find the right one for you and your setup. Once you have shot all the different tiller settings, look at the results to see what worked the best for your setup. The best setting for you will be the position that feels the most comfortable and has the best groups.

Line Tuning

Line tuning is my favorite way to tune a compound bow. I like to do line tuning at 30 or 50 meters for outdoors. If I'm shooting a 50-meter round, I will tune at 50 meters; if I'm shooting an 18-meter round, I tune at 18 meters. Tuning at the distance you will be shooting will give you the best results for the competitive round you will be shooting and will tell you exactly where your arrows are hitting. When line tuning, I start by shooting four arrows at a vertical line, with the idea to get all four arrows hitting in the width of a line or tape. You can use the top of a target face as a straight line. I use a 12-inch piece of half-inch tape, as shown in figure 2.13. Blue painter's tape works well. Once you get the vertical line where you want it, go to a horizontal line and repeat the process. Shoot four arrows at a straight line to see where they impact.

All four arrows should hit at the same elevation on the line. Make sure you shoot the arrows about two inches apart from each other so you can see a pattern. If your arrows shoot higher in the middle and the outside two arrows are lower than the group, move your nock down. If it is easier, you can move the arrow rest up; just make sure your arrow is centered in the plunger hole to start with. You can think of the line as a smile or a frown. Just move the nock the opposite direction from the farthest arrow. Make

Figure 2.13 Blue painter's tape works well for marking a line and does not damage the target when you pull it off.

all adjustments in small increments of about one thirty-second inch. Once you achieve a straight line, shoot a vertical line. To make any adjustments, move the arrow rest in or out until your arrows shoot a straight vertical line. When I shoot a vertical line, I like to start at the top and work my way down, making sure the arrows are about two inches apart. The idea again is to keep all your arrows in a straight line. If your arrows look like a parenthesis, just adjust the rest to the farthest arrow. Then retest until you get a straight line.

Bare-Shaft Tuning

Bare-shaft tuning is useful for helping you determine whether you have the correct arrows. You must have the exact same arrows (spine, length, weight and nocks, as well as the same fletchings for the fletched group) to be able to bare-shaft tune: four fletched and two unfletched arrows. There are a couple of terms associated with bare-shaft tuning. *Porpoising* is when the arrows move up and down during flight. *Fishtailing* is when the arrows move left and right during flight. You will shoot all arrows at 20 yards (~18 m) to determine whether either flight pattern is happening to your arrows.

Address porpoising first. Porpoising happens when the nock is either too high or too low. Shoot four fletched arrows and then two unfletched arrows at the target. If the unfletched arrows hit the target above the fletched arrows, move the nocking point up until all the arrows hit the target at the same height. If the unfletched arrows hit the target below the fletched arrows, move the nocking point down. It is acceptable for the unfletched arrows to hit slightly below the fletched arrows; this differential in height can help if there are problems with clearance.

Fishtailing happens when the nocked end of the arrow moves to the left and right. If the unfletched arrows hit the target to the left of the fletched arrows, the arrows are considered stiff. To correct this problem, either add a little weight to the bow if it has that type of adjustment or add weight to the points of the arrow. If the unfletched arrows hit the target to the right of the fletched arrows, then they are weak, in which case, you would make the opposite adjustments: decrease bow weight or point weight. On most bows, it is common for the unfletched arrows to hit just slightly left and low of the fletched arrows, which is perfectly acceptable. These adjustments are for right-handed shooters; if you are left-handed just reverse the process.

High-Speed Camera Tuning

I like using a high-speed camera to see whether the arrow is coming off the rest without hitting anything. To do this, have a friend take a few videos of specific parts while you are shooting. You can also check the arrow flight to see whether the arrow is kicking one way or the other. I have used a video to see whether a fall-away rest is staying down at the right time or whether it comes back up after dropping away. A cell phone works well if you don't have a high-speed camera.

Tuning Recurve Bows

For recurve bows, I use two types of tuning: bare-shaft tuning and line tuning. I like tuning at long distances. This way you can get accurate readings of what the arrows are doing. Thirty meters is a good distance at which everyone should be able to tune.

Bare-Shaft Tuning

For bare-shaft tuning, I recommend first shooting four fletched arrows at the target and then shooting two bare-shaft arrows at the target. The idea of bare-shaft tuning is to get the bare-shaft arrows in the top side of the fletched arrow group. Note that the fixes I talk about are for a right-handed shooter; for left-handed shooters, just do the opposite.

If the bare-shaft arrows hit above the fletched group, this means your arrows are porpoising. To fix this, move the nocking point up until the bare-shaft arrows hit in the same group as the fletched arrows hit. If the bare-shaft arrows hit below the fletched group of arrows, move the nocking point down until the bare-shaft arrows go into the fletched group.

If the bare-shaft arrows hit left of the fletched group, this means your arrows are a little too stiff. To fix this, either increase the draw weight of the bow if you can handle the weight comfortably, decrease the spring tension on the plunger, or increase the point weight inside the arrow. I like to have a medium to stiff plunger, so I usually increase the draw weight of the bow if possible. If the bare-shaft arrows hit on the right side of the fletched group, this means the shaft is a little weak. To fix this, you could either decrease the bow draw weight, increase the spring tension on the plunger, or decrease the point weight of the arrow.

Sometimes you might have a bare-shaft arrow hit high right or low left. If this happens, work on one fix first. I would get the nocking point set so you can focus on one item at a time. Once you get the bare-shaft arrows hitting in the fletched group, you should be ready to get your sight marks and start shooting.

Line Tuning

My favorite way of tuning a recurve bow is line tuning. Line tuning also works well after bare-shaft tuning because it helps fine-tune a recurve bow. The idea of line tuning is to get all your arrows hitting in a vertical line and a horizontal line. This tuning should be shot at 50 meters or 70 meters. The farthest you can shoot is best. I use this as a high-end tuning process. You will need some tape for this test. I use a piece of tape about three inches long of one-and-a-half-inch blue painter's tape and put it on the target. Start by shooting the horizontal line first. The reason I shoot the horizontal line first is to set the nocking point to get the porpoising action out of the arrow. Unless you have perfect tuning, you will have porpoising and fishtailing of the arrow. The horizontal line is the easier to tune because all you have to do is adjust the nocking point. If the arrows hit the target like a C facing up, just move the nocking point up. Keep making small adjustments until all arrows are in a straight, horizontal line. If the arrows hit the target with the C facing down, lower the nocking point. Keep making small adjustments until all arrows hit in a straight, horizontal line.

After you shoot the horizontal line, shoot the vertical line. Shoot six arrows at the line from top to bottom. If all your arrows hit the line, you have a good tune. If the arrows line up in a zigzag pattern, adjust the center shot. For a right-handed shooter, move the plunger out about half a turn and re-shoot the line. You should never move the plunger more than an eighth of an inch off center. If you have to move it farther than an eighth of an inch, check to make sure you are shooting the right arrows or adjust the poundage to get the arrow spine to match the poundage. For left-handed shooters, adjust in the opposite direction.

Line tuning takes time, so be patient. When adjustments to straighten out a line make the line worse, just adjust the other way. I have seen some recurve shooters, because of their form, make a bow react totally opposite from what the bow is supposed to. Many of the top shooters check their tune every time they shoot the bow. Always strive for a better tune. Remember a bow should be tuned to the arrow and the archer. Archers change day by day because some days are better than others, so the bow will react differently on those days. Just do your best to have your bow shooting the best every day.

Tuning bows takes time and patience. It is very important when tuning to make the best shots you can, which will produce the best results. Tuning is a never-ending job. Don't be afraid to make small changes to your tune when you are at a tournament. Every day your shot will change a little, so make sure your bow is performing well for your shot on that day. A well-tuned bow will make shooting more enjoyable.

3

Developing Your Shot Sequence

Guy Krueger

You've heard the phrase "Timing is everything." In archery, timing refers to the rhythm of the shot, and a consistent timing on each shot is a major key to becoming a successful archer. The more consistent your timing is for each arrow, the more consistent momentum the arrow has toward the center of the target. To develop consistent timing, you need a consistent, well-defined shot routine. This chapter provides insight into the importance of a shot sequence and briefly outlines the steps of a proper shot sequence. This chapter also establishes a foundation for the mental and physiological aspects of archery, and the following chapters go into more detail for each step of the shot sequence.

THE IMPORTANCE OF A SHOT SEQUENCE

A well-defined shot sequence, consistently followed, increases the probability that you will have a more consistent outcome. As a beginner, just learning the basic step-by-step process of shooting the arrow can be complicated because the intricate details of each step of the shot process are still unfamiliar to you and your focus is on the many details of each step of the shot. You might have difficulty performing all steps correctly and consistently. Initially, the entire shot sequence might take 20 to 30 seconds. As you become more comfortable and coordinated, the shot sequence might decrease from 12 to 15 seconds because some of these details will have become automatic subconscious actions. However, you need to have a well-defined shot process with specific steps to excel to the next level. Each step has a specific goal, and you must continue to focus on these steps of the process, especially in competition.

In intense competitions, such as in national championships, world championships, and the Olympic Games, your level of awareness can be different from that during training. Oftentimes the pressure creates a drastic change in awareness. Some athletes report feeling mentally "numb" and that they can easily forget what they are supposed to do, whereas others say they are aware of everything and feel overwhelmed. Having a well-defined shot process helps you stay focused in pressure situations and gives you a set of instructions to follow, thus allowing you to be more consistent and oftentimes to perform better in competition than in training.

THE SHOT CYCLE

Biomechanical strength plays a role in your success in high-pressure competitions. Ideally, athletes who are stronger biomechanically have an advantage in competition. A shot sequence derived from biomechanics gives you an advantage because it allows you to practice more. Proper biomechanics also decreases your probability of being injured because you are using the correct motions throughout the shot cycle.

The shot cycle provides the major steps of shooting correctly and is the foundation of the National Training System. The shot cycle is a series of actions within phases of the shooting process developed with the use of biomechanics by world-renowned archery coach KiSik Lee and first introduced to the world in the book *Total Archery*, by KiSik Lee and Robert de Bondt. KiSik Lee is one of the most successful coaches in the international archery community and has been coaching professionally for over thirty years. He has developed successful national programs in South Korea and Australia, and now in the United States. Coach Lee's athletes have won nine Olympic gold medals and numerous other Olympic, World Championship, and international medals since 1981.

The purpose of the shot cycle is to give you a set of steps to follow to create a consistent shot process and to allow your body to shoot the bow in the most biomechanically efficient manner. The shot sequence also creates a solid foundation for the mental routine you need to follow to stay focused in competition. The most important goal of the shot cycle is to allow you to shoot every shot with *holding*. Holding is the feeling of being completely braced in the bow and able to withstand its force.

Figure 3.1 shows a basic diagram depicting the shot cycle and outlining the thirteen basic steps of shooting. The diagram shows how the basic steps of the shot cycle come

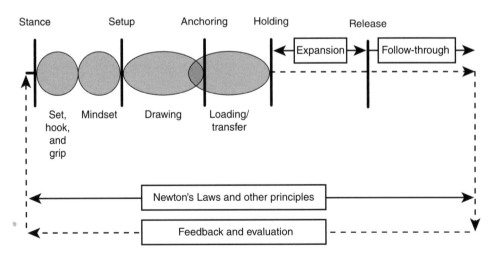

Figure 3.1 Thirteen basic steps create the shot cycle and give you a sequence of events to follow for each shot.

© 2005 KiSik Lee. Reprinted, with permission, from *Total Archery* by KiSik Lee and Robert de Bondt.

together to flow into one complete action. During the shot cycle, Newton's laws of motion play a part in describing the forces you encounter. For example, the force the bow applies on you, pulling you forward during the shot and after the release, can be described by Newton's third law of motion. The third law of motion states that every force has an equal and opposite force reacting to it. As you continue to draw the bow back, the bow continues to exert a force on you, pulling you forward. This force is also directly related to the shot process, from holding to follow-through. Holding allows you to resist that force through bone alignment, and the follow-through is a reaction of losing the force that the bow exerts on you while you increase the force applied to the bow.

The thirteen basic steps of shooting follow:

1. Stance
2. Nocking the arrow
3. Hooking and gripping
4. Set position and mindset
5. Setup
6. Drawing
7. Loading
8. Anchoring
9. Transfer
10. Holding
11. Expansion and aiming
12. Release and follow-through
13. Feedback and evaluation

Defining the Concepts

Some key concepts need to be covered before the shot cycle steps are described in detail because many of these concepts are used in this chapter and in many of the remaining chapters. The principles should be the same for everyone, but some of the details will vary for each archer because of body type, size, and strength.

A difference exists between focusing on movement as opposed to focusing on muscle contraction. Commonly, in technique sports, people focus on tightening a specific set of muscles and thus create too much tension in one area, making the movement more difficult. An excellent example can be seen in the ways you can move your forearm to your upper arm. First, focus on contracting the biceps to bring your forearm up to your upper arm. Notice this action takes a great deal of effort, causing your forearm to move to your upper arm in a slow and possibly shaky manner. Now focus on moving your forearm to your upper arm without focusing on contracting the biceps. Your forearm moves naturally to your upper arm and with less tension of the biceps. This more natural movement happens because many small muscles in your arm simultaneously contract and relax to create it.

The best archers make shooting a bow seem effortless because they are focused on the movement, not on a specific muscle contraction. Describing movement is therefore the main focus in explaining the steps of the shot cycle. Although movement is the key focus, feeling tension in specific areas is necessary for you to confirm you are in the correct position, thus allowing you to become more consistent and to coach yourself through each shot.

Figure 3.2 shows the major muscles of the back, which play a major role in many of your movements and provide you with the strength necessary to properly execute the shot. The middle and lower trapezius, the triceps, and the deltoids are the larger, stronger muscles of the back, shoulder, and arm. These muscles used in combination with the correct bone alignment give you the strength to shoot comfortably and consistently.

An important term in learning the correct shot cycle is *LAN 2*, a half dollar–sized area on the outside of the upper arm, halfway between the shoulder and elbow which you can see in figure 3.2. It is the back of the triceps, located about where the sleeve of a short sleeve shirt ends. Focusing on moving the LAN 2 area during the shot cycle allows you to use the stronger muscles of your body and facilitates the body's smooth movement.

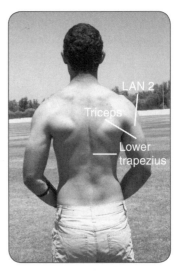

Figure 3.2 All of the muscles of the back play some role in the shot process; however, the lower trapezius and triceps are your main focus. Note the position of the LAN 2.

Stance

The stance is the first part of the shot cycle and provides the foundation for angular motion. Beginners often overlook the stance, whereas the best archers take their stances and foundations very seriously. The stance can be compared to the foundation of a house, and with archery, you are building a very big house so you need a very strong foundation. It is extremely important for you to use an open stance from day one. With an open stance, your feet should be approximately shoulder-width apart, close to parallel, and rotated about 30 degrees toward the target (see figure 3.3). Your back foot might be rotated slightly less than 30 degrees but should not be parallel to the shooting line. Your hips should stay in the same direction as your feet throughout the shooting process. You should also maintain a majority of the pressure on the balls of your feet and not on your heels while keeping both your feet flat on the ground.

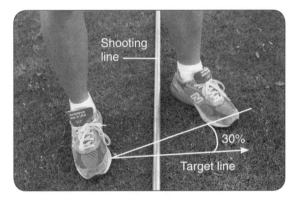

Figure 3.3 Archer in an open stance.

Nocking the Arrow

Nocking the arrow is the second and easiest step of the shot cycle. This is the moment that you attach the arrow to the string. The nock of the arrow should fit under the nock locator of the string, and you should feel the nock "snap" onto the string (see figure 3.4). Some archers prefer to hold the arrow by the nock end, and some prefer to hold

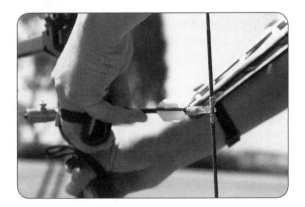

Figure 3.4 The archer places the arrow on the string, known as "nocking the arrow," the second and easiest step in the shot cycle.

the arrow by the shaft before the fletching. It is important to hold the arrow the same way every time. Nocking the arrow is not only a physical action but also marks the beginning of the mental process of the shot. After this point, you begin to focus on key elements of each step of the shot cycle.

Hooking and Gripping

The next step is the moment in which you hook the string with your drawing hand and set the grip with your bow hand (see figures 3.5 and 3.6). It is important that you set the finger position, the drawing wrist, and the hold on the string with your draw hand first and then set the position of the bow hand in the grip. It is also highly important that you visually check these placements each time to ensure consistency. You might need to set all three fingers of the hook just below the nock of the arrow on the string. After a few weeks of shooting, you should be able to use the more advanced method of hooking the string with your index finger placed over the top of the arrow nock and your middle and ring fingers on the string just below the arrow nock.

Figure 3.5   Archer hooking the string with the drawing hand.

Figure 3.6   Archer setting the grip with the bow hand.

Set Position and Mindset

Set position refers to the position of your body just after you set the hook and grip. At the basic set position, you should maintain your posture and keep your shoulders in a natural position (see figure 3.7). Your bow arm should be fully extended in a natural position, with slight tension in your bow-arm triceps, and your bow-arm elbow should be slightly pronated. Next rotate your chest slightly away from the target to create tension in your lower and middle trapezius. This rotation should open the bow, increasing the distance from the string to the grip a few inches without actually pulling the string back with your arm. Your head should be rotated toward the target and set over your chest and not over your spine. Right-handed archers should tilt their heads slightly to the right. Once your head position is set, you should not change it throughout the shooting process.

Figure 3.7 Archer in the set position after the hook and grip.

After you set the hook and grip, you begin to mentally prepare for the shot and visually address the target, an important step in keeping your head position set. This is a good time to check the wind one last time and to decide where to keep your eyes focused during aiming. During mindset, you must maintain mental focus and be fully committed to taking the shot. Any hesitation or distraction from this point forward can cause a mistake.

Setup

The next step in the shot cycle is to raise the bow from set position to setup position. The setup position refers to the final position of your body just before the drawing phase. The correct setup position requires that you not only learn the correct way to raise your bow but also how to set the correct shoulder alignment, a position called the "barrel of the gun."

To raise the bow correctly, you must utilize the stronger muscles in your body without compromising your foundation. Therefore, you must focus on maintaining the correct stance and hip alignment. The correct method of raising the bow will also allow the drawing side of your body to be in the correct position to efficiently draw the bow back. In the next part of the setup, position your bow-hand wrist, bow shoulder, and drawing shoulder in a straight line. This straight line is referred to as the alignment of the barrel of the gun. This body position not only provides bone-to-bone alignment but also provides your body with a stable base from which to draw the bow back angularly.

To set up correctly, it is important for you to do the following while going from set to setup:

1. While maintaining the stance, hip alignment, posture, hook, grip pressure, and head position set in the previous steps, begin raising the bow with your bow hand first.

2. Raise the bow with only your bow hand; your drawing hand is attached to the string from the hook and raises up naturally.

3. Continue raising the bow with your bow hand while keeping tension in the bow-arm triceps.

4. Raise your bow hand high enough so that the sight is above the target, usually around mouth to nose level (see figure 3.8).

5. Your drawing hand should remain at a level slightly lower than your bow hand, usually just at or below the level of your chin.

6. The stabilizer should point slightly up and to the left for a right-handed archer and should not be level to the target. The stabilizer will point slightly up and to the right for a left-handed archer.

7. For a right-handed archer, the drawing hand should be slightly to the right of the target line, which causes the arrow and stabilizer to be pointed slightly up and to the left of the center of the target. For a left-handed archer, the drawing hand should be slightly to the left of the target line.

8. At the end of the setup, move your drawing-side scapula closer to your spine to create a straight line through your bow-arm wrist, bow shoulder, and drawing shoulder. This is called setting the barrel of the gun and is explained in more detail in chapter 4.

Figure 3.8 Archer in the setup position.

Drawing

The drawing phase of the shot cycle is where the largest, most noticeable movements take place. Drawing can be defined as the process of moving the string away from the pressure point of the grip by focusing on moving the LAN 2 area (refer to figure 3.2) of the drawing arm back while keeping your bow-arm extended (see figure 3.9). Archery is considered a high-level, repetitive motion sport and thus carries an increased risk for sustaining a repetitive motion injury, such as bicipital tendonitis or a rotator cuff tear. It is highly important that you use the correct muscles and positioning during this phase to prevent such an injury. It is also important that aiming does not start until after you reach the holding phase. Aiming too early will lead to linear drawing, which can increase the probability of a shoulder injury. Instead, drawing should be an angular movement.

The drawing motion must also be angular and not linear. A completely linear movement requires you to draw back, with the sight and arrow perfectly in line to the target. However, as you will see later, this movement causes you to bend the wrist on your drawing hand. Biomechanically, linear drawing puts more stress on your drawing shoulder joint and thus increases the potential for injury. Angular drawing, on the other hand, means you draw the bow so that from an overhead view, your elbow appears to be rounding and not coming back in a straight line.

Figure 3.9 Archer drawing the bow.

Loading

The drawing motion leads into the loading phase and position. The loading phase refers to the action of increasing the intensity on the muscles in the lower and middle trapezius. Loading position refers to the final position of your body after drawing and before anchoring. At the loading position, you should feel almost completely braced within the bow.

The typical loading position is shown in figure 3.10, *a* and *b*. Notice that the archer's hand is typically one-half to one inch below her jaw at the loading position. Also notice that the drawing scapula is lower than the bow-arm scapula. This archer is using her lower trapezius to draw the bow, and as a result, the scapula is lower. Although you feel the tension in your lower trapezius, you should not lower your drawing shoulder. If you were to see this position from an overhead view, the archer's elbow should already be behind the line of the arrow at this point and the archer is almost completely at full draw.

Figure 3.10 Archer in the loading position from the *(a)* front and *(b)* back.

Anchoring

After you have drawn the bow to loading position, it is time to come to the anchor position. Anchoring, although subtle, is an important step in the shot cycle. While anchoring, you must maintain the load put on your lower and middle trapezius during loading while raising your drawing hand and drawing arm up to firmly contact your jawbone and neck. At this point, the bow string should be in firm contact with the front side of your chin just before the corner of the chin (see figure 3.11). If the string and anchor are too far back and on the side of the chin, you will experience "string drag" upon release. String drag occurs when the string's movement on release is obstructed by the chin and the string "catches" the skin around the chin and pulls it forward. This can cause damage to the skin in the chin area and will almost always cause tuning and grouping issues.

During the process from loading to anchoring, it is extremely important that you maintain your hook and finger pressure on the string and the pressure point on the grip. Maintaining the finger pressure and hook during anchoring allows you to increase your back tension from loading to anchoring.

Figure 3.11   Archer in the anchor position.

Transfer

Even after you have reached a solid anchor position, you are still not completely braced inside the bow. You must make a small movement to get into the holding position. The small movement, called transfer, helps you shift the tension from your arm and forearm to your back. By focusing on the LAN 2, this movement allows you to keep your elbow past the line and resist the force of the bow. To transfer, you must focus on moving the back of your drawing shoulder (LAN 2 area) slightly down and behind you.

Holding

Holding is the most important phase of the shot cycle. The concept of holding means you are completely braced inside the bow and can withstand the force of the bow pulling your arm forward (see figure 3.12) A good indication that you are shooting with holding is that no shaking is visible while you are shooting and at the full-draw position. Once you take holding, you should feel a strong connection from the tip of your elbow on the drawing side through the middle and lower trapezius on both sides of the scapulae, to the pressure point of the grip. The shot cycle allows you to set the proper bone alignment to create the strongest structure possible and to create a skeletal foundation to brace the bow. Shooting with holding prevents collapsed shots and allows you to execute the shot more consistently in pressure situations. Holding must be a conscious step in the shot cycle, even for advanced and elite archers.

Note that holding does not mean you necessarily stop your motion. Holding is a phase, and you must maintain the feeling of holding through expansion, release, and follow-through. You should also feel a percentage of holding through the shot beginning at set position, and that percentage of holding should increase through each step of the shot cycle.

Figure 3.12 Archer at the holding position. Correct bone alignment is what will create the structure to brace the bow.

SQUEEZE DRILL

Holding can easily be felt without a bow in the Squeeze Drill. To perform the Squeeze Drill, position yourself as if you were at full draw and in the anchor position. The instructor then applies force to your drawing elbow toward the target while simultaneously applying force to your bow hand away from the target, trying to make your arms come forward or collapse. At the same time, put your body in position to withhold the force of the bow, therefore taking holding. You should feel a connection between your back and arms through the muscles in the back surrounding the scapulae.

Expansion and Aiming

Now that you have consciously taken holding, expansion and aiming can begin. Expansion is the process of continuing to increase the balanced forces of the bow-arm triceps and LAN 2 in the same direction as transfer through the release and follow-through. Expansion is in the same direction of movement as transfer, but it will be a smaller, more internal movement. Intermediate- and higher-level archers should be using a clicker, a simple device that makes a small click when the arrow is pulled to the farthest position, just before releasing. The farther the bow is drawn, the more energy is put into the arrow upon release. The clicker allows you to be even more consistent upon release because you always know when you have reached your optimal draw length. However, it is important that you control the rhythm and timing of when the clicker clicks and not be controlled by the clicker. Correct expansion happens naturally while you focus on maintaining holding and moving the back of your drawing shoulder. Expansion should be maintained until you reach the end of the follow-through.

Expansion is an angular, imperceptible movement. When you expand correctly, you appear to be merely comfortably bracing the bow. However, archers new to using a clicker and new to this technique might shake or tremor slightly during expansion.

You should not begin aiming until you have achieved holding. Aiming should be done by keeping your eyes on the point of focus on the target. The target should be in focus, and the sight ring and pin should be out of focus and floating. Maintaining the correct string alignment during the aiming and expansion phase is also highly important.

Release and Follow-Through

The release is the critical instant of the shot and must be a completely subconscious, natural action, as you would do in setting down a glass of water, effortlessly letting the glass slip from your hand onto the table without any focus on opening your fingers. Consciously letting go of the string results in your fingers forcibly opening, thus reducing the consistency and force of the bow applied to the arrow. Any excess tension in your fingers can prevent the correct amount of force from being applied to the arrow in the correct direction.

Follow-through is the reaction that occurs when you let the string go while maintaining force to expand through the clicker. As you expand past the clicker, the bow exerts a force on you that is equal to the force you are applying to the bow. Once you expand past the clicker and let the string go, the force of the bow is no longer acting on you. However, you are still maintaining the expansion and force through the release, and the resulting reaction sends your drawing unit in the direction of the force being applied from expansion. Figure 3.13 shows the end of the follow-through from an overhead view. In this view, the archer has continued to focus on the LAN 2 around behind him through expansion, release, and follow-through. In this final position of the follow-through, you should feel a strong contraction in the muscles surrounding the scapulae.

Execution is the combination of release and follow-through of the shot. The cleaner your execution, the more momentum (since momentum is directional) the arrow will have in the direction of the center of the target. Therefore, the more consistent your execution from shot to shot, the more consistent the arrow's momentum, and thus you should have better grouping.

Figure 3.13 Archer's follow-through as seen from an overhead view. Note the archer has maintained tension and direction through the follow-through.

Feedback and Evaluation

Before beginning the shot sequence for the next arrow, you must take a moment to evaluate the shot and make the necessary adjustments for the next shot. Oftentimes, inexperienced archers base their feedback on the location of the arrow without first considering how the shot and execution felt. If you can keep your focus on the process of the shot during the execution, release, and follow-through, you will be more able to evaluate each shot based on what you did rather than on where the arrow landed in the target. The best archers often know where their arrows will go before they hit the target because they are focused on the feel of the shot. Through hours and hours of training, they are able to perceive the subtle difference in the feel of each shot and the outcome it will create on the target.

The general shot cycle outlined in this chapter provides you with the information necessary to have a consistent, organized shot process, which provides the foundation for a mental shot sequence. Although the main steps are the same for everyone, each archer is unique and has individual differences in his or her body shape and structure, making him or her look slightly different when completing the shooting process. Some archers might be more flexible and have a more open stance. Other archers might have a wider distance between their shoulders and a setup that is much farther back than someone with more narrow shoulders. Some archers might have a longer or shorter neck, thus affecting the height and angle of their drawing elbow at full draw. The next three chapters contain specific examples of these types of differences. The concepts are the key, and the entire process is designed around the concept of holding.

Recurve Shooting: Setting Up

KiSik Lee

This chapter focuses on the finer details of the shot cycle that set up the shot specifically for recurve archery. The farther a recurve bow is drawn back, the heavier the draw weight will be, differing from the mechanical advantage that a compound bow provides. Recurve archery and compound archery have slightly different rules regarding the supporting equipment that is allowed. For example, recurve bows cannot use mechanical releases, peep sights, or magnified sighting apertures, whereas compound bows can. These rules account for many of the differences between recurve archery and compound archery. Setting up for a compound bow is covered in chapter 7.

This chapter covers the steps of the shot process that relate to drawing the bow back with the proper bone alignment using the larger muscles of your back, thus creating a solid foundation These steps include stance, posture, hook, grip, set, and setup.

KEY CONCEPTS OF SETTING UP FOR RECURVE ARCHERY

Before I dive into the step-by-step explanation of the shot cycle for recurve archery, you must understand certain concepts and definitions. Holding, barrel of the gun, upper and middle trapezius and the LAN 2 area, and angular and linear motion are concepts discussed in chapter 3. This chapter goes into further detail about what these concepts mean and how to apply them to recurve archery. These concepts are important for you to understand because they lay the foundation for the shot cycle.

Holding

Holding is defined as the feeling of your body braced within the bow at full draw (see chapter 3). Correctly aligned, your bones are able to withstand the force of the bow, allowing you to rely on bone alignment rather than on muscle strength. The result is that you feel a full-body connection from the tip of your drawing elbow, through the middle and lower trapezius around the scapula, through the bow-arm triceps, to the pressure point of the grip. This chapter and chapters 5 and 6 discuss this feeling of holding that is created from having the correct bone alignment. Figure 4.1 shows the force of the bow on the archer.

Because holding is the most important concept of the shot cycle, you must learn it as soon as possible because it is the foundation of the shot process. One of the best ways to learn holding is to perform the Squeeze Drill (see chapter 3).

Figure 4.1 The forces of the bow pulling the archer's draw side forward while pushing the archer's bow side back. To resist these forces, the archer must feel braced inside the bow, as the line with end caps displays.

Setting the Barrel of the Gun

In the shot cycle for recurve archery, the barrel of the gun refers to the bone alignment from your bow-hand wrist, through your bow shoulder, to your drawing shoulder (see figure 3.8 on page 36). This body alignment should be a straight line for optimal stability and strength and is set from the rotation of your torso at the setup position. Do not make the mistake of trying to achieve this alignment by rolling your shoulder in. To create bone-on-bone alignment on your bow shoulder, the head of your humerus must remain in the glenoid socket. Rotating your shoulder in moves the head of your humerus out of the glenoid socket and prevents bone-on-bone contact, meaning you have to rely on your shoulder muscles to maintain your bow arm. With each shot, your muscles become more and more fatigued, resulting in your bow shoulder raising and difficulty in expanding through the clicker.

Identifying the Trapezius and the LAN 2 Area

The trapezius connects the neck and spine to the scapulae and plays a major role in how the scapulae move. Activating the upper trapezius causes your shoulders and scapulae to raise, and activating the middle trapezius causes your scapulae to come together toward your spine. Activating the lower trapezius causes your scapulae to rotate downward. It is important for you to use your lower and middle trapezius to keep your shoulders down in conjunction with your scapulae, which helps create the bone-to-bone alignment needed to create the barrel of the gun.

Although the LAN 2 area is described in chapter 3, it is important to explore this term and its effect in more detail. The LAN 2 is the area just behind your drawing upper arm (see figure 4.2). Focusing on the LAN 2 area throughout the shot process allows your scapula, upper arm, and elbow to move together as a unit. Focusing on only the scapula might not move the arm and shoulder unit together. The same holds true if you focus on only the drawing elbow because you might not move the scapula. Notice in the picture that the LAN 2 is on the triceps about where the sleeve on a short sleeve shirt would end (see figure 4.2).

Figure 4.2 The location of the LAN 2; note that it is on the triceps, and approximately located at the end of the sleeve on a short sleeve shirt.

Achieving Angular and Linear Motion

Linear motion is movement that is directed in a straight line at a constant speed. In shooting a bow, linear motion refers to the movement of drawing and executing the shot so that the bow is drawn with the arrow directly in line with the center of the target from the beginning of the shot and the string is moving at the same speed throughout the shot cycle to release. In contrast angular motion refers to movement around a fixed point. In archery this means that the drawing motion and execution are around an axis of rotation, the spine.

Now that I have reviewed the major concepts that create the foundation for the recurve shot cycle in more depth, I can explain the finer details of the shot cycle. Shooting is a three dimensional process, and I examine the steps from several angles to give a full representation of the biomechanics of the shot process.

ESTABLISHING PROPER STANCE

The basics of the stance are first mentioned in chapter 3. Your stance and hip, chest, and head positions work together to create the correct posture and foundation to shoot the bow. The stance is the first part of this unit and is very important in creating a solid foundation, which directly affects your posture. Although posture is part of the set position, I cover it here because it is integral to your stance. A correct stance positions your body correctly and provides a solid base for angular motion and for shooting with back tension (see figure 4.3).

An open stance is necessary to create a torsionally stable base and prepares your body for angular movement. If you are right-handed, your feet should be about shoulder-width apart and almost parallel to each other but not parallel to the shooting line. Your front foot, the foot closer to the target, is rotated about 30 to 40 percent toward the target, and your back foot is typically rotated 15 to 30 percent toward the target. The ball of your back foot should be on the target line, and the toe of your front foot should be just to the left of the target line. In the beginning you might have a tendency to rotate your back foot away from the target. It is very important to be aware of this foot rotation because it will cause your hips to rotate out of alignment.

The target line is the line formed on the ground from the shadow of the arrow while you are at holding. The target line should be positioned from the ball of your back foot directly to the center of the target. This line should be in the same direction of the arrow as seen from an overhead perspective once you are at full draw and have reached holding. Your stance, posture, and head position have the greatest effect on where your target line rests. If you have too much weight on your heels, the target line will be over your heels, resulting in an arched back. If you are too hunched over, the target line will be over your toes.

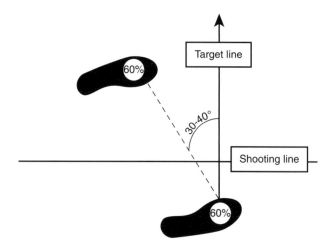

Figure 4.3 Correct stance, which forms a solid foundation for the shot, including angular motion and the ability to shoot with back tension.

Your flexibility determines how much of an open stance you can comfortably use. If you try to use a stance that is too open, you might have difficulty setting the barrel of the gun. However, the more open you can stand, the more back tension you will feel leading up to and at holding. Experiment with your stance to find the optimal amount of openness for you.

The weight on your feet should be distributed 60 to 70 percent on the balls and 30 to 40 percent on the heels. Despite the weight distribution on each foot, the entire sole of your foot should contact the ground. Your weight should be evenly distributed between your front foot and back foot, and your feet should feel as though they are gripping the ground. Bringing your chest cavity down toward your abdomen and slightly tightening your lower abdominal muscles naturally creates the 60/40 ratio of balance on your feet.

You must maintain a slight amount of tension in your lower abdomen throughout the shot to keep your back flat and chest down. However, in Western culture, people are taught to "stand tall" and arch their backs from an early age. Arching your back puts the majority of your weight on the heels of your feet. In addition, your legs should be straight and relaxed, but your knees should not be locked or bent. Locking your knees can restrict the blood flow through your legs. Your brain in turn receives less oxygen, which can cause you to faint.

Your hips and torso play an important role in creating a solid foundation. Your hips should be tucked in to create a flat back, yet must stay in the same alignment and direction as your feet are in. From an overhead view, your hips are directly above your feet. Avoid pushing your front hip toward the target.

Keep your hips in line with the 30-degree offset of your feet. At setup position, twist at the torso, just above your waist and below your rib cage, causing your chest to rotate and bringing your shoulders in line to create bone-to-bone alignment. This twisting motion connects you to the ground, creates a rigid center section in your body, and allows you to set the bone alignment of the barrel of the gun at setup position.

Creating the correct stance and posture is extremely important and must not be overlooked. Without the correct stance and posture, your ability to take holding is limited, and you will not use the correct back muscles throughout the shot. To improve your stance and posture try standing on two two-by-six-inch boards so that only the balls of your feet and your toes are on the boards. Shooting on these boards helps you develop the strength and stability to keep the 60/40 weight distribution on your feet. Or you can do the Posture Drill, described in chapter 8. Video is also an effective tool to help you maintain the correct stance and posture. A common error you might make is to rotate your hips away from the target throughout the shot process. Video feedback can help you recognize when and to what degree you are losing your hip position.

HOOKING THE STRING AND GRIPPING THE BOW

After the stance, nock the arrow (see chapter 3). The next step of the recurve shot cycle involves setting your drawing-hand hook on the string and placing your bow hand on the grip of the bow. Hooking and gripping the bow are very important steps because the hook and grip are the two main places where your hands contact the bow and they provide control over the direction of the arrow. Hooking and gripping must be a conscious activity for every shot in competition and training, even when the action becomes subconscious and second nature to you. In competition, it is easy for your hands to feel different, thus making it very important to visually check that they are set correctly each time.

Setting the Hook

Setting the hook properly is key to having a good release and execution and consists of setting the string in the correct location and having the correct finger pressure and correct thumb, little finger, and wrist positions. The correct hook also prevents possible injury and gives you a firm yet relaxed method of holding onto the string. As mentioned before, you must visually set the hook each time to increase its consistency.

Placing the fingers of your drawing hand in the correct location on the string is the first step in creating a proper hook. The string should rest just before the first joint of your index finger, just behind the first joint of your middle finger, and just before the first joint of your ring finger (see figure 4.4). Once at the full-draw position, you should have about 50 percent of the pressure of the string on your middle finger, 35 to 40 percent on your index finger, and 10 to 15 percent on your ring finger. However, because of the string angle at set position, you need to feel the majority of pressure on your index finger. The angle of the string changes from being straight (see figure 4.5) to being angled on the top and bottom (see figure 4.6) once you pull the bow back. Although the string angle changes, you must maintain the placement of the string on your fingers.

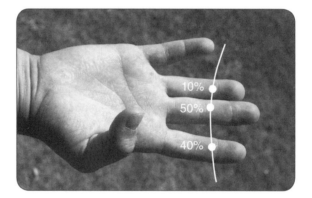

Figure 4.4   The string should rest on the fingers when setting the hook. The line is angled to demonstrate how the angle of the bow string changes during the shot process.

Figure 4.5   The archer places the fingers on the string in the correct location. Notice the thumb and little finger are in the correct position. The yellow arrows in this photo show the direction that the archer must pull the fingers to set the hook correctly.

Figure 4.6 The final position of the hook. Notice how much the fingers are curled around the string in the final position and how the tips of the fingers are curled upward.

If you set the string deeper on your hand and let the string slide into position, you will not keep the position of the string, resulting in a loss of back tension around your drawing-side scapula. In this situation the string always has the sensation of slipping and pushes skin in front of it, preventing a clean release. Instead, you must set the string in the correct position and then pull up with just the first joints of your fingers to create the hook. When pulling up, place the pressure and contact point of the string on the bottom of each finger, thus allowing your index finger and middle finger to create a horizontal gap, which gives the arrow enough clearance at full draw. This feels as though you are hooking the string upward to get the correct location of finger pressure. If you do not apply pressure to the bottom of your fingers and curl your fingertips up, most likely your index or middle finger will contact the arrow. This contact interferes with the flight of the arrow, and you might not be able to maintain the hook on your bottom finger because your hand twists out, away from the string.

Slightly squeezing your finger spacer with your middle and index fingers while keeping your knuckles in helps to keep the hook in the correct position throughout your shot (see figure 4.7). Keeping your drawing-hand knuckles in helps to maintain the gap created by your finger spacer throughout the shot cycle. Keeping your knuckles in also helps to keep your drawing-arm wrist slightly out, helping you to maintain back tension (see figure 4.8). If your knuckles are not kept in, you will release the string using finger and hand tension, which will prevent you from executing a clean shot using back tension.

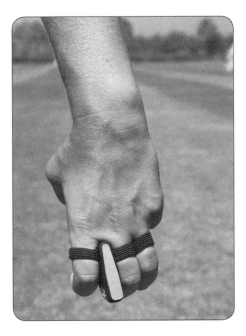

Figure 4.7 By squeezing the finger spacer and keeping the knuckles in, the hook will remain in the proper position for a clean release.

Figure 4.8 Keeping the knuckles in while squeezing the finger spacer will help the archer keep the drawing wrist out slightly and will keep the thumb and little finger back, away from the string.

Your little finger plays an important role in establishing the correct hook. Just as you pull the first joints of your fingers upward to hook the string, your little finger should also be pulled slightly upward and as far back as comfortably possible. Doing this keeps your drawing hand from rotating throughout the shot process. Your little finger, thumb, and wrist work together to create the correct wrist–forearm position. To have a clean release and execution, your forearm needs to have as little tension as possible. Placing your thumb as far back as comfortably possible while keeping your thumb bent at the first joint causes your wrist to bend out. Your thumbnail should rest on your neck when you are at anchor position (see chapter 5).

You should imagine that your forearm and wrist connection is like a "steel chain"; the connection should feel as relaxed as possible while you maintain your hook on the string. Some tension needs to be in your forearm to maintain your hook and to keep your drawing hand turned in. To get the feeling of a steel chain, you can pick up a bucket of paint or step on a stretch band, as in the Hook Drill.

HOOK DRILL

You can practice keeping your hook and the feeling of releasing the string correctly using the Hook Drill. Step on the loop of a stretch band. Notice how your wrist bends out and your thumbnail touches your thigh. This is the correct position to produce the feeling of the steel chain. You can also practice releasing the stretch band in this drill. When your wrist is in the correct position, your hand follows your upper thigh upon release (see figure 4.9); however, when your wrist is straight or broken, the follow-through is away from your thigh (see figure 4.10). Release the stretch band, alternating between your wrist out and the straight or broken wrist positions.

Figure 4.9 The correct wrist position for the Hook Drill. Notice how the wrist is slightly out. Because of the correct wrist position, once the stretch band is released, the hand slides straight up.

Figure 4.10 The incorrect wrist position and reaction upon release. In figure *a* notice how the wrist is bent in. This creates the reaction of the hand coming away from the body during the release of the stretch band, shown in figure *b*.

Gripping the Bow

After the hook and wrist are set, set the grip. The grip plays a very important role in the set process because it is the last point of influence you have on the bow as the arrow is released. Any amount of torque on the grip can cause force to be applied in a different direction, therefore taking momentum from the arrow in the direction of the center of the target. The elements of setting the grip correctly include the pressure point, hand angle, thumb position, and knuckle positioning of the fingers.

Pressure and Pivot Points

The pivot point on the grip is the deepest point of the grip. The pressure point is where the majority of the pressure from the bow hand is directed. You can see the corresponding area of the bow grip and the bow hand in figures 4.11 and 4.12.

Figure 4.11 The difference between the pivot point of the grip and the pressure point of the grip. Although the archer has contact with the pivot point of the grip, the pressure point is the location where the majority of pressure should be applied. Notice how the pressure point is to the right of center of the grip for a right-handed archer.

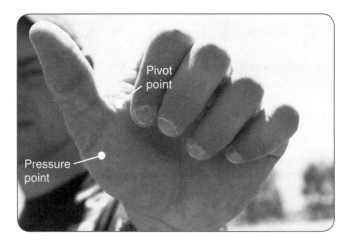

Figure 4.12 The corresponding points on the archer's bow hand.

Although the majority of pressure is applied at the pressure point, the pivot point and the web of the thumb and index fingers still maintain contact throughout the shot. To properly set your bow hand into the grip, first set the web of your hand into the pivot point of the grip (see figure 4.13a), and then set your thumb pad down to contact the pressure point (see figure 4.13b). The lifeline of your palm should be just off the left side of the grip if you are a right-handed archer. For a left-handed archer, the lifeline of the palm should be just off the right side of the grip. Your thumb should be fully extended, and the force of your thumb should be directed through the thumbprint area toward the target while your ring-finger and little-finger knuckles are pulled farther from the target. Your thumb should be closer to the target than the knuckles of your bow hand, and the knuckle of your little finger should be farther from the target than the knuckle of your index finger. Your index finger should point downward, and your remaining fingers should be relaxed and curled under.

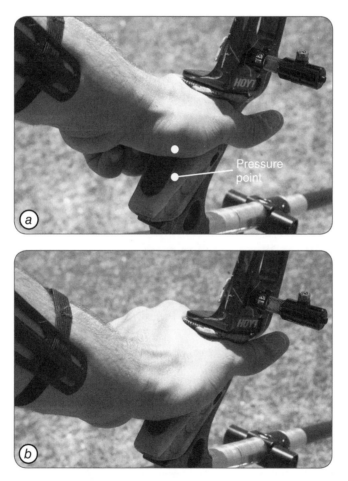

Figure 4.13 The correct method for gripping the bow: *(a)* the archer sets the pivot point into the grip and *(b)* then sets the pressure point while maintaining the direction of the center of the thumb tip to the target.

At this time pronate the elbow of your bow arm slightly so that your elbow is not facing down and is almost parallel to the ground (see figure 4.14 for an example of the correct position). The movement is centered at your elbow, and your forearm and upper arm rotate slightly, causing the head of the humerus to lock into the glenoid socket. Rolling your shoulder causes the head of the humerus to slip out of the glenoid socket and prevents bone-to-bone alignment. Your elbow should pronate only 60 to 90 degrees from the relaxed position (elbow joint pointing down). Learning to pronate the elbow can be difficult. It is important to learn this skill as soon as possible not only because of the stability the position creates but also because it will help to keep you from hitting your bow arm with the string on release.

Figure 4.14 Correct elbow rotation for the bow arm, which creates a solid bow arm and provides good clearance for the bow string.

Pitch, Yaw, and Roll of the Grip

The pitch, yaw, and roll of the grip refer to angles on three axes that affect the grip. The pitch refers to the height of the grip, the yaw refers to the palm angle of the grip, and the roll refers to the degree to which your bow-hand knuckles are rotated.

Theoretically, the higher the angle of pitch (i.e., the higher the grip angle) (see figure 4.15), the closer the pivot point and pressure point are to each other. Because the vertical distance from the pressure point to the pivot point is decreased, the result should be a more accurate bow. However, the higher grip angle also means that it will take more strength to keep the bow shoulder down while shooting; therefore, it is recommended that intermediate and beginning archers use a lower grip.

The yaw, or palm angle of the grip, is a personal preference, but the yaw should have a positive angle, meaning that the grip is inclined to the left for a right-handed archer versus declined to the left for a left-handed archer. A positive angle helps you to keep your grip from slipping and ensures proper contact of your thumb pad to the grip while you maintain pressure on the pressure point. The yaw of the grip can help you maintain the pressure point and direction of the thumbprint area to the target. The yaw should not be at so great an angle that you feel the majority of pressure on the finger side of the grip.

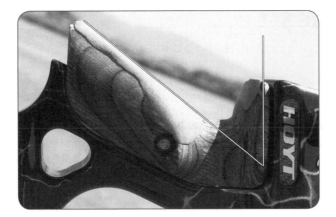

Figure 4.15 The pitch angle of the grip, commonly referred to as the grip's height.

The roll, or the degree to which your bow-hand knuckles are rotated (see figure 4.16), should be at least 45 degrees or more. If the angle is less than 45 degrees, you will have difficulty setting the pressure point and getting the knuckles of your little and ring fingers back.

Figure 4.16 A good roll angle of approximately 45 degrees.

ACHIEVING SET POSITION, POSTURE, AND MINDSET

Finally, after setting the hook and grip, you are ready to complete the set position. Set can also be described as the A spot of each shot (see figure 4.17) because it is the end of the preparation portion of the shot cycle before any major movements occur. After you set the hook and grip, look up, prepare your torso, and confirm that your stance and posture are correct. Set your head position and shoulder alignment so that your shoulder is approximately 60 to 80 percent in line with the target. Your head should sit over the ball of your back foot, thus helping to provide the 60/40 ratio of weight distribution on the balls of your feet, and must not sit over your spine, helping you to maintain a flat back and some tension in your lower abdominal muscles. It is also important that you feel a small amount of tension in the lower trapezius at the final set position.

Now that you have set the physical foundation, make the final preparations before raising the bow. Mindset refers to the final mental preparations you make prior to committing to the shot process and is the final part of the set position. Now, select the point of eye focus (i.e., location on the target at which to aim). During windy or rainy conditions, aim at a location on the target other than the center. In these weather conditions you must judge how much to aim off based on your experiences. Once you have fully committed to taking the shot, move to the setup position.

Figure 4.17 The archer is in the final set position and has finished the A spot of the shot process.

ACHIEVING THE SETUP POSITION

Setting up refers to the movements you make to achieve the setup position. Once the set and mindset are complete, raise the bow to setup position. The main goal of the setup is to set the barrel of the gun while maintaining the grip and hook positions and having your drawing scapula close to your spine. To raise the bow to setup position, initiate the movement at your bow hand. At the very beginning of raising the bow, your bow hand must raise the bow in an arcing fashion, with your bow arm extended as far away as possible from your body (see figure 4.18). Your drawing arm is merely connected to the string and is raised by this connection and not by your manually raising it or your drawing hand. Raising the bow in this manner causes the stabilizer to point up and your drawing hand to be at a lower vertical position than your bow hand at setup. As you raise up, the sight should not be in line with the target. If you are a right-handed archer, your sight should be pointed to the left of the target at the final setup position, thus preparing you for angular drawing (the position will be the opposite for a left-handed archer). You should be able to see the target slightly through the riser and string.

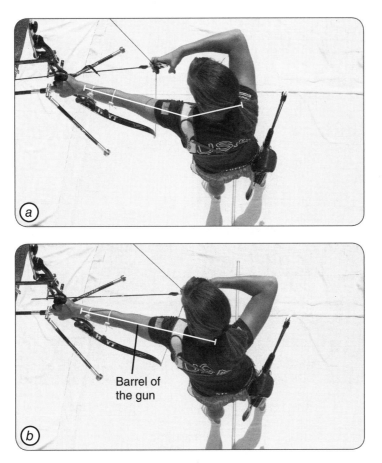

Figure 4.18 *(a)* The archer's shoulder alignment just before rotating the torso to set the barrel of the gun and *(b)* the archer's shoulder alignment and barrel of the gun set after rotating the torso above the waist.

As you raise to setup, maintain the position of your drawing forearm and wrist, and the hook and feeling of the steel chain. You should feel an increase in the tension in your lower trapezius as you rotate your chest to set the barrel of the gun. While you raise to this final setup position, take an "extra set" to create the bone alignment to achieve a perfect barrel of the gun. The extra set motion requires you to twist more at your midsection, above your waist, to get your shoulders and chest to set the barrel of the gun. Do not roll your bow shoulder forward or try to set your drawing shoulder back to set the barrel of the gun. The alignment from the pressure point of the grip through your bow shoulder to your drawing shoulder should be set from rotating only the torso away from the target. The torso rotation sets the barrel of the gun (see figure 4.18). The most important philosophy behind these steps is to create a foundation for angular drawing and loading. With angular movement, you use more efficient torque of your body's pivot point. If you are new to this setup you might have a tendency to exaggerate the position and movement. It is important to remember that the motion from set to setup should be a smooth, natural movement and not be exaggerated. If you exaggerate the motion too much, you might not be able to easily set the barrel of the gun. See figure 4.19a for an example of correctly setting the gun and figure 4.19b for an incorrect example.

Figure 4.19 *(a)* Correct setup position with the barrel of the gun set and *(b)* incorrect setup position. In the incorrect setup position, the archer does not have the barrel of the gun set because his setup position is too open and exaggerated, which will not provide him with a solid position from which to draw back the bow.

The steps of the recurve shot cycle set you up for a solid, strong foundation. Each step creates a foundation for the next step, making it particularly important to spend a great deal of time mastering each step leading to the setup position. The next chapter builds on the information in this chapter and covers the steps leading up to the execution of the shot and the motion of drawing the recurve bow in an efficient manner.

5

Recurve Shooting: Drawing the Shot

KiSik Lee

The drawing of the bow to the full draw position has a tremendous effect on which muscles you use and can greatly affect the direction in which the arrow goes after release. This chapter focuses on the most important steps and concepts of the recurve shot cycle leading up to the release of the arrow. Chapter 4 covers the steps that prepare your body for angular movement and holding. The remaining steps in the shot cycle outline the movements necessary for completing the shooting process through angular movement and executing the shot with holding. Although these steps outline the final moments leading up to the critical instant of release, it is equally important that you maintain the foundation (see chapter 4).

KEY CONCEPTS OF DRAWING FOR RECURVE ARCHERY

Before I dive into the steps of the recurve shot cycle after the setup position, you need to understand some key concepts. The first concept, maintaining the foundation, is discussed in chapter 4, but this chapter further shows how each step creates a foundation for the next step. The second concept describes the increase in muscle tension in your back throughout the shot in relation to the tension in your drawing hand.

Maintaining the Foundation

The preparation phases of the recurve shot cycle (see chapter 4) include specific tasks for you to accomplish based on specific concepts. By the time you reach the final setup position, you have set the correct hook, grip pressure point, head placement, shoulder alignment (barrel of the gun), torso twist, posture, and stance. It is important from this point on that you focus a certain amount of mental energy on maintaining these positions until the completion of the follow-through at the end of the shot.

Creating Proper Back-to-Hand Tension Ratio

Back tension refers to the activation of the lower and middle trapezius muscles in your back surrounding your scapulae (see figure 5.1). The triceps on your drawing arm and bow arm also play a key role in back tension and provide stability and a channel for connecting both arms to the back muscles. Figure 5.1 shows the lower and middle trapezius of the back, and the triceps. Notice that the drawing scapula is slightly lower than the bow-shoulder scapula. This is caused from using the lower trapezius more than other muscles to draw the bow back. This movement is most commonly felt near the bottom inside corner of your drawing scapula; however, you should always have a noticeable feeling of connection between both scapulae and the muscles between them. Back tension is a result of the correct body alignment while shooting.

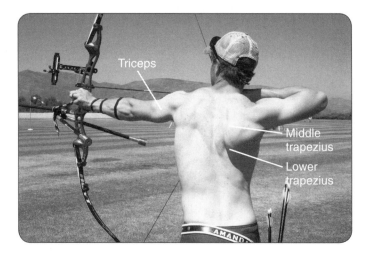

Figure 5.1 How the archer's back should look at the full-draw position. Notice that the drawing shoulder is slightly lower than the bow shoulder and the bow-shoulder triceps is tense. This picture also clearly shows the use of the lower trapezius, with the drawing-side scapula lower than the bow-side scapula.

The back-to-hand tension ratio describes the feeling of the amount of back tension and hand tension throughout the shot. During the drawing process, you should feel an increase in back tension and percentage of holding. A ratio of back-to-hand tension can accurately describe the increase in feeling braced and able to withstand the force of the bow pulling you forward throughout the shot cycle. At set position, you should feel some percentage of back tension and have about a 50/50 ratio of back-to-hand tension. At setup position you should feel a 60/40 ratio of back-to-hand tension, and at drawing/loading, an 80/20 ratio. This ratio should continue to increase throughout the rest of the shot process, and at holding, you should feel about a 90/10 ratio. Up to the point of release, you will always feel some tension in your hand to maintain the hook on the string.

Many archers believe that the biceps should relax to increase back tension. However, some biceps tension is necessary to maintain the hook on the string. Biceps tension also occurs naturally in your drawing arm because as you come to the loading and anchor positions, your upper arm and forearm come closer together, naturally activating the biceps. Your bow-arm biceps is extended but firm. Therefore, focus on the movement and not on the muscle contraction and relaxation during the shot process. The only tension you should be aware of is the connection between both your scapulae in the lower and middle trapezius and in the triceps, beginning at set position.

Now that the concepts of maintaining the foundation and the back-to-hand tension ratio have been explained, we can explore the critical steps involved in drawing the bow through expansion.

DRAWING

Drawing is the action of moving the string from setup to loading. The drawing motion of the shot process has several implications for how you shoot and directly affects the remaining steps of the shot cycle. For instance, if you begin with a linear draw movement, you will not be able to fully engage your back, you will have a difficult time achieving holding, and you will increase your chances of injuring your shoulder. The velocity at which you draw the bow and your ability to maintain your posture greatly affect the outcome of the final steps.

The drawing motion is an angular motion, centered on the focus of moving the LAN 2 area back behind you while you maintain the barrel of the gun. During the drawing motion you must maintain a 50/50 balance between your bow-arm and drawing-arm sides of your body. This balance is created by increasing the tension in your bow-arm triceps while drawing the bow with your LAN 2 area. Drawing with the LAN 2 area means that you are focused on moving your LAN 2 area behind you (down the shooting line), from setup to loading. Try not to tighten or squeeze your LAN 2, but just simply move it. In figure 5.2, the archer's focus is on moving the LAN 2 area to the left. The arrow shows the direction the archer is trying to move the LAN 2 area, from setup, as shown in figure 5.2a, to loading, as shown in figure 5.2b. By moving the LAN 2 area in

Figure 5.2 Archer at the setup position. *(a)* The dot shows the LAN 2 area, and the arrow shows in which direction the archer should move the LAN 2 area, from setup to loading. This focus causes the elbow to become almost completely in line with the arrow. Notice that the elbow is to the right of the body. *(b)* The archer is at the loading position. Notice now the position of the elbow in relation to the body.

this manner, the archer's elbow easily comes into alignment, as indicated by the dots. This is different from focusing on drawing your elbow directly away from the target.

When you reach loading position correctly, your drawing-side latissimus dorsi will rotate around to the back side. However, do not tighten this muscle; the muscle is simply a good reference point for whether you are moving correctly. You must maintain your grip pressure point, hook pressure point, and drawing-wrist position throughout the drawing phase. Although from an overhead view at setup position your draw hand is to the right of the line to the target if you are a right-handed archer (and to the left of the line for a left-handed archer), the angular drawing of your shoulder unit causes your draw hand to come in close to your neck in a straight line, from the setup position. From a profile view, the motion of your drawing hand is slightly down; however, it is critical that you keep your forearm level during the drawing/loading process. In figure 5.3, the archer draws her hand just below the chin level while maintaining a level drawing forearm.

You must also maintain your body posture and head position during the drawing motion. You might have a natural tendency to lean back to move your center of gravity to between your feet; however, your center of gravity for your entire system should remain around your front foot (see figure 5.4) because of the weight of the bow and stabilizers, which are extended away from your body. To prevent leaning back, increase the tension in your bow-arm triceps throughout the drawing process to create a balance between the front half and the back half of the shot.

Leaning back while drawing is a good sign you are drawing back linearly. The Posture Drill, described in chapter 8, is an effective way to learn to keep your head still during drawing. You can also train by pulling a stretch band or lightweight bow on a balance disc. Once you can comfortably control the position of your head while drawing with the lightweight bow or stretch band, you can start to use your normal bow. You can also gain coordination and body control within a short time by pulling the bow or using a stretch band in front of a mirror.

Figure 5.3 The correct direction and movement from setup to loading, from a side view. It is important that the archer does not draw more than one inch below the chin at loading and that he maintains a level drawing forearm.

Figure 5.4 The archer maintains his posture by keeping his center of gravity and the mass of the bow just around his front foot. The second line shows that the center of forces acting on the bow must remain at the spine to provide balance. By creating the proper balance, the archer can maintain his posture.

LOADING

Loading occurs at the end of the drawing motion and is the final position of the drawing process. As you draw to the loading position, your back-to-hand tension ratio increases from 60/40 to 80/20. At the loading position your drawing elbow should be in line with the arrow line, and your body should feel as though it is at full draw before anchoring. Your body will feel as though it has almost reached full holding.

During the end of the drawing action, continue to load the lower trapezius around your drawing-side scapula. As mentioned before, when observed in profile, this movement appears as a straight line to approximately one inch below your chin. From an overhead view, the motion is seen as drawing from outside the target line in an almost straight line to your neck. Your total focus is on feeling your body in line with the arrow line while maintaining the barrel of the gun. If your posture and head position are maintained, the string touching the corner of your chin and your drawing thumb and little finger touching your neck at the sternocleidomastoid can be excellent secondary references. Although your drawing scapula moves closer to your spine during loading, you must maintain total focus on moving your LAN 2 angularly.

You will feel a majority of the braced percentage of holding taking place at the end of loading. This feeling is where your lower trapezius meets the lower left-hand corner of your drawing-side scapula if you are a right-handed archer. For a left-handed archer, the feeling will be noticed where the lower trapezius meets the lower right hand corner of your drawing-side scapula. In other words, you will feel the tension where your lower trapezius connects to your drawing scapula (see figure 5.5). Just feel the tension at this point and do not try to lower your scapula or draw with your scapula, which will cause you to break the barrel of the gun.

Figure 5.5 The area of the lower trapezius in which the archer should feel tension through the shot process.

At the end of drawing/loading, your drawing velocity slows down as you prepare to change to a lower gear and direction at anchor. As the string comes into contact with the front of the corner of your chin, it should touch the same point of contact as the string at anchor position. You must maintain the position of your thumb, little finger, and wrist on your drawing hand. Maintaining the hook and position of your wrist is essential for a clean release. Resist the urge to drop your bow hand as you load (see figure 5.6). Dropping your bow hand at loading means you will have to raise the sight from below the target after transfer when aiming. Raising the sight from below the target in the next steps causes you to fight against gravity, making aiming more difficult. Dropping the bow hand at loading, and having to raise the sight from below the target during subsequent steps, causes you to lean back or your bow shoulder to raise, in effect causing you to lose the barrel of the gun.

Figure 5.6 The straight line indicates the correct pathway for your drawing hand to the loading position. The curved line is the incorrect pathway of your drawing hand and indicates a common mistake. Drawing incorrectly in the arcing manner will cause you to lose tension in your lower trapezius.

Loading means you are essentially increasing your back tension and preparing your body for holding. A coach can test you at loading to see whether you are loading correctly. Once in the loading position, you should be able to maintain the position comfortably for 10 to 15 seconds without coming to anchor. Although you would not normally do this during the shot cycle, it is a good exercise to improve your power and feeling at loading. Loading properly is a concept that takes time to master. Here are some of the highlights of correct loading:

- Feeling an increase in the back-to-hand tension ratio from 60/40 to 80/20.
- Feeling the tension in the lower trapezius near the bottom corner of your scapula.
- Loading position is when your drawing hand is approximately one inch below your jaw, the string is touching the front corner of your chin, your drawing forearm and wrist are maintained in position and level to the ground, and you have maintained the barrel of the gun.
- At the final loading position, you should feel braced enough to take an ever so slight pause to switch gears and direction for anchoring.

The following are a few common examples of incorrect loading:

- Dropping your bow hand and arm several inches, causing the sight to dip below the center of the target.
- Drawing to your chin directly or drawing to your chin directly and then loading by drawing directly down to the loading position.
- Loading by drawing more than one inch below your chin (see figure 5.7).
- Lowering your rear scapula too much, causing a low drawing shoulder and thus breaking the barrel of the gun (see figure 5.8).

Figure 5.7 An archer loading too low with the drawing hand while at the same time dropping the bow hand. Drawing too low at loading causes the archer to feel excess tension in the shoulder and could cause some impingement issues in the shoulder joint. Dropping the bow hand during loading also causes the sight to dip below the center of the target and the archer to break the horizontal plane of the barrel of the gun, causing him to have to fight against gravity to raise the sight to the center of the target.

Figure 5.8 Loss of horizontal shoulder alignment due to lowering the drawing scapula so much that the drawing shoulder is lowered and the bow-arm shoulder raises up, causing the archer to lose the horizontal alignment of the barrel of the gun.

ANCHORING

Anchoring is the process of raising your drawing hand and forearm from loading position to underneath your jawbone, with the string firmly contacting just the front of the corner of your chin. The physical location of the string and your drawing hand is an important detail, but maintaining your drawing scapula's position from the loading position is the key. During the drawing/loading phase, your focus is on moving the LAN 2 area, but then, from loading to anchor, your focus must shift to maintaining your scapula position and feeling an increase in your back tension. Physically, you must raise your drawing hand to firmly contact underneath your jawbone. During this motion, if you maintain your scapula position, your elbow should move slightly up and back around (see figure 5.9). This motion is called angular anchoring and should be initiated at your drawing hand and forearm and not at your elbow. Your total focus must remain on maintaining your scapula position and increasing the back tension on your drawing side, causing the intensity in the lower and middle trapezius to slightly increase during the anchoring process. In contrast linear anchoring causes you to lose back tension while you move from loading to anchor position. When you anchor linearly, your elbow raises straight up or even comes forward, and back tension is lost. Usually linear anchoring is caused when you raise your elbow up first to move your hand to the anchor position.

Now that the action of moving from the loading position to the anchor position has been described, we can examine the details related to the physical anchor position. You must consider many details when you reach the anchor position, such as string position on your face, hand position, and head position and angle. Each of these aspects plays an important role in making you as biomechanically strong as possible and in preventing interference upon release.

Figure 5.9 The archer maintaining the scapula position while transitioning from the loading position to the anchor position. Focus must be maintained on keeping the scapula position and lower trapezius tension.

Anchor Point

The anchor point is defined by the string's firm contact with your chin, just in front of the corner of your chin, and the firm contact of the second joint of the knuckle of the index finger of your drawing hand with the underside of the jaw. Your thumb should be in firm contact with your neck either on top of or just behind the sternocleidomastoid (the large muscle in your neck). Depending on the length of your hand, you might be able to fit your thumb behind the sternocleidomastoid (see figure 5.10). The pad of your little finger should also touch your neck either on or behind the sternocleidomastoid (see figure 5.11a), and your little finger should maintain its upward pull, set at the beginning of the shot (see figure 5.11b). However, anchoring with your thumb behind the sternocleidomastoid might not be necessary for you. If you have shorter hands and fingers and longer jawlines, you might not be able to anchor with your thumb behind the sternocleidomastoid. You will still be able to get a solid anchor in front of the sternocleidomastoid. If you anchor in front of the sternocleidomastoid, it is still important for your thumb to touch your neck firmly and for your little finger to touch your neck because they provide solid reference points. If you have very short fingers you might need to touch your thumb and little finger together to provide a good reference, but your thumb should still firmly contact your neck. However, touching your thumb and little finger together should be avoided because this finger position causes the back of your hand to round slightly and adds extra tension to the back of your drawing hand.

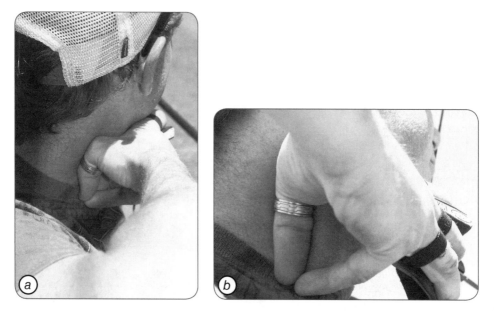

Figure 5.10 An archer anchoring with the sternocleidomastoid. The thumb behind the sternocleidomastoid provides a very solid anchor point.

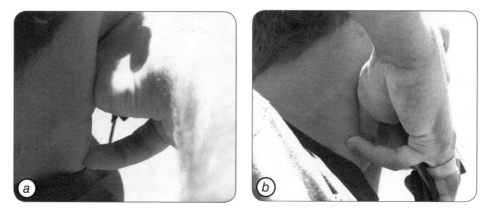

Figure 5.11 An archer anchoring in front of the sternocleidomastoid and still maintaining a very solid anchor. Notice the thumb and little finger contact in both photos.

The string's contact with your chin should fully compress the skin, creating a string-to-bone contact on your chin. The string's contact should be so firm that you can see a line on your chin after each shot but not so firm that the skin is broken or damaged. The string should also contact the center of your nose. The degree to which the string touches your nose depends on your facial structure and on the length of the bow. A longer bow creates a flatter string angle, and the string-to-bone contact on your chin is more firm, whereas a shorter bow has a sharper angle, and the string might contact your nose less firmly.

Head Position

Your head should slightly turn out, caused from your chest and the barrel of the gun being angled slightly to the right of the target if you are a right-handed archer, and angled slightly to the left of the target for a left-handed archer. From a rear view, your head should sit over the ball of your back foot (see figure 5.12), helping to provide the 60/40 ratio of weight distribution on the balls of your feet and also providing a solid jaw location to anchor under. Your head should be tilted ever so slightly toward the string, which would be to your right if you are a right-handed archer (see figure 5.13), and to your left if you are a left-handed archer. If your head is turned too far away from the string, your irises will be at the corners of your eyes (see figure 5.14). Keeping your head turned too far away does not provide an aggressive enough stance and body posture.

Figure 5.12 The archer's head is in the correct position. The line shows that the archer's head is positioned out from the neck over the ball of the back foot.

Figure 5.13 Both archers' heads are angled slightly toward the string. The circles highlight the placement of the string, which is slightly to the left of center from the reader's point of view.

Figure 5.14 The head should be turned toward the target so that the irises are close to the center of the eye openings. In this photo, the irises are too far to the edge of the eye openings, and thus the stance is less aggressive and neurological strength is decreased.

TRANSFERRING CORRECTLY

Holding is the most important step in the shot cycle, but to reach the optimal level of holding, you must shift any unnecessary tension from your drawing hand and forearm to your back muscles. Shift this tension by making a definite movement with your drawing-shoulder unit by focusing on moving the LAN 2 area back (behind you) and not by focusing on relaxing the biceps of your drawing arm or by focusing on moving your shoulder. From an overhead view the LAN 2 area moves directly behind you, down the shooting line. From a rear view, your drawing elbow and the LAN 2 moves slightly down and to the left in a straight line if you are a right-handed archer (see figure 5.15), and slightly down and to the right for a right-handed archer. From a front view, your drawing elbow should not extend directly away from the target during transfer, and from a rear view (viewing your back from the shooting line) your drawing-side scapula should move slightly closer to your spine during transfer. Transfer should be a visible yet subtle movement, with your LAN 2 and elbow not moving more than half an inch.

During transfer, maintain the length of the barrel of the gun and do not extend the barrel of the gun. The transfer causes you to increase back tension and the ratio of back tension to drawing-hand tension to approximately 90/10. It is highly critical that you maintain your hook position and finger pressure on the string. Any loss of finger pressure results in a loss of control and back tension. At this point you are mentally committed to take the shot.

Figure 5.15 Direction of transfer from behind the archer. Notice that in this photo the LAN 2 and elbow moves slightly down and back along the same plane as the upper draw arm at full draw.

TRANSFER DRILL

Transfer can be improved through the Transfer Drill, using a lightweight bow. To perform the Transfer Drill, go through all the steps of the shot cycle up to anchor. When you are ready to transfer, transfer half an inch down and back to holding position and then let up some and return to the anchor position. From the anchor position, transfer half an inch, then let up that half inch back to anchor position. Repeat this sequence three to seven times before setting down. This drill helps you to gain more confidence in the feeling of the transfer in the correct direction.

HOLDING

You know from chapter 4 that holding is defined as the feeling of your body braced within the bow at full draw. Once you have transferred and feel braced inside the bow, you have achieved the correct bone alignment to support the weight of the bow at full draw. During holding, your bone alignment allows the overall intensity of the shooting process to decrease, but the tension of the back muscles is increased. You are able to mentally and physically settle at this point, and your heart rate should slightly decrease. You should feel completely connected with the front and back half of the shot, meaning you feel the muscles in the lower and middle trapezius connected on both sides of your spine (see figure 5.16). The term *holding* might be misleading because you aren't actually stopping your movement. Although you should take a brief moment (less than one second) to feel braced, do not physically stop expanding, a concept we'll cover in the next section on expansion. In essence you have switched to a lower gear, which creates internal angular movement. Holding is the B position of the shot cycle and is the goal of the first half of the shot process for recurve archery.

Figure 5.16 The holding connection describes the feeling of being completely braced from the front half of the body to the drawing side of the body. The archer feels strong from the pressure point through the bow-arm triceps, through both scapulae, and through the LAN 2 area.

I cannot stress enough that holding is the most important concept and feeling of the shot cycle. To improve your ability to feel and take holding, you must practice holding. Holding can be felt and practiced using three different drills. The first is the Squeeze Drill (see chapter 3). The Holding and Structure Specific Physical Training (SPT) Drills also allow you to feel this braced feeling. Both drills are described in more detail in chapter 8.

EXPANDING THROUGH THE CLICKER

You are now in position to execute the shot using back tension. Angular expansion is an invisible movement made in the same direction as transfer; however, expansion is a much slower movement and should occur naturally. Expansion should not take more than three seconds. The more consistently you expand, the more consistent your arrow's momentum becomes.

Expansion occurs as your LAN 2 area continues to move in the same direction as transfer but at a much slower and steadier rate. You must maintain a 50/50 balance between the tension in the front half of your bow-arm triceps and the forces of the back half. During expansion the barrel of the gun must remain the same length and in the same direction, which is a major difference between angular expansion and linear expansion.

Because expansion is an angular movement, a very small amount of movement creates a longer linear movement of the arrow. At holding, the tip of the arrow's point should be around a sixteenth of an inch from coming through the clicker (see figure 5.17). Less than a sixteenth of an inch of angular movement is required to expand through the clicker. In an overhead view of you expanding through the clicker, the distance between your LAN 2 and bow hand decreases through expansion. A good example of rotational ratio of movement is a typical golf swing. The golf swing is created by rotation of the golfer's chest and not by a movement of the golfer's arms. A very small rotation of the golfer's chest creates a very large movement of the golf club's head. Of course, this distance is

Figure 5.17 Correct position for the clicker at the beginning of the holding step. With a sixteenth of an inch or less to expand, the archer is almost completely still, and expansion is barely perceptible.

much greater in golf than the distance from the hook to the LAN 2 in archery, but the golf swing still serves as a good example.

The C spot refers to the feeling and final position after follow-through of the drawing LAN 2 and the barrel of the gun, and the feeling of the connection in your middle and lower trapezius (see figure 5.18). Place your focus during expansion on the feeling of the C spot, but instead of focusing on each aspect of the C spot, focus on the overall feeling of those elements in the final position, which creates natural expansion.

Focus during expansion can easily be related to a sprinter running a race. As the sprinter nears the finish line, he is not merely focused on reaching the finish line but is instead focused on running through the finish line to about 10 meters past it. This holds true for most sports and is the reason follow-through is so important. In archery, follow-through is a continuation of expansion and is accomplished by focusing on the feeling of the finished follow-through position.

If you are a beginner or intermediate-level archer just learning the steps of the shot cycle, you might need to spend some time manually training yourself to focus on expansion. Expansion should be a slow, controlled movement, requiring you to develop the correct type of muscles for this action. Slow, controlled movements are performed by slow-twitch muscle fibers. You can develop this muscle fiber type through practicing slow, controlled expansion for longer periods of time than for the normal two to three seconds. The Flexibility SPT Drill, described in more detail in chapter 8, is an effective way to build slow-twitch muscle fibers and to develop the control you need during expansion. The drill requires that you expand for 10 to 12 seconds after taking holding and set down, and then repeat this action every minute for 10 to 30 minutes.

The steps of the recurve shot cycle that are described in chapter 4 prepare the body to draw the bow with angular motion through focusing on the LAN 2. This chapter focuses on drawing the recurve bow with angular motion and preparing you to execute the shot correctly at the critical instance of release. The rhythm and focus of these steps can be closely compared to the steps a bicyclist might use to climb a steep hill. In the

Figure 5.18 The C spot is the goal of the shot after achieving holding and is the focus during the expansion phase.

beginning the cyclist is on flat ground preparing to gain as much speed as possible before meeting the hill. Just before hitting the hill the cyclist is at his highest gear and fastest speed (drawing). Once the cyclist begins climbing the hill, he switches to a lower gear and begins to climb slower (loading to anchor). As the cyclist continues up the hill and begins to cross over the peak, he prepares to focus on getting over the peak completely (transfer/holding). Once he is over the peak he can focus on going past the finish line (expansion and follow-through).

These are the steps of the recurve shot cycle that prepare your body for the critical moment of truth, the execution. These steps prepare your body to make a clean, consistent execution. Chapter 6 covers the details of the execution and follow-through of the recurve shot cycle.

6

Recurve Shooting: Completing the Shot

KiSik Lee

In recurve archery, although your fingers are protected by a finger tab, they control the bow string unlike in compound archery, in which you traditionally use a release aid. Because of this difference, key differences exist between the execution phase of recurve shooting and that of compound shooting. The execution phase of the shot is especially important in recurve archery because the release must happen subconsciously for you to release the string as naturally as possible. This chapter looks at the details of the release and follow-through of the execution of the shot for recurve shooting based on the recurve shot cycle and also provides examples of how to apply the recurve shot process to different body types.

During some steps of the shot cycle, several actions must occur simultaneously, and this chapter provides insight into how to put all the steps and actions together. For example, during expansion you are also aiming with the sight aperture and maintaining the string alignment, processes very specific to recurve archery. During the entire shot process you are also performing a consistent breathing cycle, and during the release and follow-through you are not only finishing the shot on your drawing side but on your bow-arm side as well. This chapter also considers how the rhythm and velocity of motion throughout the shot ties into recurve archery.

KEY CONCEPTS OF COMPLETING THE SHOT FOR RECURVE ARCHERY

Before I introduce the details of the aiming process, release, and follow-through, it is important to look at some key concepts in more detail. After you set the barrel of the gun, several movements occur, and it is especially important to look at what should happen with the barrel of the gun through the execution. It is also important to examine how the breathing cycle is connected to the recurve shot cycle.

Barrel of the Gun Length

The purpose of the barrel of the gun has been explained in previous chapters. At setup the barrel of the gun provides your body with a stable platform for angular drawing. Once you achieve anchor and transfer, the barrel of the gun provides the bone alignment necessary for your body to take holding. Studies on biomechanics in archery at the University of Florida have shown that for some of the best archers in the world using the shot process described in this book, the barrel of the gun does not increase in length during the holding, expansion, and execution of the shot. In fact, during the follow-through (discussed later in this chapter), the barrel of the gun increases less than an inch. Some of this increase is due to the force of the bow going forward. Therefore, it is very important that you picture the barrel of the gun remaining the same length throughout all the phases of the shot process.

Breathing Cycle

The breathing cycle of the shot process is altogether another dimension of shooting. If you fail to breathe correctly yet complete all the physical steps of the recurve shot cycle, you will have a very difficult time executing a clean shot. Breathing is also an important process of the shooting cycle because it helps provide your muscles with the correct amount of oxygen throughout the shot process.

During the shot cycle, you should never reach your minimum or maximum lung capacity. Instead your breathing should be relaxed and natural; deep breathing should not be required during the shooting process. Prior to the shot cycle, you might need to take a few deep breaths to relax, but you should not inhale or exhale deeply during the shooting cycle.

At set position your breathing is slow and natural. As you raise up to setup, inhale about three-quarters of your lung's capacity and then exhale about half of the amount you inhaled. During the drawing process, inhale, and just before anchor/transfer, exhale slightly. After transfer, when you have achieved holding, hold your breath. You must hold your breath during holding, expansion, release, and follow-through. After you have reached the C spot, begin to breathe again. This is another important reason the holding/expansion phase of the shot should not take more than three seconds (see chapter 5).

AIMING

Most elite-level archers say that aiming in the traditional sense is not as important as the technical aspects of archery. Again, holding is the most important part of the shooting process; however, string alignment and eye focus are also very important aspects of the shot cycle. Aiming and setting the string alignment incorrectly can have a great effect on your shooting.

Aiming in the traditional sense refers to getting your sight set on the center of the target. However, with some trial and error, you will see that aiming in this way can be a complicated task, especially while maintaining and executing steps of the shot cycle. Because the aperture is much closer to your eyes than the target is, your eyes will either focus on the target or on the aperture. Your natural tendency might be to aim by focusing on the aperture and not on the target. This focus, however, is incorrect because you will lose the point of direction to the target and oftentimes become consumed with trying to control the movement of the aperture, which might lead to your taking too much time to execute the shot (more than three seconds after holding). The aperture will float slightly regardless of how steady you can hold.

Instead, resist the urge to control the aperture and set and maintain eye focus on the specific point on the target that you wish to hit, the point of eye focus. Pick this point at set/mindset position but do not actually focus your eyes on only that point until you have reached holding. Setting and maintaining your eye focus on a specific point on the target allows you to aim more naturally while you maintain the optimal timing and rhythm for the shot. The sight will move and float around, but maintain a determined eye focus as if you were staring through the point of focus. With time and training, your mind will automatically synchronize the sight aperture with the point of focus at the point of execution and send the arrow to the center of the target.

You can test this concept by picking an object, or "target," to aim at across the room. Shift your eye focus to the tip of your thumb and try to place your thumb over the object. After you have successfully placed your thumb over the object, try to aim with just your eye focus on the target instead of focusing on your thumb. Now, try to place your thumb over the target by just focusing on the target. Focusing on the target happens very naturally and is easier than focusing your eyes on your thumb.

Furthermore, both of your eyes should remain open during the entire shooting cycle, and the irises of your eyes should be close to the center of your eye openings. If your head is turned too far away from the target, the irises will be in the corners of your eyes, which will not provide optimal eye focus. Keeping both eyes open also helps you relax your facial muscles and focus on the target and not on the aperture. Sunglasses also help to keep your eyes relaxed and are a good tool to use when shooting. Not only do sunglasses hide the emotion of your eyes from competitors, but the frame and lenses also give you a reference as to whether your head is not turned enough toward the target. If your head is turned too far away from the target, you will not be able to shoot in sunglasses with the correct string alignment.

String alignment, or string blur, refers to the unfocused shadow of the string in relation to the sight and target while at full draw. While at anchor, the string is very close to your face; however, your eyes are focused on the target, and just like with the sight, the string is out of focus, creating a shadow or blur. The alignment of the string shadow with the sight aperture is very important and is the closest reference to a peep sight or rear sight. If you are right-handed the string shadow should sit just on the right edge of the round aperture where the aperture meets the threads of the aperture bolt (see figure 6.1); for a left-handed archer, the string shadow should sit just on the left edge.

Figure 6.1 The string alignment during holding and aiming for a right-handed archer. The blurry line of the string crosses where the circle of the aperture meets the threads of the sight pin.

This is the point closest to the center of the bow that does not cover the aperture. You do not need to observe and maintain the string shadow until you have reached holding position. At holding, the string shadow should remain in this position throughout expansion. Changing the string alignment during expansion or from shot to shot can cause the arrows to inconsistently hit in a left and right pattern on the target.

Depending on your degree of eye dominance, you might see two sight apertures while keeping your point of eye focus. If you are a right-handed archer, focus with your right eye and aim with the left sight aperture (see figure 6.2). If you are a left-handed archer aim with the right aperture over the point of focus (see figure 6.3).

Figure 6.2 The sight aperture should be out of focus, whereas the target should be focused from your point of view. Aiming in this manner allows you to maintain eye focus on the target and not on the aperture.

Figure 6.3 It is recommended to keep both eyes open for recurve shooting. This figure shows why you might see two sight pins depending on your degree of eye dominance. If you are a right-handed archer, use your left sight if you see two sight apertures while shooting. For the left-handed archer, use the right sight if two apertures are visible.

RELEASING THE STRING

Once you have expanded through the clicker, let go of the string. Letting go should be totally subconscious and happens naturally once you slightly relax the flexor muscles in your forearm. Once your flexor muscles have relaxed slightly, the string begins to go forward and around your fingertips. The movement of the string around your fingertips creates the beginning of the oscillation of the string (see figure 6.4). The cleaner the release, the less oscillation the string has, which results in less flexing of the arrow. You do not need to manually open your fingers but simply to picture the string going through your fingers. During this time, maintain expansion to the end of the shot. Although you are not consciously focused on releasing the string, you are focused on one specific thought during the execution, finishing the shot to the C spot (see chapter 5).

Maintain the length and line of the barrel of the gun through release. To maintain the barrel of the gun, release your bow grip while simultaneously releasing the string (see figure 6.5). Release the bow grip by flipping your bow hand straight down so that your bow-hand index finger points straight down while you maintain the space between

Figure 6.4 The string leaves your fingers when you release it. The string does not travel in a straight line or oscillate from side to side.

Figure 6.5 Synchronized release of your drawing hand and your bow grip.

your thumb and index finger. This movement must be straight down and not out toward the target. To do this movement, focus on the final position of your bow hand, with your index finger pointing down at the end of follow-through. Releasing the bow grip helps you maintain the length of the barrel of the gun. It is especially important to synchronize your bow-hand release with your drawing-hand release. Mimetics is the act of imitating the physical shot process in archery. Mimetics in front of a mirror without using a stretch band is an excellent method to imitate and practice this technique. Once you become more comfortable with the synchronization, you can develop this skill with stretch-band shooting.

At first, you will have to practice this movement consciously, but over time it will become more and more subconscious as you incorporate this feeling into the C spot feeling and focus. The C spot is the final position of your drawing arm LAN 2 area and scapula and your bow-arm pressure point at the end of follow-through (see chapter 5). You should feel as though your body is completely connected, from your drawing arm LAN 2, through the muscles in your lower trapezius around both scapulae, through your bow arm LAN 2, and all the way to your bow-hand pressure point. Focusing on this feeling allows you to subconsciously release the bow while maintaining expansion to the end of follow-through.

FOLLOW-THROUGH

As mentioned before, holding is the most important step of the shot cycle. Not only does holding allow you to be completely braced but also to execute the shot with back tension every time. The moment of release is the critical instant of the shot, and the smallest mistake during that fraction of a second can cause the arrow to miss the center of the target. Follow-through in essence is the continuation of the tension and direction of expansion and holding through the critical instant of release. Follow-through is not only a reaction of the sudden loss of force from the bow pulling you forward, but it is also a continuation of expansion. In theory, expansion and aiming, and follow-through are essentially the same step, and release is a subconscious action that happens during expansion. However, because of the changes in force on you created from the string leaving your fingers, these steps are actually different, which is why during expansion it is best to focus on only the feeling of the C spot. The final position should be the farthest you can expand naturally without causing discomfort (see figure 6.6).

It is easy to relate the final follow-through position to the final distance a sprinter runs. Even though a 100-meter sprinter is timed at 100 meters, the sprinter is actually focused on running well past the 100-meter mark. If the sprinter focuses on running only to the 100-meter mark, he will slow down before reaching the finish line and be passed by other runners. For you to put the maximum amount of energy into the arrow each shot, you must focus on expanding to the end of the follow-through and not just to the point the clicker goes off.

If you recall, the shot cycle is based on angular, not linear, motion. As described before, a true linear motion for archery means that your stabilizer and arrow point directly to the target through the entire shot process and your drawing hand pulls the string directly to your face (in a straight line with the target). In other words it is very similar to your aiming the entire time. The resulting follow-through for a linear shooting motion is that your drawing elbow goes straight back from the target and your drawing scapula moves away from your spine. This movement is referred to as releasing the bow

Figure 6.6 Your elbow should continue in the same plane as your upper arm is in at full draw during follow-through, which is typically down and back behind you.

with your hands (see figure 6.7). Angular motion in contrast means that your stabilizer is not pointing directly to the target at setup and the drawing motion and execution are centered around an axis of rotation. Angular follow-through causes your drawing elbow to continue around you in the direction of the shooting line behind you. Notice in the picture that the elbow follows an arc because of the existence of a center of revolution (see figure 6.8).

Figure 6.7 A typical linear release in which the drawing elbow is almost in a straight line from the target. This is a clear indication of pulling from the target as opposed to expanding angularly.

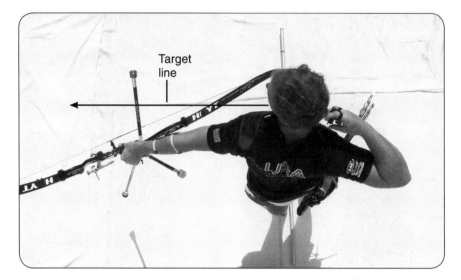

Figure 6.8 Correct follow-through position seen from overhead. Notice how the elbow is not in a straight line to the target and is in fact behind the archer.

Angular Motion and the Recurve Archer

Angular motion is described in previous chapters but it is important to revisit the topic. To paint a complete three dimensional picture of the motions described in the National Training System, the shot cycle must be explained in several different points of view. Overhead, back profile, and front profile views have been explained in detail. The observing angle from behind your draw elbow also helps to understand the correct movements of your body during the shot cycle.

From set to setup position your elbow raises up and then comes closer to your body as you take an extra set, resulting from your body's twisting at the abdominals to set the barrel of the gun. From setup through drawing/loading your elbow continues to come closer to your body in a slightly downward angle because you are drawing angularly and loading your lower and middle trapezius while drawing approximately one inch below your chin.

During anchoring, your elbow raises slightly; however, if you maintain the scapula position, your elbow will also move slightly back as a result of the angular anchoring. After anchoring, transfer in the same plane as the drawing upper arm (at anchor), allowing you to increase back tension. This movement is small but noticeable and is at most half an inch. You then feel the braced holding feeling.

Then naturally begin to expand while focusing on the C spot, the final position of the follow-through. During this focus, the tension and direction of the C spot should continue in the same angle as the angle of the transfer and your upper drawing arm.

COMPLETING THE PICTURE

The rhythm of the entire shot cycle is dependent on the rate of velocity for each step. The velocity of these steps plays an important role in finishing the action phases of the shot cycle. The more consistent your rhythm, or timing, for each shot, the more consistent the shot is. The consistency of your timing at holding and expansion is the most important aspect in putting a consistent amount and direction of momentum into the arrow. However, the timing of the steps prior to holding plays an important role in allowing you to have enough energy and oxygen to complete the shot cycle.

The movement from set to setup position must be controlled and natural. As a beginner or intermediate-level archer, you probably need to pause slightly at setup position; however, over time, as an expert archer, you will simply change your pace and switch gears at setup and not necessarily need to make a definite stop.

Drawing requires you to move the force from a slightly paused position (setup position) to another phase and position (loading). Because you are drawing the bow a great distance while the draw weight of the bow increases, you need a considerable amount of momentum to draw the bow to the loading position. A higher velocity of drawing motion allows you to get to the holding position more quickly. After loading, move to an anchoring position. In doing so you must maintain control of the scapula position. Because this movement must be more controlled than loading, switch gears and slow down. At transfer, switch gears again and move more gradually. This is also a slow movement because you must control the direction of transfer. After transfer, you can settle slightly because your bone alignment reduces your energy expenditure. Once you reach the holding position your bone-on-bone alignment greatly reduces your energy expenditure. As you begin expansion, your movement must be even slower and more controlled than the steps before it because you are maintaining the braced feeling created from your stabilizing muscles. Physiologically, your antagonist muscles (triceps) keep the bow braced while your agonist muscles (lower and middle trapezius) create the expansion. The follow-through is then a continuation of the expansion and a reaction to the sudden loss of the force of the string.

After you take holding, the expansion, release, and follow-through should take between one to three seconds total. Overall, the timing of the entire shot should not be more than 15 seconds; however, if you are a beginner archer, you might not be able to do this immediately. If you are a new or intermediate archer, learning the steps of the shot cycle might take you some time before you are able to complete all steps in this amount of time. The most important aspect to the rhythm of a shot is that the time after holding should be only one to three seconds. Holding longer than three seconds fatigues your muscles much more quickly and reduces your overall performance.

If you are a beginner or intermediate-level archer just learning the shot cycle, you will take longer to complete the shot cycle than is recommended. As you become more familiar and coordinated with the shot cycle, the length of time you take to complete the shot cycle decreases. If you are an advanced archer, see table 6.1, which lists the ideal time for each step in the recurve shot cycle. Please note that holding, expansion, and aiming have been combined in this table because holding continues through aiming and expansion.

You might notice differences between archers who use the shot cycle. For example, some archers with wide shoulders might set up farther back, whereas archers with narrow shoulders might set up more forward. Both positions are correct, but because

Table 6.1 Step Times for Recurve Shot Cycle

Step	Time in seconds
Stance	1-2
Nocking the arrow	1-2
Hooking and gripping	3
Set position and mindset	1-2
Setup	12
Drawing	1
Loading	0.5
Anchoring	1-1.5
Transfer	0.5
Holding, expansion, aiming	2-3
Release and follow-through	1
Evaluation	2-3

of the archers' individual body types, each has a different setup position. Some archers with long necks might have a higher drawing elbow at full draw than archers with short necks. Although the elbow positions are different, both are biomechanically correct. Because of flexibility, archers might vary in the degree to which their stances are open. The manner in which an archer raises from set to setup position might vary for each as well. Some of these differences exist because of personal preferences. In these instances, the most important thing to consider is the concept and not the details.

Your rhythm from shot to shot also plays an important role in consistency. Because feeling is such an important part of the shot process, the sooner you shoot the next arrow, the easier it is to replicate your first shot. Ideally, if each shot feels the same, you should be consistent. Decreasing the amount of time between shots also reduces the time you have to think, thus benefiting you mentally by putting less pressure on you. However, this does not mean that you must shoot six arrows in a row quickly with no rest. The rhythm of the entire end is up to your personal feelings, physical endurance, and mental state.

The weather is also a factor in determining your strategy for the end rhythm. For example, on very windy days, most likely you will have to shoot at a faster pace than you would on a less windy day, and you might have to vary the time between shots because of wind gusts. In this scenario, you need to develop a strategy to execute the shot consistently in the wind. If you do not adjust your rhythm for each shot and vary your time between shots, the wind gusts could cause you to make several mistakes. In this situation, wait for lulls in the wind and then enter into your shot process. Depending on the frequency of the wind gusts, increase the rhythm of each shot by increasing the speed of each step of the shot process to execute the shot before the wind gusts. The most important aspect to consider in dealing with the end rhythm is that you try to replicate that rhythm as much as possible. See the sidebar "Mastering Wind Shooting," for more information on this subject.

You should also have other contingency rhythm strategies for various situations such as rain, team rounds, and finals rounds. In rainy weather, decrease your exposure to the rain as much as possible. Not only is this important to keep you healthy so you can

Mastering Wind Shooting

Most of the time in outdoor shooting, wind will be blowing. When this is the case, you must select your point of eye focus (where to aim off of the center) so that the arrow drifts to the center of the target. It is critical that you maintain your eye focus on the point of eye focus after reaching holding, through follow-through, until the arrow has hit the target. Especially when it is windy, losing your eye focus to watch the arrow's impact can cause your body to slightly shift at the moment of execution and cause the wind to carry the arrow even more than it should have. Your gut instinct of where to aim off in windy conditions is usually fairly accurate. However, use the wind flag, wind sock, and surrounding trees to your advantage when taking the wind force into account. It is also very helpful to think of the gust of wind as movement of waves. In other words The wind blows very hard at some points, and then usually immediately afterward, the wind gusts calm down slightly before the next gust. This is a prime time to shoot, and it is highly recommended to feel the wind and shoot at the moment of the lightest wind as long as you stay within the time limit. The time limit for rounds depends on the type of competition. For example, for outdoor World Archery qualification rounds, you must shoot six arrows in a four-minute time limit, and for elimination matches, you have two minutes to shoot three arrows.

Sometimes you might have to shoot in extremely heavy wind. In this situation, make sure you shoot a strongly executed shot; otherwise the wind will carry the arrow. Aiming close in the general area and executing a strong shot yields better results more consistently than focusing too much on aiming and executing a weaker shot, especially for recurve archery.

perform at your best, but it also allows you to keep your finger tab as dry as possible. The finger tab is made of leather, and once the leather begins to absorb water, it stretches and causes you to lose your feeling of the tab and might change the tune of the bow.

In team and finals rounds you have less time than in qualification scoring rounds to complete each shot. This is another scenario for which you have to develop a modified strategy. In team rounds your team, comprised of you and two other archers, is given two minutes to shoot six arrows (two arrows each), and only one of you is allowed to shoot at a time. This leaves you with an average of only 20 seconds per arrow to step onto the line from the one-meter line (one meter behind the shooting line), pull your arrow out of the quiver, nock the arrow, and complete the shot. In finals rounds, you and another archer alternate shooting arrows and have a maximum of 20 seconds to complete each shot. The fast pace of both of these rounds requires that you be prepared for a quicker rhythm.

All the steps of the recurve shot cycle have been explained in detail. Now it is up to you to learn those steps and become proficient in the specific technical skills for recurve archery. The most important thing to consider is that the pictures and definitions explain concepts. The concepts are the key, and the application of those concepts might look slightly different for you based on your physical structure, age, and strength.

For you to become highly skilled in the steps that make up the shot cycle, it is extremely important that you very deliberately practice and train. Deliberate practice means that you consciously focus on the actions of the shot and try to accomplish specific technical goals at each training session. This type of mental focus separates training from merely practicing without direction. As you become more comfortable with the steps of the recurve shot cycle, picture the steps as part of a continuous shot process that continues from one shot to the next. With correct training and mental focus you will become comfortable with all of the steps of the recurve shot cycle.

7

Compound Shooting: Setting Up and Completing the Shot

Mel Nichols

In this chapter I discuss setting up and completing the shot for compound shooting. There are many ways to shoot a compound bow, but the way I discuss works well and helps prevent injury caused from using bad form. You will see some differences from recurve form as outlined in previous chapters, but compound form uses basically the same muscles and movements.

Before I go into compound setup and completing the shot, however, I want discuss the main differences in compound and recurve bows. The greatest difference between them is that compound bows have cams, which allow them to have a draw weight of 60 pounds but for which you hold only a percentage because of cam let off. Another difference is that recurve bows are shot with your fingers and most compound bows are shot with releases. A compound bow can be shot with your fingers, but shooting with a release is more accurate. In compound target archery the rules allow you to use peep sights, which are not allowed in recurve target archery. Peep sights give you an advantage over the recurve archer when aiming. Peep sights allow you to center your scopes or pins, giving you a more consistent aiming spot. Recurve archers do not have peep sights with which to aim, so they have to use the anchor point, making a consistent anchor very important to a recurve archer. You on the other hand need good anchor points, but with the use of peep sights, you can use floating anchors. Both compound and recurve archers need to get the best anchors they can. Compound bows are considered easier to learn to shoot compared to recurve bows. This is because during the shot with a recurve, the archer must hold the full draw weight of the bow, and the recurve bow, released with fingers, is less forgiving than the compound. I like compound shooting because I can get results much faster than when I shoot a recurve bow.

The steps I discuss as part of setting up for compound shooting are stance and posture, and mindset. Stance and posture make up the foundation of the shot. A solid stance and proper posture brace your body for the draw cycle and shot. A good mindset keeps you focused on the process of the shot and helps you achieve an accurate and strong shot.

STANCE AND POSTURE

Before you start the shot you need to have proper footing to establish the foundation of the shot and keep you in good balance. Set your upper-body position before you start drawing the bow. Open your lower body and hips at the same angle to the target as your feet. Your upper body needs to be in line with the target and your head, in a natural position. Your head should be as straight to the target as possible. The stance and posture are the foundation of a good shot.

Stance

The stance is one of the most important components of your shot because it sets the foundation and is the first thing you address when you step up to the shooting line. There are three types of stances: straight, open, and closed. In the straight stance your feet are parallel to the target line (see figure 7.1a). Imagine a line going from the shooting line to the target and put your toes on the edge of the line. I try never to shoot a straight stance because it is less stable than the open stance. Your front foot is slightly forward of the target line, and your rear foot is still on the line in a closed stance (see figure 7.1b). In the open stance your front foot is slightly behind the target line, about four to five inches (~10–13 cm) (see figure 7.1c). In an open stance you should feel a backward twist in your body when you draw the bow. A slightly open stance gives you the most stability during the shot. An open stance is how I like to see every shot set up. Keeping your waist open and aligning your shoulders to the target creates a little pressure in the core of your body and gives you the strongest body position for your shot.

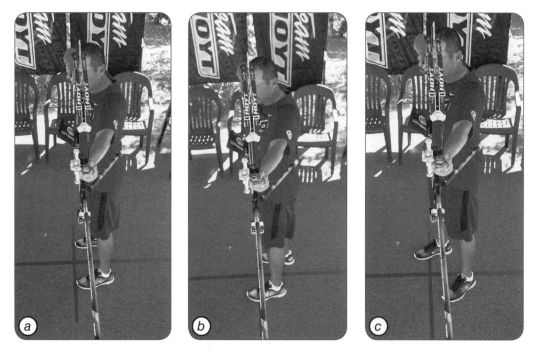

Figure 7.1 Stances for compound shooting: *(a)* straight, *(b)* closed, and *(c)* open.

Stand on the shooting line in a relaxed manner, with your feet about shoulder-width apart. An open stance gives you more stability and control in unfavorable conditions such as wind and also gives you more string clearance if you hit your arm during your shot. Very rarely will you get your shoulders in full alignment with the target because this is how the open stance allows for string clearance. In other words, by keeping your shoulders slightly open to the target, while still preserving solid upper body alignment, you will allow the string of the compound bow to clear the chest and shoulder area. Your rear foot is closed and parallel to the shooting line. Your front foot is open from the center to the heel of your rear foot, at about a 45-degree angle. Distribute your weight evenly on both feet, with at least 60 percent of your weight forward toward the balls of your feet, keeping your knees slightly bent and relaxed, not locked.

Pay attention to how you set your stance on the line and try to duplicate the same stance each time, ensuring that you maintain consistency at the beginning of your shot cycle each time you step up to the shooting line. A good training tool to help you get the correct weight distribution on your feet and the correct posture is the stability disc. These discs are 14 inches (~35.5 cm) in diameter and about three inches (~7.5 cm) thick. They are filled with air so that when you stand on them the air moves around. The idea is to stand on the stability disc (one per foot) and keep as still as possible in the proper stance. Doing this a few times before each training session gives you a better feeling of your stance, which helps you with the foundation of your shot. The idea is to tighten the core of your body and reduce any excess movement.

Posture

Like the stance, the correct position of your upper body, or posture, keeps you stable. Maintaining good posture is critical in the development of the proper shot sequence.

Keep your upper body in a tall and straight position, and anchor your body into the ground by keeping your back flat. A slight pelvic tilt helps keep your back flat. You should have a solid feeling in your chest. Imagine yourself anchoring your chest to the ground with an imaginary chain going through your body. Keep your waist even with your feet and twist with your upper body. See figure 7.2 for an example of the proper upper-body position.

Figure 7.2 Archer assuming the proper upper-body position.

Keeping your back as straight as possible is the key to helping you execute a strong shot. Keep your shoulders and neck as relaxed as possible, without any tension. When I talk about shoulder position just remember, the lower, the better. Any movement in your shoulder should be a pivot motion and not a lifting motion. This one movement has the most effect on your shot. Keeping your shoulder down allows your shot to go off naturally and in a good rhythm. A low shoulder helps you move through the shot cycle in a more controlled manner. Practice setting the proper upper-body position with a stretch band and a mirror before every practice session.

Head Position

Your head position is crucial to your shot. Set your head before you start the shot process. Eliminate excess head movement, which can cause added tension in your neck. Keep your head in a relaxed and neutral position, centered over your spine (see figure 7.3). Proper posture lessens the likelihood of fatigue while shooting. Do not tilt your head to the left or right, or tilt it forward or backward. Keep your head as straight as possible while looking toward the target. When you draw your bow, bring the string to the tip of your nose, allowing you to have a clear picture through your peep sight. You might have to adjust your anchor slightly to maintain the proper head position.

Figure 7.3 Archer's head is positioned directly over the spine.

PELVIS TILT DRILL

The most important part of the stance is a solid body anchor. What I mean by solid body anchor is that you feel as if you are anchoring yourself to the ground. An effective drill to help create a solid body anchor is to perform a slight pelvis tilt when standing tall. Just rotate your hips backward while maintaining a tall body position. You should feel your glutes pinching together.

WAIST TWIST DRILL

A good way to get a feeling of anchoring yourself to the ground with your stance is to stand on the shooting line in an open stance. Twist at your waist and get in shooting position, with your shoulder parallel to the target. Have someone push on your upper shoulder and upper back to see whether you can maintain the stance without moving your feet. Now do the same test with your feet parallel to the target. Notice that it is more difficult to maintain the stance and your balance. This test shows why an open stance works well, especially in the wind.

HEAD MOVEMENT DRILL

Check for excess head movement by standing ready to take a shot and having someone place a cup of water about three-quarters full on your head (see figure 7.4). Then draw your bow. Keeping the cup on your head throughout the shot process indicates you most likely have a good head position. This exercise provides instant feedback and is a fun game to play in a group.

Figure 7.4 A cup of water is placed on the archer's head. This demonstrates the Head Movement Drill—a fun way to determine if the correct head position is being used.

Shoulder Position

Proper shoulder position is important to maintaining the proper alignment for your shot. Your shoulders should be parallel to the ground and kept as low as possible to allow you to get a better bone-on-bone contact and help prevent injury (see figure 7.5). You should feel like you are holding your shoulders down. Maintain this low shoulder position during the drawing process and the shot; this position removes stress from your shoulder muscles and allows your shot to be much stronger. Leaning your shoulders back can be caused from shooting too much poundage, lengthening the draw and making it difficult to get the shot off. Keep your shoulder and bow arm (discussed in the next section) in as straight a line as possible to your anchor point (see figure 7.6).

Figure 7.5 Proper shoulder alignment is critical. Keep the shoulders parallel to the ground and as low as possible, without "forcing" the shoulders down.

Figure 7.6 The straight line from the archer's anchor point to the bow shoulder and bow arm demonstrates proper upper-body alignment.

ARM RAISE DRILL

Stand in front of a mirror and raise both arms straight out toward the mirror. Keep a close eye on the top of your shoulders to make sure they do not raise up. Keep raising and lowering your arms; each time you raise your arms move them apart a few inches so that after about six or seven raises, your arms are out to your sides. Now notice the position of your bow shoulder. This position should be the bow-shoulder position during your shot cycle. With your release hand still out to your side, bend your elbow and touch your hand to the front side of your shoulder and go to your anchor position. This movement puts your draw arm in the same position it is in when you shoot. Take note of your shoulder position and try to get this feeling every time you take a shot.

Bow-Arm Position

The difference between holding steady and moving all over the target is the strength of your bow arm. When lifting your bow, keep your arm fully extended and your shoulder as low as possible (see figure 7.7, *a* and *b*). Your arm pivots up at your shoulder joint, like it is on a hinge. Keep your lats and triceps tight to keep your bow arm in a strong position. Keeping the lats and triceps tight also keeps your elbow in a vertical position to the ground and allows you adequate string clearance.

Figure 7.7   The "hinging" motion used to raise the bow allows the archer to maintain a proper shoulder position and correct posture while raising the bow.

If your bow string hits your arm, rotate your elbow in an outward direction, putting your elbow in a more vertical position to the ground. You should clear your arm if you are shooting the correct draw length. Remember to keep your shoulder low and relaxed and to pivot at the joint. Do not grip the bow tightly to create a strong bow arm because tightly gripping the bow actually makes your bow-arm weaker. Your grip should always feel relaxed; keep your bow arm strong by keeping your triceps tight. A low shoulder and tight triceps are the key to a strong bow arm.

SET: HOOK AND GRIP

The hook and grip, as in recurve shooting, refer to the two main points of contact between the archer and the bow: where the release is hooked onto the string and where the bow hand makes contact with the grip. Here, we'll review the correct procedures for each position.

Hook

Hooking means attaching a release aid to the string. Recurve archers attach their fingers to the string with a piece of cordovan placed between the string and their hands. Some compound archers shoot with their fingers, but most shoot with release aids.

There are three types of releases for a compound bow: trigger (see figure 7.8a), thumb (see figure 7.8b), and back tension (see figure 7.8c). The setup of all three of these releases is similar. A key to a good release is to keep the back of your hand flat so that it's in a strong and neutral position. Do not grip the release as if you were making a fist. Hold the release with just enough tension in your finger that the release does not slip out of your hand when you draw the bow.

When you set up using a trigger release, lead with your elbow, taking almost all the involvement of your biceps out of the draw. Then, all you have to do is rest your finger on the trigger and use your back to make the release go off. Make sure you can feel the trigger with your finger. Triggering the release when the pin or dot is on the target creates a type of target panic because when your mind knows it has to do something, it starts anticipating it. When you put your aiming devise on the target, let your shot happen naturally. The release is supposed to be a smooth and natural motion, not a surprise action. Overall, the trigger release is an effective all-around release; it is good in windy conditions when you have to be more aggressive because your sight picture is moving around a lot. You still need to back tension the release, but you can be more aggressive.

The thumb release is set up the same way as the trigger release, the only difference being that the biceps

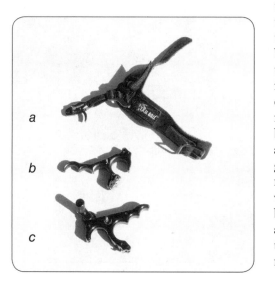

Figure 7.8 Compound bow releases: *(a)* trigger, *(b)* thumb, and *(c)* back tension.

is used because you have to hold the release with your fingers. Use just enough finger pressure to hold the release, then put your thumb on the trigger and squeeze your back until the shot goes off. If you are a right-handed shooter, visualize your right scapula moving toward your spine to squeeze your back. For left-handed archers, the left scapula will move toward the spine to squeeze the back. The trigger release is very good to use, in the sense that it gives the archer more control over the shot, but can be tricky to use in windy conditions. The thumb release is a trigger-style release. A thumb release can be shot aggressively if needed. The benefit of the thumb release is that it gives you a more controlled feeling because you have to apply pressure to the release to get it to go off.

The back tension release is my favorite. Under good shooting conditions you should know where each arrow is going to hit. Set up a back tension release by keeping your hand flat and just enough tension in your fingers to hold the release in a relaxed manner. Once you grip the release your fingers do not move; keep the same amount of tension on your fingers during the entire shot cycle. The back tension release is ideal when you do not have windy conditions. You should have a feeling of just aiming and staying into your back with this release style.

Grip

An often overlooked step in setting up is the grip position. Proper grip position is important to getting a consistent shot. An inconsistent grip can cause your arrow not to hit anywhere near your pin, even with a great shot.

The grip is one of the two points at which the bow is contacted, so it is very important. A good grip is a relaxed hand without tension, not a hand clutching the bow. You can use a finger sling to help you keep a relaxed grip (see figure 7.9). Finger slings give you the confidence of knowing you can relax your bow hand and that the sling will catch the bow on release. Using a properly set finger sling allows the bow to jump about one inch (~2.5 cm) at the shot, allowing the bow to react to the shot naturally, and catches the bow upon release, keeping it from being damaged. Finger slings also keep the bow from falling and hitting the ground at the end of your shot.

Grip the bow the same way every time; a quick visual check helps you accomplish this. Make sure the edge of your grip is not too far away from your lifeline so that you start to twist your wrist. If you set up too far away from the lifeline, you will feel like the bow could come out of your hand at any time. You will need to determine the proper pressure point which is the point of contact between the hand and the grip. A good way to find the proper pressure point is to do a push-up and feel the spot on your palm that has the most force on the ground. You should have the same feeling when the bow is at full draw.

Figure 7.9 Archer using a finger sling to help keep a relaxed grip.

COMPOUND BOW GRIP DRILL

If you have a problem gripping your bow, try this exercise with someone's help. Take off the finger sling; tell the other person you are going to shoot the bow and that she is to catch it under the stabilizer about two inches (~5 cm), which is an easy place to catch a bow. Now shoot the bow, keeping your bow hand relaxed. The bow should jump out of your bow hand. Do this for a dozen shots, then go back to using the finger sling. The idea is to get used to relaxing your bow hand. This exercise helps tighten up your groups and improves your shot.

SETUP

The first part of setup is to put a little pressure on the grip of the bow to engage your triceps; you should feel like you are extending your bow arm. Next hook the release to the string. Now lift the bow in a forward motion, making sure to keep your bow shoulder down and your triceps tight (see figure 7.10a). Your bow hand should be relaxed during the lifting of the bow. Raise your bow just above shoulder height, with your release hand following your bow hand (see figure 7.10b). Your release hand goes up only because it is connected to the bow by the string; you should not feel muscles engage in your release arm. Keep your lats tight at all times to help keep your posture straight. Lifting your bow this way helps keep your hand relaxed, takes off any pressure that might build up due to gripping the bow, and helps you stay steady when aiming.

Figure 7.10 Archer setting up by lifting the bow. Note that the bow arm extends toward the target, and the bow is lifted in a forward motion, with the shoulder low. The release hand follows the bow hand and the posture remains straight.

If aiming is an issue and your pin is floating around in a large group, keep your triceps as tight as you can. Maintain the same distance between your bow shoulder and grip hand at all times during lifting. Lifting should feel like you are pushing the bow away from you in a scooping motion (see figure 7.11a). This pushing motion is an internal feeling. Do not extend your shoulder; your arm should feel rigid. Lift your bow just high enough so that your bow hand covers the target. Do not lift your shoulder; it should be pivoting upward at the joint as if it is on a hinge. Maintain the same distance from your shoulder joint to the grip position, putting you in a good position to draw your bow (see figure 7.11b). Keep your shoulders down at all times. Your bow hand should feel connected to your body with bone-on-bone contact. Inhale a deep breath at this point. Your release hand should be about even with your nose before you draw, allowing you to draw the bow in a slightly downward motion.

Figure 7.11 The archer raises the bow in a "scooping" motion, with the draw hand following the bow hand, and the shoulders remaining low throughout.

DRAWING

Drawing is the pulling of the string back to the bow's maximum draw length. When preparing to draw the shot, your shoulders should be slightly open to the grip of your bow. When you start to draw, your rear shoulder moves in an angular direction to help set the barrel of the gun (i.e., the alignment of shoulder to shoulder to pressure point of the grip) (see figure 7.12). The barrel is in a straight line facing the target when at full draw. Your draw shoulder moves toward your back with an angular draw. A great way to get a feel for angular movement is to stand against a wall and move your draw shoulder toward the wall. Your shoulder should move the rest of your body off the wall. Now practice drawing with this same movement, and you will be using an angular draw.

You should be able to feel the muscles in the middle of your back when you draw. Pulling the bow straight back is called linear drawing. Linear drawing means drawing with your arms. It is very hard to duplicate this type of draw, and it puts a lot of stress on your shoulder muscles. An angular draw allows you to take any extra muscles out of your shot and to get to the hold position easier. Start with your release hand moving in a slightly downward angle to get your scapula in a good position (see figure 7.13). When you start drawing your bow you can slowly start exhaling. Draw with your LAN 2 area and feel your back muscles when drawing. If you do not feel your back muscles, you are probably drawing linearly and not angularly.

Figure 7.12 The bow is drawn using angular motion, which allows the archer to maintain the barrel of the gun while building back tension through the drawing process.

Figure 7.13 The release hand moves in a slightly downward angle, which helps the scapula to move into the correct position.

Keep the biceps and triceps out of your draw. Imagine yourself drawing by leading with your elbow (see figure 7.14). When you get to full draw you should feel the solid wall of the bow. The wall of the bow is defined as hitting full draw; the cables will stop on one of the smaller parts of the cam (depending on how the bow is designed). The wall should feel solid. If the wall feels spongy or soft, look at the timing of your cams. From this point on, the amount of pressure in holding the bow should increase only slightly. You should feel this slight increase of pressure until you get to transfer. The amount of pressure should never decrease because decreasing the pressure creates a soft-feeling shot. When the pressure decreases, the shot tends to take a few seconds longer, and the arrow groups get larger.

Figure 7.14 The archer draws by leading with the draw-side elbow.

ANCHORING

Anchoring happens when your scapula moves to the final position. Bring up your release hand in one smooth motion (see figure 7.15a). Where your drawing hand touches and is flat against your face is called the anchor point (see figure 7.15b). You should not have to move your hand around the side of your face to find your anchor point. If your anchor is not solid and not in the same position every time, your hand will float around the side of your face, causing inconsistent shots and large groups. A good anchor point position feels natural. But remember, everyone's face is different, so you need to find the most comfortable anchor point for you. You might need to adjust your equipment if you are having difficulty finding a comfortable anchor point. A consistent anchor results in tight arrow groups and a smooth-feeling shot.

When you hit the wall of your bow, bring it to anchor. Maintain consistent pressure on the bow when moving to anchor. Do not increase your back pressure at this point. You want a solid anchor that you can easily duplicate and be comfortable with. You should feel a little more of your back in the shot right now because of the angular anchor.

Remember a good anchor has your hand in a position against the side of your face. Make sure you get a good reference point. The jawbone is a good reference point because it is in the same position during every shot. You can get a good pressure-point feeling when you anchor in the same spot every time.

Figure 7.15 (a) Correct technique for bringing the release hand up at anchor, and (b) achieving a solid anchor point against the face.

TRANSFERRING

Transfer refers to the motion of transferring 100 percent of the draw load onto your back muscles in an angular movement. Focus on your back muscles and on moving your LAN 2 area away from you and parallel to the shooting line. The tension in your back starts to increase, and your scapula moves toward your spine. Think about the tension in your back as if your back is a piece of paper you are trying to crush in your hand. The back tension you feel is a crushing-type tension. A good feel for back tension makes the shot feel smooth and effortless.

HOLDING

Holding feels like you don't have to do anything to get your shot to go off. When holding, your alignment is perfectly straight, and your elbow is in line with the line of the arrow (see figure 7.16). Proper holding feels like the bow is working for you.

Once you are holding, start the aiming process. From this point on, your focus is on only aiming so that your shot happens subconsciously. Your aiming device (dot or pin) floats over the 10 ring, but do not try to hold the dot still on the target because doing so causes unneeded tension in your bow arm. Letting your dot or pin float feels like it is moving slowly around the 10 ring. Your holding position controls how well you aim and how smooth your shot is. When you get to proper holding it feels like you are doing nothing but aiming.

Figure 7.16 In this photo, the concept of holding is illustrated; this is the state of being in perfect alignment, with the bow working for the archer.

COMPOUND AIMING DRILL

A good exercise for aiming is to see how long you can hold on the target. Start by holding your pin or dot on the target for five seconds. Do this five times in a row without leaving the 10 ring. After you can successfully do this, hold for a few more seconds, working up to 10 seconds each try. If you can get up to 10 seconds of holding on a target without moving your pin or dot out of the 10 ring, you should be in good shape for making a shot.

EXPANSION

Expansion is the step in the shot cycle that allows your shot to go off and includes breathing. Deeply inhale and exhale before you start your execution. When you lift the bow up to draw, take a breath in and start exhaling it slowly as you draw all the way through expansion. When you get to expansion, stop exhaling. At this stage of the shot, you should have exhaled half your breath. Now stop exhaling, hold your breath, and allow your chest to expand and your bow arm to rotate at your shoulder, making your release go off. The shot should be a surprise when it goes off. Think of expansion with a back tension release, like the release is on a hinge just about to go off; all that is needed is a little more movement to get the release to go off, and the expansion of your chest is just enough to make it fire. This movement is so small, but when executed properly your arrow is likely to hit right behind the pin. You cannot see this movement, but you can feel it inside your body.

RELEASE

The release should feel like a surprise. Do not make your shot happen; just let it happen. Trust that the moment of release is a natural feeling. It's a good feeling knowing your arrow will hit right where you want it to hit. The feeling of release is a feeling of control. A good release follows your jawline back over your draw shoulder (see figure 7.17). If you have good back tension, the release goes toward your draw shoulder. Without back tension, the release comes off your anchor to the side and then moves in a backward motion. Practice the release with a stretch band that has a draw stop on it and add a string loop so you can hook a release to it. Now draw and anchor in the same way you would with a bow, and shoot the shot. This exercise gives you a good feel for your release.

Figure 7.17 Notice the direction of the release and follow through, a natural result of the back tension used to execute the shot.

FOLLOW-THROUGH

It is very important to finish with good, strong form to make the shot go off effortlessly. The reason follow-through is so important is because when you finish strong, all steps leading up to the follow-through will more likely have been good. A good archer looks like a shooting machine. Everything is smooth and effortless because you finish with good follow-through.

At follow-through, movement of your bow arm is toward the target, and movement of your release arm is away from the target (see figure 7.18). Just remember that with the expansion of your chest on release, your follow-through will be slightly toward your back on your bow hand and release hand.

Figure 7.18 The movement of the archer's bow arm is toward the target, and the movement of the release arm is away from the target. The expansion on release creates this natural follow-through.

REAFFIRMATION

After the conclusion of the shot, take a moment to reflect on its strong parts. During this time release any tension created from the shot to prepare for your next shot. Use this time to think about and take in the feeling of your shot and make any adjustments needed for your next shot. If you need to make a specific part of your shot stronger, visualize yourself executing that part of your shot flawlessly so that you are both mentally and physically ready for your next shot. Make sure everything you do or think about in the reaffirmation phase is positive and like you. For example, if you need to improve the tempo of your shot, you might say to yourself, "I have a strong five-second shot," or "It's like me to shoot my shot in five seconds." Hearing, saying, or writing something makes it more likely to happen. Protecting and building your self-image during this process helps you become a better archer. Just make sure you keep a positive attitude no matter what happened in the shot before. The only thing you can control is the process, so focus on good reinforcement.

The compound setup is the foundation of the shot. With everything in the right position you should feel confident in taking the shot, and when you shoot, you should know that you executed the best possible shot you could. If you can do this for every shot you should have good results. Focus on the process and not on the outcome. Compound bows seem fairly easy to shoot, but don't let them fool you. They magnify the mistakes you make. Try to make the same shot every time, and you will enjoy shooting a compound bow.

8

Making Practice More Effective

KiSik Lee

Chances are you have heard the phrase "Practice makes perfect." There might be some truth to this statement, but in reality, much more is involved in improving performance. This chapter focuses on all aspects of training, including SPT (specific physical training) drills and execution improvement drills and also covers warm-up routines and how to combine all training aspects to create an individual training program to improve your skill level. Also included are training drills and activities to help you develop and improve your archery skills to become a better archer and competitor. Technique, physical training, mental training, and equipment also play a key role in improving performance and are tied in with some aspects of your practice.

DEVELOPING A TRAINING PROGRAM

What is the difference between simply practicing and training in archery? Practice generally refers to repeating an action or group of steps to improve performance ability. Practice in archery means simply picking up the bow a certain number of times per week and just shooting, with no real goal. Training generally refers to a structured plan that includes a combination of meaningful practice and instruction designed to improve your performance. Training in archery means having planned, meaningful practice activities centered around instruction designed to improve specific performance objectives. Merely practicing might help you improve, but with no clear direction of where you are going, the probability that you will achieve your potential is greatly reduced. Training on the other hand allows you to continually track progress and provides direction.

Ideally for archery, the training program should be designed to improve technical skills, competition skills, and mental toughness. To be most effective, each training program should become more individualized the more advanced you become. Generally a group of beginning or intermediate archers might have the exact same training program, but as the archers progress, each will have different strengths and will need to address different areas of deficiency. Numerous studies have shown that specific, meaningful training greatly improves the probability that potential is reached. Meaningful, deliberate training means that you are consciously focused on developing specific technical and mental skills during training.

Periodized Training

Most sports scientists and studies on training suggest that a periodized training program is ideal for keeping athletes motivated and increasing athletes' ability. A periodization training program is a type of planned training program in which the year is divided into different cycles in order to vary the intensity and volume of the training. In a periodized plan, the year, called the macrocycle, is divided into several mesocycles, which can be anywhere from four to eight weeks. The mesocycles are further broken down into four to six microcycles, which are typically each a week in length. Consecutive mesocycles can create phases of the competition year, which include the off-season, precompetition, and competition phases.

This process of constantly varying the intensity and volume of training requires you to become more adaptive and helps prevent stagnation. The best athletes are usually the ones who can adapt quickly to new situations, stimuli, and pressures. The wind, the weather, the altitude, and the pressure are all different at each competition venue. The better you are able to adapt to these stimuli, the better you will perform.

Another important concept of periodization is supercompensation. After a period of training has been placed on you and you have been given a recovery period, your capacity to perform the trained skill increases slightly. Because of the recovery time, your skill supercompensates from its original performance state. Planning for recovery time is a must! Recovery time is important in keeping you healthy and injury free, and increases the probability that you will supercompensate. Recovery, even a day off or a reduced volume, allows you to bounce back and perform at a higher level.

Following are a sample mesocycle (see figure 8.1) and a sample microcycle (see figure 8.2) for a beginner archer advancing to the intermediate level who is still attending school.

Figure 8.1 Sample Preparation Phase Mesocycle for Beginner or Intermediate Archer

	Microcycle 1	Microcycle 2	Microcycle 3	Microcycle 4
Volume (number of arrows)	1,008	1,075	1,140	900
Intensity	60%	65%	70%	75%
Focus	Strength and technique	Strength and technique	Technique and mental preparation	Technique, mental preparation, and score

Figure 8.2 Sample Week 1 Microcycle for Beginner or Intermediate Archer

Time	Monday	Tuesday	Wednesday	Thursday	Friday	Saturday	Sunday
Morning	School	School				Warm-up: 20 reps of luggage strap, 20-30 reps of light bow drawing	Off
						30 Arrows blank bale	
						30 Arrows longest distance	
Afternoon (after school)						72 Arrows FITA long distances	
	Warm-up: 50-60 reps of stretch-band shooting, 30-40 reps of light bow drawing	Warm-up: 20 reps of luggage strap, 20-30 reps of light bow drawing	Warm-up: 50-60 reps of stretch-band shooting, 30-40 reps of light bow drawing	Off	Warm-up: 50-60 reps of stretch-band shooting, 30-40 reps of light bow drawing	50 Arrows personal training	
	20 Arrows Formaster	50 Arrows blank bale	50 Arrows blank bale		30 Arrows Formaster		
	70 Arrows blank bale	72 Arrows scoring	60 Arrows Gold Game		50 Arrows blank bale		
	100 Arrows Four-Minute Drill	80 Arrows distance blank bale	72 Arrows short distances		100 Arrows distance training		
SPT	Holding (20 min)	Power (20 min)	Structure (20 min)		Flexibility (20 min)	Holding (20 min)	
Volume: 1,008 arrows	190	202	182		180	254	
Physical training		Yes			Yes		

Individualized Training

Your training program must be tailored to you and your schedule. Factors that affect the look of your training program are whether you work full-time or part-time, are a student, have a family, or train full-time. Your schedule might be dependent on when training times are available at your local archery range or club and whether equipment and coaching are available. You can supplement training activities that do not include shooting, such as SPT, stretch-band shooting, and Shot Trainer (by Astra Archery) or Formaster (by Range-O-Matic) by shooting without an arrow when actual target shooting is not available.

Figures 8.3, 8.4, 8.5, and 8.6 are examples of possible individualized training programs for beginner, intermediate, advanced, and elite archers. These are just samples, and the activities, volume, and frequency will have to be adjusted for you. The sample training programs do provide an idea of the volume and intensity of training required to excel to the next level. For example, if you are an advanced-level archer you might want to increase your training to mirror that of an elite archer to develop into that level. As a beginner archer you would not start on an advanced archer's training program because this could cause severe fatigue and injury. You should consult a qualified archery coach or slowly ease into a training program if the volume and intensity of training are more than the amount you are currently doing. Notice that in the sample training programs, mental training and physical training are included in the planning process and elements of both of these types of training are included in the beginner and intermediate training programs. It is especially important to include these types of training from the beginning; they will not only affect your archery but also your life.

Also, it is important to follow several guidelines when developing a specific training program. First, planning ahead gives your coach insight into your plans. For example, will you be competing at three local competitions this month, or will you be preparing for a national or international competition? The higher the desired level of competition, the further in advance you should plan. If you are a beginner or intermediate archer you might not need to plan out a training program until a month or a couple of weeks prior to competition. However, if you are an advanced or elite archer you should plan your events and schedule a year to four years out if you are training for an event such as the Olympics.

The plan must also be adaptive. Remember that nothing ever goes as planned and it's vital that the plan not be too strict. Especially when planning far in advance, you cannot foresee exactly where you will be in your progress. Progress is rarely a steady linear increase, but instead you will experience ups and downs along the way.

You must plan for recovery time when you develop a program. The concept of supercompensation was explained previously, and supercompensation is one of the biggest mistakes most athletes make in their training when striving to reach the next level. Recovery reduces the probability of injury and allows you to increase performance. However, because archery is a "feeling" sport, it is important for you not to take more than two or three days off in a row because your fine muscles begin to lose strength and you might lose your feeling. After the completion of the competition season you can take a few weeks off to recover completely from the competition year.

Figure 8.3   Sample Beginner Training Schedule

Time	Monday	Tuesday	Wednesday	Thursday	Friday	Saturday	Sunday
Morning	Off					Warm-ups 1 and 2	
						20-30 Arrows blank bale	
						USA Archery Adult Archery Achievement scoring round	
						Cool-down	
Afternoon							Warm-ups 1 and 3
							20-30 Arrows blank bale
							30-50 Arrows distance blank bale
After school or work		Mimetics imagery (5-10 min)		Action meditation (5-10 min)			Cool-down
		Warm-ups 1 and 2		Warm-ups 1 and 3			Review weekly goals
		50-100 Arrows blank bale		30 Arrows drills	Jogging (15 min)		
		Cool-down		30-50 Arrows target shooting		Shoulder strength-ening exercises	
		Stretch-band shoot-ing at home (10-30 min)		Cool-down			
Total arrows: 250-330		100		80	70	80	
Warm-up 1	Light run, arm circles, helicopters, windmills, side stretch, hamstring and quad stretches, arm across stretch and elbow stretch, neck and wrist stretches (2 min)						
Warm-up 2	Squeeze Drill, stretch-band shooting, and light bow (10 min)						
Warm-up 3	Squeeze Drill, shooting mimetics, and form step (10 min)						
Cool-down	Jumping jacks, side stretch, hamstring and quad stretches, arm across stretch and elbow stretch, neck and wrist stretches (10 min)						

Figure 8.4 Sample Intermediate Training Schedule

Time	Monday	Tuesday	Wednesday	Thursday	Friday	Saturday	Sunday
Morning	Off					Focus training (10 min)	
						Warm-ups 1 and 2	
						50 Arrows blank bale	
						JOAD/adult achievement scoring round	Warm-ups 1 and 3
Afternoon					Video training or distance training	50 Arrows execution drills	
					Cool-down	50 Arrows blank bale	
		Review new weekly goals				50 Arrows distance blank bale	
		Mental imagery (10 min)		Action meditation (10 min)		Cool-down	
After school or work		Warm-ups 1 and 2		Warm-ups 1 and 3		Weekly training goals review	
		30 Arrows execution drills	Jogging (15 min)	30 Arrows drills	Cardio (20 min)		
		50-100 Arrows blank bale	Shoulder strengthening exercises	60 Arrows target shooting	Shoulder strengthening exercises		Basic exercise program
		Cool-down	Stretch-band shooting at home (30 min)	40 Arrows Four-Minute Drill			
				Cool-down			
Total arrows: 610		130		130		200	150
Warm-up 1	Light run, arm circles, helicopters, windmills, side stretch, hamstring and quad stretches, arm across stretch and elbow stretch, neck and wrist stretches (2 min)						
Warm-up 2	Squeeze Drill, stretch-band shooting, and light bow (10 min)						
Warm-up 3	Squeeze Drill, shooting mimetics, and form strap (10 min)						
Cool-down	Jumping jacks, side stretch, hamstring and quad stretches, arm across stretch and elbow stretch, neck and wrist stretches (10 min)						

Figure 8.5 Sample Advanced Training Schedule

Time	Monday	Tuesday	Wednesday	Thursday	Friday	Saturday	Sunday
Morning	Off					Focus training (10 min)	
						Warm-ups 1 and 2	Mental imagery (10 min)
						50 Arrows blank bale	Warm-ups 1 and 3
						50 Arrows distance training	20 Arrows execution drills
Afternoon		Review new weekly goals	Cardio (15 min)			50 Arrows video training	72 Arrows score 70 m
		Mental imagery (10 min)		Action meditation (10 min)		144 Arrows FITA scoring	50 Arrows OR Set Play training
		Warm-ups 1 and 2	Warm-ups 1 and 3	Warm-ups 1 and 2		Flexibility SPT (15 min)	Cool-down
		30 Arrows execution drills	40 Arrows blank bale	50 Arrows execution drills		Cool-down	
After school or work		30 Arrows blank bale	80 Arrows Four-Minute Drill	100 Arrows target shooting			
		100 Arrows practice FITA distances	100 Arrows aim-off training	90 Arrows Four-Minute Drill	Jogging (25 min)		Exercise bike (20 min)
		80 Arrows Four-Minute Drill	50 Arrows distance blank bale	50 Arrows personal training	Specific weight training program		Specific weight training program
		Holding SPT (20 min)	Flexibility SPT (20 min)	Pumping SPT (15 min)	Shoulder strengthening exercises		Weekly training goals review
		Cool-down	Cool-down	Cool-down			
Total arrows: 1,240		240	270	290		300	140
Warm-up 1	Light run, arm circles, helicopters, windmills, side stretch, hamstring and quad stretches, arm across and elbow stretch, neck and wrist stretches (2 min)						
Warm-up 2	Squeeze Drill, stretch-band shooting, and light bow (10 min)						
Warm-up 3	Squeeze Drill, shooting mimetics, and form step (10 min)						
Cool-down	Jumping jacks, side stretch, hamstring and quad stretches, arm across stretch and elbow stretch, neck and wrist stretches (10 min)						

Figure 8.6 Sample Elite Training Schedule

Time	Monday	Tuesday	Wednesday	Thursday	Friday	Saturday	Sunday
Morning	Off						Focus training (15 min)	
							Warm-ups 1 and 2	
							30 Arrows blank bale	Mental imagery (15 min)
							80 Arrows distance training	Warm-ups 1 and 3
Afternoon		Review new weekly goals				40 Arrows video training		20 Arrows execution drills
		Mental imagery (10 min)	Cardio (15 min)			144 Arrows FITA scoring		72 Arrows score 70 m
		Warm-ups 1 and 2	Personal mental training (10 min)	Action meditation (10 min)		Flexibility SPT (25 min)		50 Arrows OR Set Play training
		30 Arrows execution drills	Warm-ups 1 and 3	Warm-ups 1 and 2			Cool-down	Cool-down
After school or work		30 Arrows blank bale	20 Arrows blank bale	50 Arrows execution drills				
		150 Arrows practice FITA distances	144 Arrows FITA scoring	60 Arrows increased heart rate training	Jogging (25 min)			Exercise bike (20 min)
		90 Arrows Four-Minute Drill	50 Arrows aim-off training	100 Arrows Four-Minute Drill	Specific weight training program			Specific weight training program
		Cool-down	110 Arrows personal training	130 Arrows personal training	Shoulder strengthening exercises			Weekly training goals review
		Holding SPT (25 min)	Flexibility SPT (25 min)	Pumping SPT (20 min)				
		Cool-down	Cool-down	Cool-down				
Total arrows: 1,500		300	320	340	100	300	140	
Warm-up 1	Light run, arm circles, helicopters, windmills, side stretch, hamstring and quad stretches, arm across stretch and elbow stretch, neck and wrist stretches (2 min)						
Warm-up 2	Squeeze Drill, stretch-band shooting, and light bow (10 min)						
Warm-up 3	Squeeze Drill, shooting mimetics, and form strap (10 min)						
Cool-down	Jumping jacks, side stretch, hamstring and quad stretches, arm across stretch and elbow stretch, neck and wrist stretches (10 min)						

TRAINING DRILLS AND ACTIVITIES

This section outlines various types of training drills and activities that you can do to develop skills, improve scores, and prepare for competition. Many of these training drills and activities are helpful for you to do at various points in the yearly training cycle, and some might be used regularly year-round. Skill development drills aim at developing specific technical or mental skills, whereas competition preparation drills might be more difficult than the format of actually competing. All of these drills will be helpful to you at some point in your development. You can use the following levels to clarify your level of development:

- Beginner archer—shooting three to six months
- Intermediate archer—shooting six months or more
- Advanced archer—can shoot over 1,200 points in a FITA scoring round or compound
- Elite archer—can score over 1,300 points in a FITA scoring round

Warm-Up Shooting Activities

It is always best to begin the training session on the right track. After not shooting for a day or even several hours, it can be difficult to get the feeling of the shot back quickly if you go directly into training with a normal bow. You can also cause injury to your muscles if they are not properly warmed up. This section highlights a few activities you can do to warm up your muscles for shooting.

Typically it is recommended to do a combination of stretch-band, light-bow, and form-strap activities during warm-up sessions. Here is an example of a good warm-up for you to follow: On Monday, Wednesday, and Friday, do stretch-band shooting for 10 minutes at five to six repetitions per minute (50–60 total reps), followed by 10 minutes of light-bow (four–five reps per minute) or some variation of light-bow SPT. On Tuesday, Thursday, and Saturday, use the form strap for 10 minutes with two to three repetitions per minute (20–30 reps total), followed by 10 minutes of stretch-band shooting at five to six repetitions per minute (50–60 total reps) in front of a mirror.

STRETCH-BAND SHOOTING DRILL

A stretch band is a great training tool not only because it gives you the ability to warm up by pulling it back, but it can also simulate the feeling of a bow. You can draw the stretch band back and shoot it just like a bow at a fraction of the weight. If you are a beginner or intermediate archer, stretch bands are great for learning the steps of the shot cycle because they give some resistance yet not enough that you will be fatigued. You can practice drawing stretch bands and releasing them in front of a mirror to get a better idea of what your body is doing. If you are an advanced or elite archer, stretch bands are good to use between ends at competitions to help regain the feeling of the shot (see figure 8.7).

Figure 8.7 Practicing with a stretch band is an excellent way to learn new skills and to get a better feeling for the shot process.

LIGHTWEIGHT BOW TRAINING DRILL

A lightweight bow is also an excellent tool to use when warming up and is simply a bow with a very light draw weight (10–20 lb). Light bows help replicate the weight of the mass of the bow as well as the feeling of the string. Light bows can be drawn in front of a mirror without the use of an arrow so you can visually check your technique. When using a light bow, however, it is important not to dry fire the bow, which means letting go of the string without an arrow. When a bow is released, the stored energy in the bow is directed to the arrow. Releasing the string without an arrow does not allow this energy to be redirected away from the limbs, which can cause the bow to explode or break and potentially to cause injury. So it is especially important to maintain a strong hook on the string to prevent dry firing.

STATIC STRAP TRAINING DRILL

A luggage strap or Form Strap (by Easton Archery) is also a good tool to use (if you don't have access to either of these, a rope tied in a loop will also work). This kind of device is a good tool to use for isometric exercise to develop strength at a specific location in the drawing cycle or at full draw. Isometric exercise can be especially helpful in developing flexibility and strength in the LAN 2 area during the drawing phase. To use a luggage strap correctly, the strap should be set at 80 percent of your draw length, meaning that you will not quite reach the anchor position. Then go through the steps of the shot cycle until you have reached the maximum draw length of the strap (see figure 8.8). This is usually between setup position and loading. At this point, pull as hard angularly as possible. Hold this position for five to 10 seconds each time.

Figure 8.8 The archer uses a strap at approximately 80 percent of the full draw position so that the archer's hand is in front of his full draw position and not quite to the anchor position yet.

BLANK BALE

Blank bale shooting refers to shooting at a target mat without a target face, usually at a close distance (see figure 8.9). The point of this type of training is to focus on the shot cycle and improve specific steps without complicating the shooting process with aiming or the pressure of dealing with results from scoring. In essence, this type of training allows you to prepare for shooting at a target face. This is also a good warm-up after stretch-band and light-bow exercises.

Blank bale is usually shot at a distance of five meters (~16.5 ft) but can be shot at much farther distances. Your bow arm must be at a slightly higher angle to reach the longer distances, and this higher angle might make you feel uncomfortable. At longer distances your mind naturally wants to aim too hard, which increases the timing and prevents you from shooting at the right rhythm. Shooting at blank bale at distance can help you master shooting longer distances with the same feeling as you have shooting up close because you do not have the pressure of the target.

Figure 8.9 Shooting blank bale is an excellent way to practice the shot process and feeling of the shot without aiming. This allows you to focus more clearly on the technique and not on the end result of the arrow in the target face.

Execution Improvement Drills and Activities

Developing a clean execution is very important because execution plays such an important role in the direction the arrow goes. All the steps of the shot cycle are designed to allow you to execute the shot as clean as possible. The actual execution and release should be subconscious actions. There are a few activities and drills that help in developing clean execution.

EXECUTION DRILL

One drill involves using a training aid such as a Formaster (by Range-O-Matic) or the Shot Trainer (by Astra Archery). This training aid attaches the bow string to your drawing elbow (see figure 8.10). When you release, you must continue to expand and increase your back tension to resist the force of the bow and cord from pulling you forward. It can be used with or without an arrow. This type of training aid is excellent in improving reaction time of the release when using a clicker, and it is preferred to use this training aid while aiming at a target. This training aid can also be used indoors without using an arrow and is an excellent way to train when weather or time prevents outdoor target training.

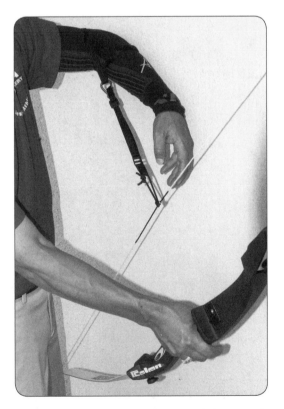

Figure 8.10 The Execution Drill utilizes a training aid that attaches the bow string to your drawing elbow. Upon release you must increase your back tension and angular follow-through to keep the force of the bow string from pulling your elbow forward.

BOW RELEASE DRILL

The Bow Release Drill teaches you how to correctly release the bow. A correct release requires you to release both the bow string and bow grip simultaneously to consistently put a constant amount and direction of momentum into each arrow and to maintain the barrel of the gun through the release. The Bow Release Drill can be practiced first without a bow or stretch band. Mimic the action of the steps of the shot cycle. At release, try to synchronize the release of your drawing hand and bow hand. Notice that your thumb and index finger are pointed straight down. After you have developed the ability to synchronize the release of your drawing hand and bow hand without using a stretch band, you can start doing the same drill with a stretch band. Next perform this drill with the bow. To perform this drill with a bow, shoot without a finger sling; have your coach catch the bow where the stabilizer connects to the riser (see figure 8.11). *Caution:* Do this drill only with a qualified coach and take all necessary precautions.

Figure 8.11 In the Bow Release Drill your coach stands slightly in front of you and catches your bow just where the stabilizer meets the bow. Then execute the shot without the finger sling on, and the coach must pay attention to the bow to catch it without letting it hit the ground.

POSTURE DRILL

The Posture Drill is excellent for helping you maintain your head position and posture throughout the shot and can be used while you are using a stretch band or shooting. To perform this drill, your coach rests her hand slightly on your head while you are going through all the steps of the shot cycle (see figure 8.12). If your coach feels your head move, he presses down firmly on your head, enough to prevent you from moving your head throughout the entire shot process for a few shots. After a few shots, your coach then presses down firmly on your head just from set to setup position. After setup your coach removes his hand to see whether you can better control your body and head. Do this drill only if you are having trouble controlling your head and posture during the shooting process.

Figure 8.12 The Posture Drill is a good way for you to develop awareness of where your head is during the shot cycle. Your coach simply applies a small amount of pressure to the top of your head throughout the shot process.

SPT DRILLS

SPT stands for *specific physical training* and is designed to improve specific skills for shooting. The most notable SPT drills are Flexibility SPT, Holding SPT, Structure SPT, and Power SPT. You can do these drills with a light bow or stretch band if you are a beginner, and if you are an intermediate to elite archer you can do these drills with your actual bow. It is highly important that you have a solid technical foundation before attempting SPT drills with your actual bow.

Flexibility SPT Drill

Flexibility SPT helps you improve execution by teaching you to continue to use back tension through expansion to follow-through. In this drill, you go through the entire shot process with an arrow at five meters (~16.5 ft) blank bale. After you take transfer and holding, expand very slowly but controlled for 10 seconds. During this time the clicker will go off, but it is important for you to continue expanding smoothly up to a quarter inch past the clicker (see figure 8.13). When the clicker clicks, maintain expansion and do not flinch. This drill allows you to control the clicker and not let the clicker control you.

Figure 8.13 Flexibility SPT requires that you continue expanding after the clicker goes off for a total of 10 seconds. Notice the point of the arrow is as much as a quarter inch past the clicker at the end of the 10 seconds.

Holding SPT Drill

Have your finger tab, arm guard, and finger sling on during this drill. Draw the bow back to the holding position without an arrow in a safe direction. Remain braced in the holding position for 15 to 45 seconds. Then take a one-minute rest between each repetition. This drill can be done for 30 minutes to one hour and can be an excellent substitute for shooting if you have limited training time. No matter your skill level, this exercise should be performed often and is usually done toward the end of training.

Structure SPT Drill

You need your finger tab, arm guard, and stretch band or lightweight bow for this drill. Draw the stretch band or lightweight bow behind your head with your hook and grip set correctly and your little finger resting on the back of your neck (see figures 8.14 and 8.15). In this position, you feel braced and completely connected. The Squeeze Drill, described in chapter 3, is also a good method for feeling this position, but this Structure SPT Drill can be substituted whenever a coach is not present to perform the Squeeze Drill with you.

Figure 8.14 The archer is preparing to draw the bow back with his drawing hand behind his head.

Figure 8.15 The archer has drawn the bow back with his drawing hand behind his head. The archer's bone alignment allows him to feel a very strong holding feeling in this position and gives the archer an idea of what holding should feel like.

Power SPT Drill

You need your finger tab, arm guard, and finger sling for this drill. Draw the bow back to the holding position (see figure 8.16a). After holding for three seconds, slowly let down to the setup position while keeping the barrel of the gun set (see figure 8.16b). Then draw back to holding again for three seconds. Repeat this action between 6 and 10 times and then rest for two minutes before beginning the next set. Do between 8 and 15 sets.

Figure 8.16 Power SPT creates power in the drawing phase of the shot. *(a)* The archer follows the steps to achieve holding and then lets up a few inches to the setup position while maintaining the barrel of the gun. *(b)* The archer then draws back to anchor to the holding position and repeats this for 6 to 10 repetitions.

COMPETITION TRAINING

In training it is a good idea to prepare yourself for the competition you will be competing in. For example, if you are a male outdoor recurve archer, you need to practice shooting FITA of 90, 70, 50, and 30 meters or, if you are female, 70, 60, 50, and 30 meters. Shooting in the same format that you will compete in helps prepare you for the competition. If you are an advanced or elite archer, there are some highly intense training days during which you might shoot as many as two or more scoring FITAs in that day. It is a good idea to practice shooting competitions and scoring in training to improve your competition performances.

DISTANCE SHOOTING
(100 METERS/80 METERS)

The longest distance you shoot is usually your most difficult distance. The longest distance is usually the distance that you can make the greatest percentage of points in your competition. Shooting a longer distance than the distance you will compete at is a good way to improve your longest distance shooting. For example, in a FITA round, if you are a male the longest distance you will shoot is 90 meters and if you are a female, 70 meters. Male archers can train at 100 meters, and female archers can train at 80 meters. By spending some time doing this, you will begin to feel more comfortable at your longest distance.

FOUR-MINUTE DRILL

The Four-Minute Drill requires you to shoot 10 to 12 arrows each end within a four-minute time limit. If you are an intermediate or advanced archer, this very physically intense drill is excellent for trying to make it to the next level. It also requires that you spend very little time at holding/aiming. This drill is also a good way for you to increase your rhythm and endurance while focusing on executing good shots. During this drill, you must execute the shot within two to three seconds, or you will fatigue very quickly.

GOLD GAME

As previously mentioned, some drills are designed to be harder than the format of competition, and the Gold Game is one such drill. Gold Game is designed to help you deal with the pressure of limited timing in Olympic round match play and the pressure of needing to win the match. In Gold Game, you are given only 10 seconds to shoot each arrow at 70 meters. You receive one point for each arrow you shoot in the yellow (9 or 10 ring). You receive no points for any arrow in the red and receive a minus one point for each arrow that is not within the 7 ring. The penalty can be adjusted depending on your skill level.

AIM-OFF TRAINING

Most of the time in outdoor archery, wind is blowing. With experience you can determine where you need to aim in various types of wind shooting. As mentioned before in chapter 6, aiming off in the wind requires a great deal of eye focus. Because you have to maintain your eye focus outside of the gold until the arrow hits the target, it is a good idea to deliberately practice aiming off. In aim-off training you can simply pick different locations on the target face to aim at. Try to get your arrows within a group the size of the gold in the location you are aiming at. For example, you could pick to aim off at a position at two o'clock in the 5 or 6 ring (blue ring), or you could even draw a circle the size of the gold and see how many arrows out of 100 you can get to land inside the circle.

1,000-ARROW CHALLENGE

You should not attempt the 1,000-Arrow Challenge unless you are an advanced- or elite-level archer whose coach has approved you to attempt the challenge. The 1,000-Arrow Challenge is an endurance drill that pushes your body's limits physically and mentally. It can also teach you to shoot with a lower overall intensity effort because you have to conserve your energy. In the 1,000-Arrow Challenge you shoot approximately 10 to 20 arrows per end continually throughout the day to reach the goal of 1,000 arrows in a day. Typically it takes about 10 to 12 hours to complete and is usually performed only once per year. If at any time you feel pain, stop shooting and seek medical advice from a qualified consultant.

INCREASED HEART RATE ACTIVITIES

The pressure of competition might have several effects on you. You might experience sweaty palms, butterflies in your stomach, or uncontrollable nervous tremors in your arms and legs. These reactions are normal, but the common denominator in feeling the effects of pressure is an increased heart rate.

Train to handle these effects by learning to shoot with a higher heart rate during pressure situations. Following are a few activities to help you learn to shoot in this way. Also note that you can increase your heart rate by doing either jumping jacks or push-ups quickly and then picking up your bow and quiver immediately and shooting. Although increasing your heart rate in training only simulates, not totally replicates, the feeling of nervousness in competition, it still provides you with a new situation to adapt to. You also have to learn to breathe correctly to lower your heart rate and to help control the shot.

OLYMPIC ROUND PRACTICE

In the current format for Olympic and finals rounds, you alternate shooting and have 20 seconds or less to complete each shot. Often this is not enough time for you to slow down your heart rate significantly. Practicing Olympic Round (OR) Set Play is another important training drill to do regularly if you are an intermediate- or elite-level archer. In most competitions, OR Set Play ultimately determines the champion, and this type of competition puts even more pressure on you. By routinely shooting OR Set Play in training, you can practice with some pressure but considerably less than that during a high-level competition.

TRIALS EVENT FORMAT PRACTICE

If you are an advanced- or elite-level archer training to make an Olympic or World team, you should run through a simulated competition of the format of the trials in training. This ensures that you understand the selection process and format and helps you feel more prepared for the trials event. If you train alone, you can always imagine shooting against opponents and draw scores out of a hat for your opponent.

VOLUME PRACTICE

As mentioned before in the explanation of periodization and supercompensation, your volume and intensity of training should fluctuate on a periodized basis. The volume, or number of arrows you shoot in a training session, can have a great effect on the progress you make. If you are a beginner spend more time learning technique through the use of stretch bands, mimetics, and light bows than through actual shooting. This is similar to many martial arts practices that teach the athlete technique first before the athlete is able to enter a sparring match. As you progress, your volume of actual shooting increases while your volume of stretch-band and light-bow use decreases. If you are a beginner archer do not shoot more than 100 arrows per day. This number of arrows allows you to learn the correct technique and limits the probability of developing bad habits.

If you are an intermediate-level archer you should ideally be shooting between 100 and 250 arrows per day, but this number is dependent on your technique, strength, endurance, and age. You should not shoot more than is comfortable for you. If you feel pain at any time during the training session, consult a qualified coach or physical trainer. If you are an advanced or elite archer, ideally you should be shooting between 200 to 400 arrows per day; however, there might be times that you shoot many more than 400 arrows in a day. On lighter volume days, you might shoot around only 100 to 150 arrows.

INTENSITY PRACTICE

Intensity in archery refers to the amount of mental and physical effort required to complete a task. For example, blank bale shooting at five meters is a very low-intensity drill, whereas simulated OR Set Play is a much higher intensity training drill. Generally, the closer you get to competition, the higher the intensity of training becomes. This of course depends on your skill level and goals for the year. The time of the year also affects the amount of high-intensity drills incorporated into your training program. If you were to maintain a very high level of training intensity year-round, your motivation would drop, and your productivity would begin to diminish. For example, in the off-season, your training would incorporate more lower intensity drills and focus more on technical improvements as opposed to focusing on scoring.

This chapter provides a number of drills and training activities that you can use to improve specific skills in archery. You can use these drills at any skill level and they can provide a solid foundation for any training program. This chapter also provides a foundation for you to develop individualized training programs, catering to your specific needs. Creating an individualized training plan requires time and the understanding that adjustments will need to be made throughout the year. Your training plan depends on your skill level, fitness level, age, and the time available for training. Refer to chapters 9 and 10 for how to incorporate physical and mental training into your overall training program.

9

Nutrition and Physical Training for Archers

Guy Krueger

In addition to the technical aspects of archery, proper nutrition, hydration, and physical conditioning play major roles in developing a successful archer. Nutrition and hydration will help you maintain energy levels throughout training and competition, and a consistent physical conditioning program can help you increase strength and improve your heart's and the lungs' ability to process oxygen. The information in this chapter is beneficial to archers of every skill level. However, you should consult with your physician before beginning any physical training or conditioning program.

If you have specific physical deficiencies, a professional physical trainer can help develop a plan to improve your weaker areas through weight training. Cardiorespiratory training can also provide several benefits, including reducing stress and helping reduce the possibility of injury.

This chapter covers

- nutrition and hydration,
- preshooting warm-up,
- cardiorespiratory conditioning,
- weight training,
- shoulder strength training, and
- balance training.

PROPER NUTRITION AND HYDRATION

Proper sport nutrition and hydration play a key role in helping you maintain consistent energy levels during training and in competition. Maintaining a healthy, balanced diet gives your body the nutrients it will need to recover quickly from strenuous workouts and shooting sessions. Eating the right foods during travel will also help your body recover from jet lag more quickly and can help with acclimation.

Nutrition is probably the most overlooked aspect of performance archery. In most other high-level sports, nutrition is highly regarded and monitored, and specific nutrition guidelines are created for athletes. Archery incorporates characteristics of an endurance sport, a power sport, and a skill sport, and nutrition can be a determining factor in all of these types of sports. Furthermore, with the increasing problem of obesity in the Western world, it is important to take a closer look at nutrition, examine the foods that you consume, and create a nutrition plan.

Examining Macronutrients, Fluids, and Supplements

The types of food you consume have a great effect on energy levels and health. The three types of macronutrients are carbohydrate, protein, and fat. This section also focuses on fluids and supplements and the role they play in an athlete's nutrition plan.

Carbohydrate

Carbohydrate provides the athlete with the majority of her energy and is vital for athletes training more than a couple of hours at a time. Elite athletes need a diet high in carbohydrate, especially complex carbohydrate such as pasta, potatoes, cereal, bread, and starchy vegetables. Simple carbohydrate (such as that found in fruit and milk) is broken down and used for energy quickly by the body, whereas complex carbohydrate is stored in the body for energy and nutrients to keep the body healthy. Diet plans such as the Atkins diet are not recommended for athletes because of low or nonexistent carbohydrate.

Protein

Protein is an important macronutrient for athletes. During exercise muscle tissue is broken down, and during recovery muscle tissue is repaired and increased. Adequate protein intake is important in this process of building muscle or even for maintaining the current level of muscle in the body. However, too much protein can also be an issue and can cause the body to store the protein as fat. Adults should get 10 to 35 percent of their total caloric intake from protein, which equates to 46 to 56 grams of protein per day (Nierenberg 2011).

Fat

Fat comes in two forms: saturated and unsaturated. Saturated fat is typically found in animal products such as meat and dairy and in processed foods. Saturated fat is not considered healthy fat because it raises LDL (low-density lipoprotein) cholesterol levels. Unsaturated fat, on the other hand, is found in fish, nuts, and avocados; it raises HDL (high-density lipoprotein) cholesterol. HDL is considered healthy cholesterol for the heart. Fat does provide a source of energy to the body; however, athletes should limit their saturated fat intake. The American Heart Association recommends less than 7 percent of an individual's daily calories be from saturated fat and that a person's average fat consumption be 25 to 35 percent of total caloric intake per day.

Fluids

Sport drinks and energy drinks dominate the beverage market these days. A growing number of children regularly drink energy drinks that contain higher amounts of caffeine than what's contained in soda as well as a host of supplements. Sport drinks contain a lot of sugar. The best fluid for the body is plain water. Eight ounces (240 ml) of a liquid carbohydrate (such as a watered-down sport drink) can be good for a high-level elite athlete within 30 minutes of beginning and ending a workout, but the majority of children and young adults who shoot archery who are not at the elite level most likely do not need the electrolytes in sport drinks. Again, water should be the main fluid you consume. Athletes should drink 8 to 15 cups (~2-3.5 L) of water a day depending on the intensity of training. Approximately 60 percent of the body's weight is from water, and it is important to replenish the body's lost water supply. Consuming water can also help remove toxins from the body and help prevent dehydration.

Supplements

Supplements are also another area of concern. Archers who are selected for international competition can be routinely drug tested for banned substances. If an archer tests positive, he can receive a suspension for two years or even for life. Supplements in the United States are not regulated by the U.S. Food and Drug Administration (FDA) and therefore do not necessarily have to contain the ingredients listed on the label. There have been cases in which athletes have tested positive for traces of banned substances while taking supplements. Furthermore, because these supplements are not necessarily tested by the FDA, there is no way of actually knowing the health risks involved in taking them. Interestingly, some energy drinks also contain supplements.

Creating a Nutrition Plan

You most likely can get the nutrients you need from a well-balanced meal. The USDA recently released the new MyPlate, which shows the basics of a well-balanced meal (see figure 9.1). It is also important to include colorful fruits and vegetables in your diet because they contain antioxidants and nutrients to keep the body healthy and to help prevent diseases.

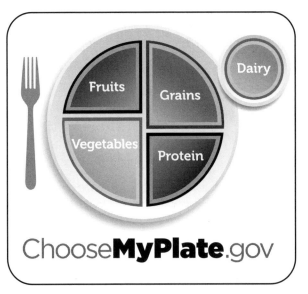

Figure 9.1 MyPlate shows the correct portions for a well-balanced diet.
© US Department of Agriculture

The frequency of meals is also an important part of the nutrition plan. You should eat three to five meals per day to stay fueled for the day. Most archers training full-time will eat breakfast before training, then eat a small 100-calorie carbohydrate snack about one and a half to two hours later, and then eat lunch around two hours after that. The afternoon eating pattern will be similar, consisting of a small 100-calorie fruit or granola bar around two hours after lunch and then dinner around two hours later. To reduce fatigue and soreness, it is a good idea to drink a liquid carbohydrate that contains protein, such as chocolate milk, within 30 minutes of finishing a workout or training session.

You should develop a nutrition plan for travel and competitions. Without a plan in place, it will be easy to resort to unhealthy fast foods for meals. You should pack some healthy snacks such as fruits, nuts, and even peanut butter and jelly and plenty of water for the competition. Once you find a nutrition plan that works for you during competitions, consistently use that plan for all competitions.

PRESHOOTING WARM-UP

A proper warm-up is important before shooting and for performing a safe and healthy physical training program. One of the biggest mistakes most archers make is that they do not have a consistent, well-planned warm-up before they begin shooting and training. A warm-up prepares the muscles for shooting and lifting weights. A good warm-up consists of dynamic exercises that get the blood flowing in the legs, core, chest, back, arms, and neck. Here is a simple 10-minute routine to follow before shooting. Note that this is the minimum of stretching recommended. You can include other stretches and do two sets of 20 seconds for each stretch if time permits.

LOW-INTENSITY ACTIVITY

First do two minutes of a low-intensity activity before stretching to increase the body's temperature and to promote blood flow. You can use a variety of exercises, including an easy jog, jumping jacks, jump rope, and twisting the body like a helicopter. Remember that whatever the exercise is, it must be low intensity.

SIDE BEND WITH STRAIGHT ARMS

Stand with the feet crossed (right over left), interlacing the fingers with the palms away from the body. Reach upward with straight arms and lean from the waist to the left (see figure 9.2). Hold for 20 seconds, and then switch sides for a total of one minute.

Figure 9.2 Side bend with straight arms.

HAMSTRING STRETCH

This is a simple stretch. Stand straight and then bend down and try to touch the toes (see figure 9.3). Do not bounce; simply reach to the floor or toes until you feel a stretch. Hold for one minute.

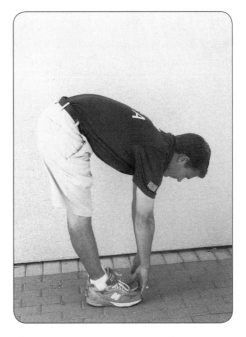

Figure 9.3 Hamstring stretch.

QUAD STRETCH

Stand balanced on the left foot, keeping the left foot pointed forward and left knee straight. Then grasp the right foot or ankle and bend the right knee so that the foot is behind the thigh (see figure 9.4). Pull the right heel backward and upward until you feel a stretch. Hold for 30 seconds, and then switch sides for a total of one minute.

Figure 9.4 Quad stretch.

ARM ACROSS THE CHEST

Grasp the elbow of the right arm with the left hand across the chest parallel to the ground to stretch the back of the shoulder (see figure 9.5). Hold for 30 seconds, and then switch sides for a total of one minute.

Figure 9.5 Arm across the chest.

ELBOW OVER THE HEAD

The athlete will hold the right arm directly up with the elbow bent so that the right hand rests on the upper back below the neck. The athlete will then grasp the right elbow with the left hand and push the elbow farther back and over the head (see figure 9.6). Hold the stretch for 30 seconds, and then switch sides for a total of one minute.

Figure 9.6   Elbow over the head.

NECK STRETCH

Stand straight and place the left hand on the top of the right side of the head. With the shoulders relaxed, apply a gentle stretch to the right, tilting the head toward the shoulders while maintaining focus forward (see figure 9.7). Hold for 30 seconds, and then switch sides for a total of one minute.

Figure 9.7   Neck stretch.

WRIST STRETCH

Hold the left arm out with the elbow straight and the palm facing up. Then bend the left hand down with the right hand until you feel a gentle stretch (see figure 9.8). Hold for 30 seconds and then bend the hand and wrist in the opposite direction (toward the top of the wrist) until you feel a gentle stretch; hold for 30 seconds. Switch sides and repeat for a total of two minutes.

Figure 9.8 Wrist stretch.

Working With a Personal Trainer

To make the best improvements and to ensure a safe and productive weight training program, you should work with a certified personal trainer or strength and conditioning coach. When searching for a personal trainer, keep several things in mind. First, ask the trainer whether she is certified by a legitimate sports medicine or exercise academy. Not everyone who works as a personal trainer is certified; a trainer's lack of credentials could have an adverse effect on your health. It is also essential to have an idea of the goals you want to accomplish with weight training. Communicate with the personal trainer about your goals for archery. Also, inform your trainer about your health history and current health conditions. These suggestions will help you find the right personal trainer to work with in a safe and organized environment.

CARDIORESPIRATORY CONDITIONING

Cardiorespiratory conditioning plays an important role in almost every sport. In high-level national and international archery competitions, archers might reach heart rates up to 150 beats per minute. This is especially true in set play elimination-round matches used in the Olympic Games. In the set play matches, archers might have only 20 seconds to shoot their arrows at a distance of 70 meters. The better the archer's cardiorespiratory conditioning, the better the archer will be able to handle the stress of competition.

Incorporating a consistent cardiorespiratory, or cardio, program into your training program can also benefit your archery performance in several other ways. Cardio training is a natural way to decrease stress and improve moods. It also helps the body regulate oxygen and has been shown to reduce the probability of injury. Cardio training is a good way to increase the strength and stability of the legs and core. The recommended amount of cardio per week depends on each athlete's age, health, and performance level. For example, an athlete in his 20s with good health and shooting at an advanced level might do cardio training three or four times per week at 20 minutes each session, whereas an athlete who is only 13 years old, in good health, and at an intermediate level might do cardio training only one or two times per week for 15 minutes each session. All athletes need to consult their medical professionals for advice on quantity and duration of cardio training before beginning any program.

A good program for archery would consist of varying distances and intensities throughout the year and even varying the exercises, from cycling on an exercise bike to running, walking, and swimming. Other sports such as basketball, football, or soccer are not recommended as a cardio exercise for archery because these sports increase the likelihood of injuring the body or hands, which are vital for archery.

WEIGHT TRAINING

There are two basic ways to increase shooting strength. One way is to improve technique, and the other is to simply build and strengthen muscles. Weight training is a deliberate way of strengthening the muscles and is essential in developing a champion archer.

Weight training is also a great mental training tool because it can boost confidence and help relieve anxiety. Physical activities such as weight training cause the pituitary gland to release a substantial amount of endorphins, which block pain and provide the body with a sense of bliss. Athletes who work out regularly also see some improvements in physical appearance, which can improve confidence. Weight training also has several benefits for older athletes, such as reduced risk for heart disease and osteoporosis.

The type of weight training should vary throughout the year. Strength training, circuit training, power training, and resistance training might be used as key elements of an overall yearly workout program. Age, experience in weight training, and phase of the competitive year will have an effect on which elements are used in the program. Age in particular will play a key role in determining the composition of the weight program. Athletes younger than 14 years should consult a physician before physical training and do only body-weight exercises. And all athletes, especially those over the age of 50, should consult with physicians and work with a certified personal trainer or strength and conditioning coach to develop a specific weight training program.

For archery specifically, weight training will serve mainly as a means of strengthening the entire body. Although the muscles in the back and triceps are important for holding the bow, the legs, core, chest, arms, and back all play important roles. Endurance also is a key to consistent competition. Unless you are focused on developing a specific set of muscles, your weight training program should be geared toward overall strength and fitness.

The actual amount, type, and intensity of the weight training program should vary throughout the year. If you did the same workout each day, you would improve in strength for a short period. Eventually you would reach a point of diminishing returns, and your effort would create less and less improvement of strength. A periodized weight training program, on the other hand, involves varying the intensity, volume, and types of weight training throughout the year and divides the year into distinct cycles and phases. Through variation in training cycles, your body will continue to adapt. Periodized programs divide the year into microcycles (one-week intervals). Four to six microcycles make up a mesocycle, and multiple mesocycles constitute phases such as the off-season, precompetition, and competition phases.

In the off-season, your weight program might consist of more strength training elements to build strength and endurance. This will have to be balanced with the need to focus on developing shooting technique at the same time. If you are too sore to comfortably work on technique throughout the off-season, this could present a serious issue for your development because the off-season is a particularly important time to develop as much technical expertise as possible. During this time you should plan to work out two or three times per week.

During the precompetition season, weight training should shift to more of a focus on both strength and endurance training. This means that you will probably incorporate more circuit training days into your weight program. You might also begin to shift from a three-day-per-week workout to a two-day-per-week workout.

The focus during the competition season is staying healthy and maintaining physical fitness. The workout frequency should switch to no more than twice a week, and the intensity should be much lower than in the previous phases. You might need to add some strength training if there is a long competition season or a long gap between major competitions. Cardio will play a much larger role during this time frame.

Three sample weight training programs are provided. If you don't have experience with weight training, you should spend four to six weeks in a general preparation phase. This phase prepares you for weight training through a variety of body-weight exercises and cardio and conditioning drills. The general preparation phase would be a very low-intensity program that includes basic cardio of varying durations two or three times per week and basic body-weight exercises and dynamic exercises. In the first couple of weeks the exercises will be very general and low intensity, and you might have only two training sessions per week. For example, an athlete might start off by just doing a warm-up routine followed by some walking or light jogging for 10 to 15 minutes. By the end of the six weeks, that athlete might be doing a warm-up followed by body-weight exercises such as pull-ups, push-ups, and squats, and finish with 15 to 20 minutes of cardio. The point of this type of training program is to get the body used to doing some movements and in good enough shape to help prevent severe soreness or injury.

Once you are prepared for actual weight training, you can enter into an off-season phase. During the off-season phase, the objective is to develop technique and strength. The strength program cannot be too intense, or the time and physical energy taken away from shooting will limit your technical development. See figure 9.9 for a sample off-season weight training program. In the precompetition phase, you must switch focus to preparing for competition, and physical training becomes a tool for maintaining good fitness. See figure 9.10 for a sample precompetition weight training program. During the competition phase the main goal is to be prepared for competition while maintaining as much fitness as possible. Because of frequent traveling and competing, it is a good idea to reduce the number of workouts to two per week. See figure 9.11 for a sample weight training program in the competition phase.

Figure 9.9 Sample Off-Season Weight Training Program

	REPS AND SETS			
Day 1	Week 1	Week 2	Week 3	Week 4
Warm-up program	1 set	1 set	1 set	1 set
2 Shoulder strength exercises	2 sets of 8 each	3 sets of 8 each	3 sets of 8 each	3 sets of 8 each
Medicine ball slam	3 sets of 10	3 sets of 8	3 sets of 10	3 sets of 10
Single-leg squat	3 sets of 10 each (75% 1RM)	3 sets of 8 each (80% 1RM)	3 sets of 6 each (85% 1RM)	3 sets of 4 each (90% 1RM)
Push-up row	3 sets of 10 each (75% 1RM)	3 sets of 8 each (80% 1RM)	3 sets of 6 each (85% 1RM)	3 sets of 4 each (90% 1RM)
Lat pulldowns	3 sets of 10 each (75% 1RM)	3 sets of 8 each (80% 1RM)	3 sets of 6 each (85% 1RM)	3 sets of 4 each (90% 1RM)
Back extension	3 sets of 12	3 sets of 14	3 sets of 14	3 sets of 16
V-up	3 sets of 14	3 sets of 16	3 sets of 16	3 sets of 18
Russian twist	3 sets of 25	3 sets of 30	3 sets of 30	3 sets of 35
Light jog	5 min	7 min	10 min	10 min
	REPS AND SETS			
Day 2	Week 1	Week 2	Week 3	Week 4
Light jog	5 min	5 min	5 min	5 min
Jump rope	1 min	2 sets of 1 min	2 min	2 min
Stretch-band training	2 sets of 8 each	3 sets of 8 each	3 sets of 8 each	3 sets of 8 each
Kettlebell swing	3 sets of 12 (70% 1RM)	3 sets of 10 (75% 1RM)	3 sets of 8 (80% 1RM)	3 sets of 6 (85% 1RM)
Dumbbell Romanian deadlift	3 sets of 10 (75% 1RM)	3 sets of 8 (80% 1RM)	3 sets of 6 (85% 1RM)	3 sets of 4 (90% 1RM)
Dumbbell fly	3 sets of 10 (75% 1RM)	3 sets of 8 (80% 1RM)	3 sets of 6 (85% 1RM)	3 sets of 4 (90% 1RM)
Push-up negatives (slow push-up—down in 4 sec, up in 3 sec)	3 sets of 8-10	3 sets of 10-12	3 sets of 12	3 sets of 12-14
Plank hold	3 sets of 30 sec	3 sets of 45 sec	3 sets of 1 min	3 sets of 1 min
Bicycle	3 sets of 16	3 sets of 20	3 sets of 20	3 sets of 24
Windshield wiper	3 sets of 14	3 sets of 16	3 sets of 16	3 sets of 18
Exercise bike (low intensity)	5 min	7 min	10 min	10 min

(continued)

Figure 9.9 *(continued)*

Day 3	Week 1	Week 2	Week 3	Week 4
	REPS AND SETS			
Warm-up program	1 set	1 set	1 set	1 set
Jumping jack	3 sets of 15	3 sets of 16	3 sets of 16	3 sets of 16
Walking lunge	3 sets of 10 each (75% 1RM)	3 sets of 8 each (80% 1RM)	3 sets of 6 each (85% 1RM)	3 sets of 4 each (85% 1RM)
Chair dip	3 sets of 10 each	3 sets of 12 each	3 sets of 14 each	3 sets of 16 each
Incline press	3 sets of 10 (75% 1RM)	3 sets of 8 (80% 1RM)	3 sets of 6 (85% 1RM)	3 sets of 4 (85% 1RM)
Bent-over dumbbell row	3 sets of 12 each (70% 1RM)	3 sets of 10 each (75% 1RM)	3 sets of 8 each (80% 1RM)	3 sets of 6 each (80% 1RM)
Superman	3 sets of 10	3 sets of 12	3 sets of 14	3 sets of 16
Leg lift	3 sets of 14	3 sets of 14	3 sets of 16	3 sets of 18
Decline sit-up	3 sets of 10	3 sets of 12	3 sets of 14	3 sets of 16
Brisk walk	5 min	7 min	10 min	10 min

Figure 9.10 Sample Precompetition Weight Training Program

Day 1		Week 1	Week 2	Week 3	Week 4
		REPS AND SETS			
Light jog		10 min	10 min	10 min	5 min
Mountain climber		16 total	16 total	16 total	10 total
Circuit	Jump rope	30 sec	45 sec	1 min	30 sec
	Exercise-band training	8 reps	8 reps	8 reps	8 reps
	Kettleball swing	3 sets of 8 (80% 1RM)	3 sets of 10 (75% 1RM)	3 sets of 12 (70% 1RM)	2 sets of 6 (75% 1RM)
	Romanian deadlift	3 sets of 6 (85% 1RM)	3 sets of 8 (80% 1RM)	3 sets of 10 (75% 1RM)	2 sets of 6 (75% 1RM)
	Dumbbell fly	3 sets of 6 (85% 1RM)	3 sets of 8 (80% 1RM)	3 sets of 10 (75% 1RM)	2 sets of 6 (75% 1RM)
	Triceps extension	3 sets of 6-8 (80% 1RM)	3 sets of 8-10 (75% 1RM)	3 sets of 12 (70% 1RM)	2 sets of 6 (75% 1RM)
	Plank hold	3 sets of 30 sec	3 sets of 45 sec	3 sets of 1 min	2 sets of 45 sec
	Crunch with twist	3 sets of 14	3 sets of 16	3 sets of 16	2 sets of 14
Exercise bike (low intensity)		5 min	5 min	5 min	5 min

		REPS AND SETS			
Day 2		Week 1	Week 32	Week 3	Week 4
Warm-up program		1 set	1 set	1 set	1 set
Circuit	Jumping jack	3 sets of 15	3 sets of 15	3 sets of 15	2 sets of 10
	Barbell lunge	3 sets of 8 (80% 1RM)	3 sets of 10 (75% 1RM)	3 sets of 12 (70% 1RM)	2 sets of 6 (75% 1RM)
	Biceps curl	3 sets of 6 (85% 1RM)	3 sets of 8 (80% 1RM)	3 sets of 10 (75% 1RM)	2 sets of 6 (75% 1RM)
	Incline dumbbell press	3 sets of 6 (85% 1RM)	3 sets of 8 (80% 1RM)	3 sets of 10 (75% 1RM)	2 sets of 6 (75% 1RM)
	Bent-over dumbbell row	3 sets of 6-8 (80% 1RM)	3 sets of 8-10 (75% 1RM)	3 sets of 12 (70% 1RM)	2 sets of 6 (75% 1RM)
	Ab wheel	3 sets of 10	3 sets of 12	3 sets of 14	2 sets of 10
	Leg throw-down	3 sets of 10	3 sets of 12	3 sets of 14	2 sets of 10
	Side crunch	3 sets of 10	3 sets of 12	3 sets of 14	2 sets of 10
Brisk walk		5 min	5 min	5 min	5 min

		REPS AND SETS			
Day 3		Week 1	Week 2	Week 3	Week 4
Warm-up program		1 set	1 set	1 set	1 set
Circuit	Medicine ball slam	3 sets of 8 (80% 1RM)	3 sets of 10 (80% 1RM)	3 sets of 12 (70% 1RM)	2 sets of 6 (75% 1RM)
	Single-leg squat	3 sets of 6 each (85% 1RM)	3 sets of 8 each (80% 1RM)	3 sets of 10 each (75% 1RM)	2 sets of 6 each (75% 1RM)
	Push-up row	3 sets of 6 each (85% 1RM)	3 sets of 8 each (80% 1RM)	3 sets of 10 each (75% 1RM)	2 sets of 6 each (75% 1RM)
	Lat pulldown	3 sets of 6-8 (80% 1RM)	3 sets of 8-10 (75% 1RM)	3 sets of 12 (70% 1RM)	2 sets of 6 (75% 1RM)
	Back extension	3 sets of 12	3 sets of 14	3 sets of 16	2 sets of 12
	Alternating V-up	3 sets of 8 each	3 sets of 10 each	3 sets of 12 each	2 sets of 6 each
	Russian twist	3 sets of 15 each	3 sets of 15 each	3 sets of 18 each	2 sets of 14 each
Light jog		5 min	5 min	5 min	5 min

Figure 9.11   Sample Competition Weight Training Program

Day 1		REPS AND SETS			
		Week 1	Week 2	Week 3	Week 4
Light jog		5 min	10 min	10 min	5 min
Mountain climber		10 total	12 total	14 total	10 total
Circuit	Stretch-band training	8 reps	8 reps	8 reps	8 reps
	Kettlebell swing	2 sets of 8 (80% 1RM)	2 sets of 10 (75% 1RM)	2 sets of 12 (70% 1RM)	2 sets of 6 (75% 1RM)
	Dumbbell fly	2 sets of 6 (85% 1RM)	2 sets of 8 (80% 1RM)	2 sets of 10 (75% 1RM)	2 sets of 6 (75% 1RM)
	Triceps extension	2 sets of 6-8 (80% 1RM)	2 sets of 8-10 (75% 1RM)	2 sets of 12 (70% 1RM)	2 sets of 6 (75% 1RM)
	Plank hold	2 sets of 30 sec	2 sets of 45 sec	2 sets of 1 min	2 sets of 45 sec
	Crunch with twist	2 sets of 12	2 sets of 16	2 sets of 16	2 sets of 14
Exercise bike (moderate intensity)		15 min	20 min	20 min	5 min

Day 2		REPS AND SETS			
		Week 1	Week 2	Week 3	Week 4
Warm-up program		1 set	1 set	1 set	1 set
Circuit	Barbell lunge	2 sets of 8 (80% 1RM)	2 sets of 10 (75% 1RM)	2 sets of 12 (70% 1RM)	2 sets of 6 (75% 1RM)
	Biceps curl	2 sets of 6 (85% 1RM)	2 sets of 8 (80% 1RM)	2 sets of 10 (75% 1RM)	2 sets of 6 (75% 1RM)
	Dumbbell bench press	2 sets of 6 (85% 1RM)	2 sets of 8 (80% 1RM)	2 sets of 10 (75% 1RM)	2 sets of 6 (75% 1RM)
	Seated row	2 sets of 6-8 (80% 1RM)	2 sets 8-10 (75% 1RM)	2 sets of 12 (70% 1RM)	2 sets of 6 (75% 1RM)
	Leg throw-down	2 sets of 10	2 sets of 12	2 sets of 14	2 sets of 10
	Side crunch	2 sets of 10	2 sets of 12	2 sets of 14	2 sets of 10
Jog (moderate intensity)		5 min	10 min	15 min	5 min

You can use these programs as is, but it is important to develop a plan that increases your personal strengths and strengthens your weak areas. Your weight training program should be individually tailored to your goals and needs. Your health and medical history can affect the makeup of your weight training program.

You might not have access to a weight room, gym, or personal trainer. However, this chapter has some training exercises that anyone can do at any location. Many of the exercises listed in the weight training program have body-weight substitutes or can be done using stretch bands. The shoulder strengthening stretch-band exercises are a must for all archers at any level and can be performed anywhere.

SHOULDER STRENGTH TRAINING

Shoulder strengthening exercises are important for archers of all ages and at all skill levels. Strengthening the shoulder girdle prevents acute injuries to the rotator cuff and chronic conditions such as tendinitis. These exercises also strengthen the fine muscles in the shoulder and scapula area, which allow you to shoot without shaking or trembling. Strengthening these muscles at an early age is essential to developing a solid shoulder foundation. Following are a few exercises for strengthening your shoulders.

EXTERNAL ROTATION

This exercise works the rotator cuff. Stand with the active shoulder farther from the stretch band's attachment. Hold on to one end of the tubing just at lower chest level, slightly forward from the body (see figure 9.12a). Rotate the active shoulder outside, away from the stretch band's attachment (see figure 9.12b), and slowly return to the beginning position.

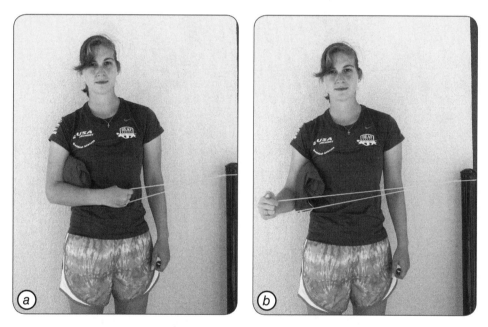

Figure 9.12 External rotation.

INTERNAL ROTATION

This exercise also works the rotator cuff. Stand with the active shoulder closer to the stretch band's attachment. Hold on to one end of the tubing, just at lower chest level, slightly forward and out from the body (see figure 9.13a). Rotate the active shoulder inside, away from the stretch band's attachment (see figure 9.13b), and slowly return to the beginning position.

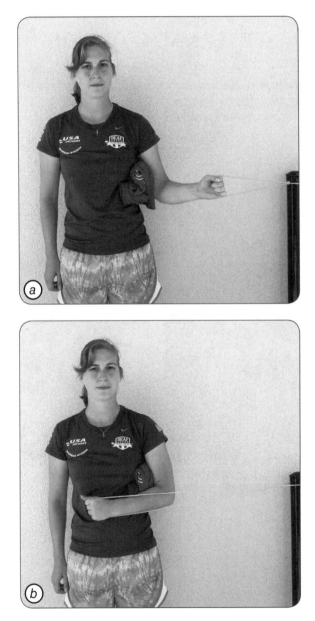

Figure 9.13 Internal rotation.

SCAPULAR PROTRACTION

This exercise works the muscles around the scapula. Stand with one arm up in front of you at shoulder level with a stretch band around your back or tied to a pole or door (see figure 9.14a). While keeping the arm straight, move the hand forward by letting the scapula slide forward (see figure 9.14b), and then bring the scapula back into position.

Figure 9.14   Scapular protraction.

SCAPULAR RETRACTION

Stand with one arm in front of you at shoulder level with a stretch band tied to a door or pole in front of you (see figure 9.15a). Keep your arm straight, and squeeze the scapulae together, which will bring the scapulae back (see figure 9.15b). Then relax and let the arm and scapulae go forward.

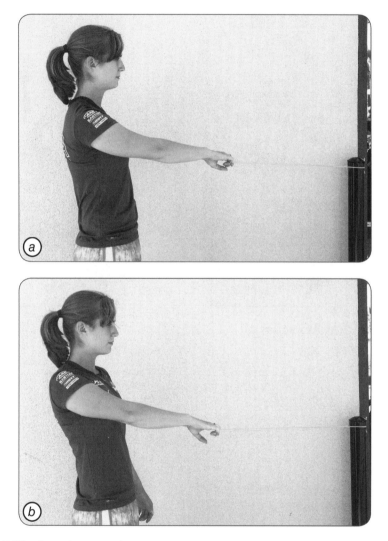

Figure 9.15 Scapular retraction.

SHOULDER EXTENSION

Hold the stretch band in one hand with the arm forward (see figure 9.16a), and then pull the arm back while keeping the elbow straight (see figure 9.16b).

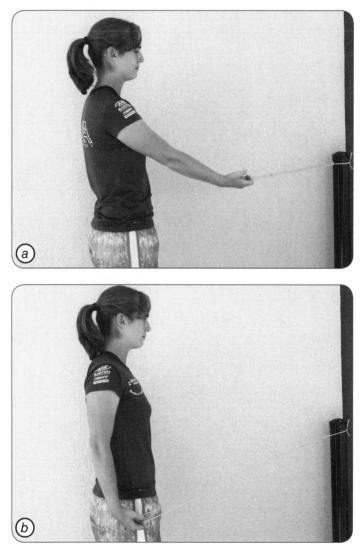

Figure 9.16 Shoulder extension.

SYNCHRONIZED EXTERNAL SHOULDER ROTATION

Stand up straight with the stretch band in both hands and elbows at the sides and bent to 90 degrees, with the hands forward. First pinch the shoulder blades together (see figure 9.17a), then rotate the forearms out while keeping the elbows at the sides (see figure 9.17b).

Figure 9.17 Shoulder external rotation.

EXTERNAL SHOULDER ROTATION AT 90-DEGREE ABDUCTION

Begin with the elbow and arm elevated to 90 degrees at shoulder height and with the arm slightly forward about 30 degrees (see figure 9.18a). Externally rotate your shoulder against the resistance from the stretch band to an almost vertical position (see figure 9.18b). Then hold for one second, and slowly return to the start position.

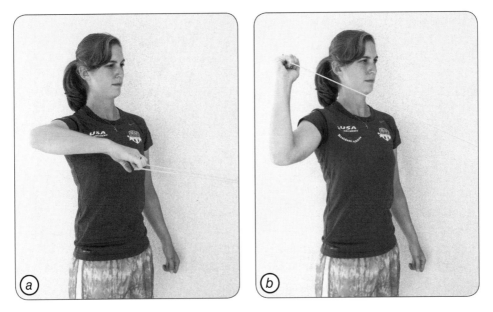

Figure 9.18   External shoulder rotation at 90-degree shoulder abduction.

INTERNAL SHOULDER ROTATION AT 90-DEGREE ABDUCTION

Begin with the elbow and arm elevated to 90 degrees at shoulder height and with the arm slightly forward about 30 degrees (see figure 9.19a). Internally rotate the shoulder such that the wrist is almost parallel to the ground (see figure 9.19b). Hold for one second, then return to the start position.

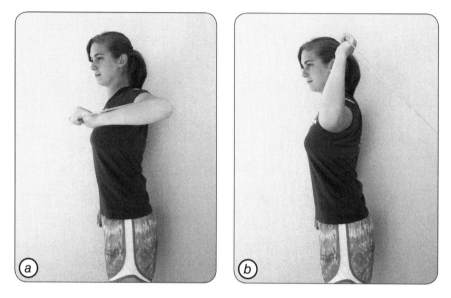

Figure 9.19 Internal shoulder rotation at 90-degree abduction.

BALANCE TRAINING

Balance training should periodically be included in your physical training program. Balance exercises can help increase stability, core strength, flexibility, and coordination.

A variety of balance training exercises, drills, and products on the market can help you develop your balance. Learning to balance while standing on balance discs is effective training. Balance discs require that the legs adjust independently to create the balance. One-leg squats can also increase stability and balance. Although balance exercises might seem simple and unnecessary, they can greatly increase stability; regular practice will help you feel connected to the ground.

Nutrition and physical training are key factors for your health and overall performance. Proper nutrition in training and in competition provides energy for training and competing at the highest levels. Physical training, including cardiorespiratory training, can make you stronger and better at handling the stress of competition. Incorporate a personalized nutrition plan and physical training plan into your overall training to maximize your skills and provide the archer with the best opportunity for success.

10

Mental Training for Archers

KiSik Lee

This chapter focuses on the mental aspects of archery not only in training but also in more critical moments during competition. Mastering the mental aspects of archery is essential to optimal performance under pressure because your mental ability works hand in hand with your physical abilities to perform under pressure. Without a strong and well-practiced mental routine you cannot achieve your peak performance when it is necessary. Luckily, developing a strong mind and mental routine is not all that difficult and can often be built on during training drills and through various mental exercises.

You might find that you can perform well in practice, but when it comes time to compete, your performance waivers. This could be because you panic, try too hard, or have an incorrect focus during the competition. With strong mental abilities you will perform consistently well in competition and will either score up to or above your average in competition. Champions exhibit the ability to stay focused under pressure and often make competing in pressure situations seem natural. They also generally have high self-confidence in their abilities, continue to lift themselves up, and are aware of their feeling and technique under pressure. All of these areas can be improved in training exercises. Just like with the technical steps of the shot cycle for recurve and compound archery, it is very important for you to train your mind to prepare yourself for competition.

REASONS FOR MENTAL TRAINING

Sports, although physical in nature, require a great deal of focus because your mind controls your body's actions. When you are placed under pressure, the stimuli of pressure have effects on your sympathetic nervous system. Your body reacts by releasing adrenalin into your bloodstream. This positive effect of the release of adrenaline includes improved reactions and reflexes, increased awareness, and increased energy; however, the negative effects include sweaty palms, shaking, nervousness, increased heart rate, and digestive problems such as diarrhea or constipation. In the Olympic Games in Olympic Round Set Play matches, athletes might experience heart rates up to 150 beats per minute!

One of the keys to shooting archery in competition is the ability to stay focused during a match or in a qualification round. A common misconception is that for you to perform at your peak you must stay calm and collected. While this certainly helps to a certain degree, in the current finals format, you might have only 10 or 15 seconds to lower your heart rate closer to your resting heart rate. Although you are in good physical shape and your resting heart rate might be between 60 and 70 beats per minute, you simply do not have enough time to lower your heart rate a significant amount. However, you are able to shoot very high scores under intense pressure. The ability to stay focused on your mental routines and technical processes is what enables you to shoot such amazing scores under these conditions. This pressure is similar to what biathlon athletes experience. Because they are scored both on their time for skiing and their accuracy with a rifle, they do not have enough time to lower their heart rates. Instead they must learn to shoot well with higher heart rates.

Improving your mental capabilities takes dedicated work and mental effort. U.S. culture and sports programs do not place enough importance on developing skills to handle pressure. Coaches receive very little instruction for how to teach methods to their athletes for coping with the pressure of competition. In fact, most athletes would agree that competing at a high level requires a great deal of mental ability, yet many of these same athletes fail to incorporate mental training into their training regimens. This is most likely one of the reasons some archers win frequently, whereas other archers of similar talent and skill level have difficulty reaching the medal podium.

This chapter provides some exercises practiced by some of the best athletes in the world. However, you will have to tailor these mental training drills to your particular training needs. Ultimately, it will take determination and dedication from both you and your coach to use these exercises to improve mental abilities.

MENTAL IMAGERY

Mental imagery is the process in which you imagine performing in training or competition from within your own body while attempting to include as many of the five senses as possible. The better you are able to "picture" the feeling, sights, sounds, and even the smell and taste of the experience, the more realistic that imagined experience is. Mental imagery is an effective tool to use to develop confidence and to help prepare you for a situation you have yet to experience. This could mean experiencing a technical change and the resulting feeling, shooting a certain score, beating a certain opponent, or even winning an event such as the World Championships or Olympic Games. This is one of the more powerful exercises you can do to prepare for a tournament; however, very few athletes actually spend enough time mentally imagining these situations.

Mental imagery is easy to practice, but it takes some time to develop your imagery skills. To practice imagery, sit down with your back flat and eyes closed. Rest your hands in a comfortable position such as on your knees. Relax your face by slightly smiling then begin to breathe slowly from just below your belly button. As you relax, begin to focus on the venue and surroundings. As you focus, try to imagine all your senses coming alive (taste, smell, touch, sight, and sound). Picture yourself shooting from within your own body as if you were actually shooting at that exact moment. Picture every aspect of the shot cycle, from pulling the arrow out of the quiver and nocking it, to transfer and holding, to your focus on the C spot. You must maintain your focus in the imagery on your technique and not on the result. Although you can picture the result and experience, your main focus has to be on performing technically under pressure.

Use this type of training to develop new technical skills as well. Before beginning a training session, it is highly beneficial to spend a few minutes rehearsing what you want to accomplish. If you are working on a specific skill, imagine yourself performing the skill correctly and the feeling of the correct action. This will help you connect your mind to the actions of your body, and the actions will become easier and more natural to perform. This technique can also be used in competition between ends and while you are walking back from the target. Also use mental imagery to prepare for different situations in a positive manner such as shooting in cold or rainy weather, shooting in a finals match, or defeating a highly ranked opponent.

Mental imagery can be performed anywhere, but it is highly recommended to set a specific time and location to practice mental imagery. You might attempt to practice mental imagery just before going to bed; however, this is not recommended because most of the time you will simply fall asleep or forget to practice at this time. Specific, dedicated time should be planned and set aside to practice mental imagery when you are awake and alert.

MEDITATION

Archery, in a sense, is a martial art, and awareness is key in becoming a successful archer. Awareness of your body and mind is key in developing the technical skills of archery and in performing the same physical actions in training and in competition. Meditation is a good way to strengthen and improve your mental awareness in training and before competition.

Meditation is an activity and a skill that you can learn to do very quickly; however, just like with mental imagery, meditation must be deliberately practiced often to become an expert. If you practice meditation regularly you can quickly relax and focus on your breathing to bring yourself into the present moment in competition. In archery, this could mean that if you shoot a bad shot or are in a high-pressure situation, you have the ability to simply close your eyes and within 10 or 20 seconds regain your focus on the present time.

Ideally, proper awareness means that you are focused on this moment right now, and now, and so on. This simply means you are focused on what you are doing physically and mentally at each moment. Meditation can help you develop this type of awareness and can be done a number of ways.

Breathing-Centered Meditation

To practice breathing-centered meditation, sit down with your back flat either in a chair or on a pillow with your eyes closed and your hands in a comfortable position such as on your knees. Relax your face by smiling slightly and then begin to breathe slowly from your diaphragm. As you inhale, slowly count up to five, and then as you exhale, slowly count down from five to one. The entire time focus on only the inhalation and exhalation of air in your body and the numbers while counting. When your mind begins to drift from your focus on the timing and breathing, simply bring your focus back.

With practice, you will increase your endurance and breathing capacity. Eventually you will be able to count slowly up to 10 and down from 10 during inhalation and exhalation. If you are new to meditation it will take some time to maintain your concentration for an extended period of time. The key concept is that meditation is not only about being able to focus on the moment but also about being able to bring your focus back when it fades away.

Thought-Centered Meditation

Thought-centered meditation is slightly different from breathing-centered meditation. To perform this type of meditation sit in the same position as you do in the breathing-centered meditation with your eyes closed and a slight smile on your face. Slowly relax and try to quiet your mind. Do not focus on any thought intentionally but instead, try not to focus on anything at all. When a thought comes into your mind, recognize the thought and be aware of it, yet do not judge it as right or wrong. After you have recognized the thought, just let it go and repeat this process for each thought that comes to mind. Eventually you will focus on nothing at all.

Mindfulness Meditation

Mindfulness meditation is a great skill for you to refine. According to Dr. Peter Haberl, senior sports psychologist for the U.S. Olympic Committee, athletes should practice awareness and attention with mindfulness exercises, and understand how the mind works. Mindfulness meditation can be practiced formally by focusing on your breathing or the sensation of walking for example, or it can be practiced informally with almost any activity. For example, mimicking the shooting process with just your hands or with a stretch band can be a method of practicing mindfulness. Attempt to fully focus on just these movements of your hands and practice, noticing when your mind wanders off from attending to these movements. Gently bring your attention back once you notice your mind wandering. To perform this type of training activity invite the use of all your senses and attempt to focus on the feeling of each movement to stay completely in the moment.

This form of meditation, just like with other forms of meditation, requires that you merely observe and do not judge each feeling, thought, or action. If your mind wanders (which it will), simply bring your focus back to the action. This kind of exercise is especially good for preparing for major competitions and learning new technical skills because it allows you to anchor your attention on every intricate detail of each step. It can be especially helpful to practice mindfulness for 10 minutes prior to competing or even between scoring ends to bring you back to the present moment. Shooting archery itself can be a form of mindfulness if it is approached with the right mindset. The key here is that you are attempting to totally focus on observing the movements and feeling of each action and not on judging them while also noticing any distracting thoughts arising in your mind and then letting these thoughts go by refocusing again on the movements.

FOCUSING

Focusing can be the most personalized mental training that you do. Focus training exercises are best when you and your coach work together to develop a specific focus exercise to help you develop your focus strength. Focus exercises are usually 5 to 15 minutes in length and can range from staring at a single object and noticing every small detail about the object to picking numbers out of a number-search puzzle. It can also include timing yourself looking at a single object several meters away. Focus training can also be developed to include some type of change such as watching the second hand of a clock for an extended period of time. Focus training should be aimed at improving mental focus and eye focus ability.

Here are a couple of examples of focus training exercises:

- Read while playing your favorite music CD and try to maintain your focus on reading for 15 minutes. Each time you catch your focus drifting to the music, simply bring it back to the reading.
- Visually focus on a tree branch, preferably in a busy park or location, and try to maintain visual focus on only the tree branch. Notice every small detail about the branch—the way the branch moves in the wind, the leaves, the bark, and so on—and try to maintain eye focus for 10 to 15 minutes.

DISTRACTION TRAINING

Almost certainly circumstances will not turn out the way you or your coach plans. Unexpected events will occur, whether a bow case is lost or a flight is delayed on the way to a competition. The conversation at the target while scoring can also be a distraction. Imagine you are shooting on record-setting pace at a competition and another archer mentions the possibility of your breaking a record with just a few ends left. The pressure on you to break that record has now been amplified, and you might be thinking of what the other archer said when you shoot the next end. You might not be prepared to handle distractions like this well.

Distractions such as loud noises, wind, a close competition with a competitor, or even an announcer speaking over a PA system can have an effect on your performance if you are not prepared to handle distractions. Conversations with other archers are usually the greatest distractions. Many competitors love to talk about the mistakes they have made, and these thoughts can creep back into your mind at the most inopportune times. Sometimes distractions can even come from not being able to sleep well the night before a competition or from something that happened in your personal life. Training for distractions is an effective way to be completely prepared to compete at a consistent level throughout an entire day.

Distraction training exercises give your coach the freedom to create a specific exercise to help you develop the ability to be more adaptive and handle distractions. Anything that can throw you out of your zone is a good place to start in developing a personalized distraction training exercise. This kind of training can include playing loud music or talking near you while you are shooting. You might be distracted in competition by the sound of other archers' clickers or release aids, so distraction training for you might include those types of sounds. A strategy or action plan can also involve how to handle distractions when they occur. Gold Game is described in chapter 8 and is an effective distraction training drill because the decreased amount of time creates an obvious distraction for you. Meditation, as previously described, can help bring you back to the right focus after being distracted and can be used within a recovery strategy.

GOAL SETTING

Imagine that two drivers are going to drive across the United States in two different cars and that driver A plans out his route, whereas driver B intends to journey with no map and no plan. Driver A might use a map or even a GPS, but he will know which city he is starting in and in which location he will end his journey. Along the way he will take various routes to complete the journey, and he will plan for refueling stops, food, and sleeping arrangements. Somewhere along the way, he might experience a flat tire or might accidentally get off track, but he will always have an idea of where he is supposed to be. Driver B on the other hand might never really know whether she is on track to her final destination. She might reach her final destination but will inevitably be driving around hoping to get to it. This process of traveling can be compared to your progress in archery. Which driver would you rather be?

Setting goals is a very similar process to that of creating a road map of where you want to be and where you should be along the way within a given time frame. Setting goals properly can help you plan your progress and provides an itinerary of where you started, where you are currently, and whether you are on track to accomplish your long-term goals.

When you begin to plan out your goals it is best to start with long-term goals first and work your way backward to short-term goals. Long-term goals are typically two to four years from being completed, intermediate are typically six months to a year away, and short-term goals are usually to be accomplished within three to six months.

When setting goals, typically you might be tempted to set score goals. Score goals do provide an idea of your competitive level, but it is better to set process-oriented goals, which define the skills you must typically have to compete at a certain level. Process-oriented goals lay the foundation for setting up a long-term training plan and prioritize the skills you need to develop along the way. Process-oriented goals are much more suitable for developing skills and developing character than are outcome-oriented goals. Character goals are aimed at developing character and life skills. Archery is also a unique sport in that you are always competing with yourself and striving to improve, and character goals will make the long, arduous hours of training worth the journey in the end.

Long-term goals are typically set two to four years in advance and might include your ultimate goal, and you can have more than one long-term goal. Long-term goals must be continually renewed and set, and it is highly recommended that you always allow for changes even in the long-term goals. Unexpected events do occur in life, but adversity creates a pathway for you to change and grow. Long-term goals are normally outcome-oriented goals, such as "I want to be the Olympic gold medalist" or "I want to be the compound World Champion," but they should include character goals too, such as "I want to be a consistent example of a good sportsman and exhibit humility in any circumstance."

Intermediate goals provide support for your long-term goals. For example, if your long-term goal is to shoot a 1,320 FITA in two years, then your intermediate goal might be to master all the steps of the National Training System within the next 10 months. If your long-term character goal is to use archery to better other people's lives, then your might have an intermediate goal to set up a local junior archery club for disadvantaged youth in the next year. You can have more than one intermediate goal, but it is important that your goals provide support for your long-term goals.

Short-term goals are most commonly set as daily and weekly training goals. They include what you want to focus on for the week, which skill you want to improve, or possibly what mental skills you want to be able to perform in the next local competition. Short-term goals ultimately lay the foundation for your long-term goals. Short-term goals should be process and character oriented, and you should review the progress of these goals regularly. Do not make the mistake of constantly setting goals but never evaluating the results. Short-term goals should be attainable yet require that you put in a genuine amount of effort to accomplish them. Short-term goals should be set by priority of which skills or tasks are most urgent and will have the greatest effect first.

Ultimately, setting goals helps you only when you regularly set goals and evaluate the progress of those goals. At times you might have trouble achieving your goals, which could be a sign that you need some recovery time, you need to set goals to focus on a different skill, or you simply have set too high a goal. Although the inability to achieve a goal might be frustrating it is a natural part of the process of planning and goal setting.

LOG BOOKS

Goal setting is a great way to track progress along the way, but to see this progress first-hand you need to continually track your progress. It is a good idea to track the volume of arrows shot in a day, types of shooting, personal best scores, and any new mental or technical skills learned. You might find yourself learning and relearning some of the same answers to questions you have simply forgotten because you didn't write them down. A log book is an organized binder of records of your shooting and mental and physical training. A log book must be personal and to be effective must be continually reviewed. Keeping log books filled with information that you never track and never review will not help you learn or improve in the long run.

You might prefer to journal, which can be a form of mental training in itself because it allows you to process and be aware of your thoughts, much like in meditation. However, unless you highlight specific information, it is difficult to retrieve information from a journal without reading all the material. A log book on the other hand can be more effective if you organize each day into a section or page that is in the same format for each page. You can neatly organize the training events by date, and it's best to include any information you will review at a later time. Review your log book at the beginning and end of the training week to provide an idea of what you accomplished and learned from the previous week and to give you an idea of what you need to accomplish during the next week. Log books should clearly outline long-term, intermediate, and short-term goals. Record your plan and goal(s) for the day prior to beginning training, and record any important information after you have completed training. Here is a list of information that is important for you to keep in your log book:

Date	Volume
Mood	New information learned
Daily plan and goal(s)	Focus for next session
Weekly goals	Coach's comments

Of course you can include more information if you believe it will help you. Each athlete is different, and no one format will work for everyone. Work closely with your coach to develop a specific format that is meaningful to you. Several computer spreadsheet programs make creating log book entry pages very simple. You can record your information on a computer, but it is wise to back up the information often. Keeping a log book up to date should not take more than a couple of minutes if it is done regularly; however, it is ultimately up to you to make keeping your log book up to date a priority.

BELIEF STATEMENTS

Do you dream of your ultimate pursuit of excellence? Whether you have just begun a journey into archery and dream of representing your country at the highest level or whether you have been on the brink of winning an elusive state title for years, you ultimately want to improve and grow. Modern science is constantly revealing new information about the power of the mind and what the mind believes. This is probably why many Olympic athletes tape note cards to walls, refrigerators, and dashboards of cars, and on bathroom mirrors in their homes. These statements often outline habits, skills, and achievements that these athletes want to accomplish.

Belief statements often change when you have accomplished the feat or added the skill to your repertoire. These statements not only motivate you but also change and mold you into a new person each day. You might agree that it is important to be positive in your life and in sport, but what does that mean—to be positive? It means that to have a profound effect, you need to saturate yourself with meaningful, positive beliefs that directly relate to your goals. To change habits and beliefs to make you stronger and tougher, you need to believe to your very core that you are capable of new feats. These types of statements also provide you with confidence and help you feel more comfortable about reaching new goals and higher scores.

A belief statement is a statement written by you in your own handwriting outlining in a positive manner either the goal or habit you would like to have. Again this statement should be personal and in a sense becomes your personal mantra or motto. You can maintain this belief statement until you believe that you have accomplished the goal or habit, and it is recommended that you have only one or two belief statements at a time. Lanny Bassham, an Olympic gold and silver medalist, from Mental Management Systems, refers to statements like these as directive affirmations in his book *With Winning in Mind*. In the book he explains that the directive affirmation can help people improve their self-images. Here are some examples of belief statements:

"It is like me to take clear transfer and holding each shot because I focus on the process consciously" –*John Smith*

"December 25, 2012—I keep my hips open to the target and maintain my posture and balance on my feet during the shot process." –*Karen McCalister*

"August 5, 2013—I shoot 1,320 on FITA scoring rounds because I focus on taking holding consciously each shot and run my mental routine each and every shot." –*Jane Williams*

The mental drills and exercises provided in this chapter help you build a strong foundation to become a highly competitive archer. Along with these skills, you need to consider your mental attitudes while training and competing. The National Training System actually does most of the work for providing you with a specific technical shot routine. The same routine provided by the National Training System also doubles as a mental routine for you to follow each step along the way. In other words, you only need to focus on completing each step as it occurs. This process gives you a definite and consistent way of thinking for each shot.

As mentioned earlier, one of the biggest problems you might face while incorporating mental training is that you either do not plan it into your training program or you plan it at a time when your mind is not fully engaged. It takes effort to do mental training exercises, but putting in that effort will give you confidence, especially if you know a majority of the athletes you are competing against are not training mentally. You can also create your own mental training activities to improve key areas. Staying motivated is key, and training with other individuals at a similar skill level can be beneficial. Having a training partner to compete against on a regular basis will help motivate and push you.

The mental drills and techniques covered in this chapter provide you with several different types of mental training. To see a significant improvement, spend a minimum of 10 minutes, four or five days per week, doing mental training. Mental training must be deliberate, planned ahead of time, and done at a time when you are alert and awake. Mental training can also be incorporated into your actual archery practice by using specific drills, and several of these examples are described in this chapter. The beauty of these exercises is that they can be practiced and utilized if you are either a beginning or elite archer. However, the most important concept involving mental training is that you focus on the process and be in the present moment.

11

Planning to Win

Butch Johnson

Does the competitive archer really plan to win? The answer is yes and no. Every archer, as we have discussed in this book, should have a process, both mental and physical, in shooting an arrow. The process must be the same in both practice and competition because it must become part of the subconscious memory. This chapter focuses on the premise that if you want to win, you must focus on the process during practice, and you practice the process because you crave the win.

WHAT DOES WINNING MEAN?

In a sense, you do plan to win. You embrace the feeling of winning—of feeling successful—and want to repeat that feeling. Winning can mean different things at different stages of your shooting career. For example, at a first-ever competition, winning might mean simply completing the tournament and learning how to shoot in competition. During a time when you are absorbing a change in form, which changes the process, you may decide that a winning tournament is to repeat the process correctly for 90 percent of your shots. With time, winning may be competing at a new kind of tournament—for example, an Olympic Trials event—and repeating the process consistently throughout. Winning may also be defined as setting a new personal best. Finally, when you are both experienced and comfortable with competition, winning may mean earning a gold medal in your category. The definition of winning depends on your level of experience, possibly your age, and your goals.

To win in any of the ways listed previously, you must decide that you want to win. This may sound like an obvious statement, but in actuality, sometimes archers are afraid to win. Others may doubt themselves enough that they don't believe they deserve to win. In the next sections, we highlight a few areas that are critical to planning for success. We focus on getting out of your comfort zone to help you prepare for stressors in competition, talk about the value of experience, and explore how you can use a support team to help you. Finally, we review the importance of finding the correct equipment.

Shooting Outside the Comfort Zone

The best competitive archers prepare well enough that they are self-confident, practice their process enough that they are comfortable with it under pressure, and always challenge themselves do their very best, which sometimes means competing outside of their comfort zone.

There are a few factors to consider. Some archers who achieve a lot very early in their careers locally are afraid to challenge themselves to accomplish something bigger. Others may reach a scoring plateau—that is, they reach a certain level and feel that they always shoot that score. For some, the comfort zone is related to environmental cues—they may be comfortable with the process and want to win, but they don't necessarily challenge themselves to experience new environments that pose different kinds of distractions. For example, an archer who shoots scores at local or state events that are consistent with national-level winning scores may be concerned about journeying outside of his physical comfort zone to compete in another state, with different people, and in a new facility. The key to establishing a plan to win is to go outside of your comfort zone and to challenge yourself to do more.

Learning From Experience

Experience, technical process, and a strong mental game are key to winning. Remember that in many ways, the mental game is having a process, but it also goes beyond the process of shooting an arrow from start to finish. For example, you must exercise the mental muscles required for processing distractions and concentrating, and this mental workout is just as necessary to winning as physically shooting arrows or doing physical training. Though we talk about mental training in depth in this book, mental training is key to your plan to win. In my experience, the best archers on the field at the Olympic Games and other major events are the archers who can shut out distractions and run a consistent mental program. Archers who are consistently positive in their approach—visualizing and telling themselves what they are going to accomplish instead of focusing on not doing something—are almost always more successful.

Creating the Ideal Support Team

Your support team is key to assisting you. Enlisting the help of experts can help you cross the threshold from local to national competition. The support team becomes a team and family commitment that includes working hand in hand with you, the coach, parents, and sometimes even siblings and close friends to ensure that the plan to win is carried out. For me, the support team involved my parents from a young age and has grown over the years to include coaches, friends, extended family, and even archery friends with whom I compete on a regular basis. Remember that a good support team member will always be honest with you and will have your best interests at heart when helping you reach your goals.

Using the Correct Equipment

In planning to win, remember that equipment is a critical piece of how you perform as an athlete. Could you imagine a guitar player walking into a big concert with a broken guitar string? Can you picture that musician not knowing how to tune his guitar? Accordingly, any competitive archer must know how to set up and tune her own equipment. Not only is it important not to be completely dependent on others, but when you know how to repair and retune your bow, it instills a sense of confidence that is simply irreplaceable. Consider the archer whose coach can't be at an important tournament and who doesn't know how to replace and set up her cushion plunger or repair a broken serving or arrow rest. Suddenly, that archer is at the mercy of others, hoping that someone nearby will have the knowledge—and the willingness—to set up her bow correctly. Additionally, think of trusting someone else to fletch your arrows—as many archers do—and then having those arrows fly poorly in a tournament because the person fletching them made a mistake. The reality is that regardless of how much you trust your coach, your coach should be in a cooperative or even advisory role when it comes to your equipment, and you should have the knowledge and willingness to do the work on your own. If you don't know how to set up your bow from scratch or aren't sure how to tune it without help, work with your coach to learn techniques for setup and tuning. Learn how to fletch your own arrows correctly from the start, and take responsibility for them. Do the work yourself and have your coach double-check your progress. However you approach the process, remember that there is no substitute for feeling confident that you can rely on your own knowledge and experience in dealing with equipment.

MANAGING NERVES AND HANDLING PRESSURE

People sometimes ask about becoming nervous in competition. How do you prepare for being nervous? The answer is to experience nervousness and then channel it productively to prepare for the next competition. The most nervous I can ever remember being in archery was at the Olympic Games in Atlanta in 1996. We were shooting the team round, and we were shooting for a gold medal in front of the home crowd. The stakes felt so huge that there was nothing I could do but focus on making strong shots and continue to run my mental program. For that match, I had to stay focused despite the other team's scores, despite what my teammates were doing or saying, and despite having my family in the stands along with millions of Americans watching. In the end, our team won the gold medal for the United States. Although I have never been quite as nervous at a tournament since, the nerves are always there, even at a national qualifier. However, I treat those nerves as an opportunity to concentrate on the task at hand and maintain proper focus.

Another valuable lesson that you must learn when preparing to win is to remain in the moment and not get ahead of yourself. In competition, it becomes easy to become overconfident when you establish a lead, and consequently you can lose focus on the process and individual shots. Frequently, archers will hear the advice to shoot one arrow at a time, and this is very true in high-level competition. Tournaments are won one arrow at a time rather than as the result of focusing on the ultimate outcome, which can cause you to commit errors that cost crucial points.

At the 2011 Pan Am Games Team Trials, there was a lot of pressure to be the best among all of the competitors present. The Olympic Trials were just two months away, and all of us were Olympic hopefuls as well as potential members of the Pan Am Games team. The Pan Am Games are widely considered the Olympic Games for the Americas, and the same team would compete at the Olympic Test Event in London. It was a critical confidence builder and opportunity to work together for those who made the team. During much of the competition, I had a solid placement in the third spot.

As it came down to the final matches, however, I got a bit ahead of myself. I made the mistake of looking at the standings and was also a bit frustrated with my shooting. It was also later in the day, and we were competing after our National Target Championships. For all of us, this was the sixth consecutive day of competing. I was physically and mentally tired. As we shot the last match, I thought I had the third spot locked up and allowed my frustration and fatigue to affect the way I competed. I thought I had made the team, but I lost my final match—a loss that kept me off the team. You must stay on top of every single arrow during every single moment. During tournaments you must know what to think about because you must practice the mental routine as much as the physical process during each arrow of every training session. Practicing under pressure—and learning to embrace pressure as part of the process—is one of the best things that you can learn to do.

SHOOTING YOUR OWN GAME

One topic that is discussed among high-level archers is whether they win because they try harder during some tournaments. Though archery is a very individual sport, the answer lies in how the archer thinks about trying harder. If you apply an inconsistent amount of focus to different tournaments or opponents, you may encounter difficulty because you begin shooting down to lower-level scores when the pressure is not high enough.

This kind of issue can be environmental. For example, you may not be as focused in a venue you're familiar with or when shooting with close friends. You must plan for environmental contingencies and prepare your mind so that when you are in competition you are not awestruck by the environment. There is absolutely no substitute for experience in this regard. Many archers need opportunities to compete at major events before you truly have an opportunity to win at them because you must absorb the differences in competitive environments and then practice what it feels like to encounter different distractions and issues. It is very difficult to prepare for something you have never seen or can't grasp; as such, you will have feelings that you can't even imagine before you have tried your first national or international competition. Gaining that experience so that you can take it home and incorporate it into your training regimen is crucial to your ability to succeed.

In match play there is also danger in shooting based on the performance of your opponent rather than focusing on your own process. The reality is that you will not truly know any other archer well enough to estimate how well prepared or underprepared your opponent is. Rather, if you are a successful competitive archer, you will treat each tournament, match, and shot the same way, with the same tenacity and the same focus on process that you do in training. The environment and opponents become irrelevant in this scenario. The advantage to this way of processing pressure is that there is no cause for alarm in shooting against a much more experienced opponent and no cause for worrying about shooting in an unfamiliar environment, because all opponents and environments are the same—and irrelevant. To be successful, you will shoot consistently from event to event and from opponent to opponent, concentrating completely on process and focus.

It is important to note the distinction between shooting differently because of the circumstances or opponent and being motivated to do well in a given competition. A good example of this is an ability to take significant pressure during a high-level event and channel it productively to help you focus more carefully or feel more tenacious about achieving excellence. As long as this increased focus does not change the way you think or shift your focus from process to winning, you can benefit from maintaining this delicate balance.

So, what happens when things don't go as planned at tournaments? Sometimes, despite your best efforts at preparing and training, you encounter difficulty in competition. The golden rule of competitive shooting is that the form is never changed during a tournament. Regardless of what is going on around you, you must understand that sometimes, for a variety of reasons, things do not go as planned. When this occurs, it is doubly important to simply work with the established process and routine. At such a time, it is critical to think of the time and preparation that you have put into getting ready for the competition, check with a trusted coach for advice, and remember to remain calm and stay focused on the process.

When you are struggling—especially under pressure—it becomes easy to let negative thinking take over and lose focus on the process. During times like these, take a deep breath, recover from the issue that has occurred—whether mental or physical—and then return to the process in which you have developed confidence. Remember that this is where the trusted coach and experts come into the picture. A great coach will be adept at recognizing when you are struggling and know how to occupy your thoughts. Additionally, it is often a worthwhile investment to work with a coach during tournaments on a fairly frequent basis so that a trust is built between you when you are under significant pressure. If you are shooting without the help of a coach, it can be difficult to manage issues such as these by yourself. Making sure that there is a plan for coaching during high-level competition will go a long way in helping you become successful.

From a state championship all the way to the World Archery Championships or Olympic Games, know that you will encounter various kinds of pressure. One of the best things you can do is to plan for pressure and commit to the plan. If you remain committed to the plan at the event, you will have one fewer concern to think about. Be honest with yourself. If you find yourself unfocused or allow nerves to take over, call yourself on it or be willing to enlist your trusted support team members to help you regain your focus. To improve at what you are doing and reach your goals, you must have and maintain your commitment to your training, process, and long-term objectives.

ANALYZING YOUR SHOTS

Analysis of both the shooting technique and the performance of your equipment is a powerful tool in helping you to win. Training logs, which detail the practice regimen as well as your progress in competition, can help you map goals and measure progress over shorter and longer periods. One of the most important aspects of keeping a training log is to be honest in writing it. If you are showing the training log to a coach and embellishing your commitment to training, it is extremely counterproductive for both you and the coach. Some younger archers express frustration with remembering to keep an accurate log of training activity. If this is the case, try keeping the log on a mobile device such as a smartphone or computer, and use the variety of apps, such as Evernote, which can assist with keeping notes from day to day and week to week. If you are working with a coach, such as you would in completing a goal-setting worksheet, it is always preferable to review the training log together. But remember that the training log is for your reference and that you are keeping it for yourself, not the coach. If you are struggling to keep a training log and are still in the early stages of athletic development, another good option is to put a calendar somewhere where you can't miss it (such as on the refrigerator) and write your daily information there. By putting this training log in a place where you have to look at it, you are more likely to be honest with yourself about your training, the goals you have set, and whether you are training correctly in order to reach the goals.

In analyzing competitive performance, determine whether trends are occurring over the course of the season or over the course of multiple years. Keep track of tournaments (including locations, weather conditions, other environmental variables, and scores) in order to have an honest assessment of whether trends are present. If trends exist, determine what they are telling you. An example is if you begin the season with a tournament at which there is severe wind and other adverse weather conditions. As you continue in the season, you compete in four additional national events in which weather conditions are favorable and wind is light. During these additional events, you see an improvement in scores and even in confidence, and you have an overall sense of making solid progress. As you begin the following season, however, you notice a drop in scores at the same tournament where conditions are traditionally windy and difficult. Should you assume there is a change in your shooting ability or attribute the difficulty to your equipment? Not necessarily. When looking at trends, note weather and other conditions as well as the time of year so that you can objectively evaluate the event. If you live in the northern part of the country and are able to shoot outdoor distances for only a week before your first national outdoor event, you can consider lack of proper training as well as adverse weather conditions as factors that could affect your score. In this case, you would then continue to map trends throughout the rest of the season. If the difficulty continues despite improved conditions and time to practice outdoors, you should meet with your coach to discuss the concerns and perhaps evaluate the setup of your equipment.

In evaluating the equipment, just as in analyzing training and competition trends, remember the importance of objective analysis. An excellent way to analyze the performance of your equipment, particularly when comparing different setups or different components to the equipment, is to plot the groups produced by the various variables being tested. Plotting sheets—or event apps for smartphones—can help you keep track of the tune of your bare shaft, how the arrows are grouping, and whether a given setup is working better or worse than another. The most important thing to remember about training logs, trend tracking, and plotting is to keep these critical data with you. If you develop plot sheets while working with your coach, remember to bring them home with you to analyze. If you keep a training log, be consistent about it and look at it critically to determine whether there is room for improvement. Finally, if you are tracking trends in your competitive performance, remember to keep a consistent record of data that will help you to evaluate your performance objectively. Analysis is a great tool that can help you to refocus after an event (whether you were happy or unhappy with your performance) and help you to identify the next course of action.

TAKING A BREAK

When you have done all of the preparation, put time and effort into training, gained experience, and won and lost tournaments, sometimes it is time to take a break. How do you know when the time has arrived? In short, if you feel burned out for any length of time, it is often time to take a step back. Remember that this chapter is predicated on the belief that, in order to win, you must *want* to win. When you stop wanting to do better—when shooting becomes a chore—it's time to give yourself a break. If you are a parent, coach, or support team member reading this chapter, know that when an archer really needs a break, there is no substitute for it and no point in pushing archers to do what they can't or don't want to do. If you, as a parent or coach, have expectations of the archer in terms of performance, practice habits, or other aspects of archery, know that it can and will lead to burnout. If your mood changes based on whether the archer is willing or able to compete or practice, you have become too emotionally invested in the archer's own dreams. Breaks can be necessary for archers, parents, and coaches. If it seems that you are in need of a break as the archer, know that the sport you love is always here for you. Archery is a sport in which you can be competitive at any age. The only requirement for continuing to compete is that you continue to have a love for archery and continue to be interested in shooting arrows. If not, take a break, knowing you can come back when you're ready. If, as the parent, you need a break or some distance, it's a good idea to have an open discussion with your child and let him or her know why you're taking a walk during tournaments. For example, you might need to allow your archer the time to focus on competition without the pressure of your expectations. However, be sure to make arrangements for your child to find you at an event if help is needed, or designate someone else that the archer is comfortable with to help with tournament trips.

Many top competitive archers take time off from training. For some, it's a short period at the end of a big competition season and then a quick return to training after a week or a few days off. Others take a month after a very hectic season, depending on what lies ahead in the following year. For example, archers in the running after a first Olympic Trials event might not want to take more than a week off when they have five or six months between trials events, knowing that more than a week off may set them back weeks or even months in training. In archery, muscle memory—and mental memory—are quickly lost, so you must consider the goals you have set for yourself in determining how much of a break to take. If you make the decision to take a more extended time off, especially after an intense period of competition, such as the quadrennial leading up to the Olympic Games, you may wish to switch from competitive to recreational shooting, or you may wish to make a clean break from the sport entirely. The important thing to remember is that it's perfectly fine to take time off. If you're a parent or coach, remember that this must be solely the archer's decision regardless of the expectations or dreams of others.

I use the late fall for projects around the house, shooting a bit with my compound bow, and other pursuits outside of archery. During this time each year, I continue practicing but on a lighter schedule, prioritizing other things so that I am practicing because I really want to rather than because I should to stay in competitive shape. This time allows me to clear my mind, look at potential changes in form, and then start to build back up to a regular training regimen. However, it is a vicarious balancing act between taking enough time off and taking too much time off. Your goals in the sport coupled with your need for a fresh perspective should help determine that balancing point.

When you plan to win, there will be triumphs and setbacks over the course of a career, no matter how long or short. Often, younger or newer archers will be fearless compared to older or more experienced competitors, and that sort of confidence can help carry them to the next level. That initial win is how you can become used to winning, which breeds confidence and sometimes more success. However, the longer you continue to compete, the more experiences (both good and bad) you gain. These experiences can haunt you and begin to trouble your mind at the least opportune moments, such as during a critical match in a challenging national or international tournament. Questions can pop into your mind, and doubts can become harder to keep at bay. More work is required to help your brain process experiences positively and productively, and this is why a good mental program and consistent shot cycle are so critical. At all times, you must remember why you love the sport, which often translates into very good competitive shooting. The more experienced you are, the more stability you have in competition, literally and figuratively. But it becomes more difficult to improve scores, and those improvements will be further apart and often small. The important thing to focus on is your love of the game—it's what will drive you to train long and hard hours. The pursuit of excellence is what will keep you on the field longer than your competitors, and it's what will make you try one more time to reach that new personal best or make that correction in form.

Planning to win is a team effort, one that requires consistent focus. It requires starting with a goal in mind and continuing to re-evaluate short-term, midrange, and long-term goals. Planning to win requires that you focus on your technical and mental process consistently both in practice and in competition. It is a team effort that will mean commitment from you, your family, and your coach. Finally, planning to win means taking mental pressure and challenges, accepting that they will happen, and channeling that emotion into the tenacity and desire to win.

12

Preparing and Peaking for Competition

Sheri Rhodes

Competition is the ultimate test of training. Did you train hard enough, long enough, and smart enough? There are lessons you will learn in competition that no training scenario or practice session can adequately simulate. The best thing about lessons learned in competition is they are deeply embedded and stay with you for a very long time. If you think you are ready for the ultimate test, here are some things to think about: The best place to start a journey into the competitive arena is at a local event. You are more likely to be familiar with the climate and the venue, and you might even know some of your competition, making for a less stressful situation. Note that for simplicity, preparing for competition is broken down into local events and out-of-town events.

PREPARING FOR LOCAL EVENTS

If you are new to competition you should begin your journey at a local tournament or club shoot. An event at this level is usually less stressful, making many variables that surround a tournament unimportant.

Tournament Dates

Generally, I suggest that you begin the preparation phase for local events *no fewer than 21 days* out to experience a full three-week training cycle. If you can outline a plan that is a year out from the event, that would be even better. Nevertheless, whether the event is 30 days or 365 days away, the general process is similar. Get out a calendar or work from a spreadsheet, and mark the tournament date(s). Working backward from the tournament, mark the current date. Now, mark off any days between the current date and the tournament date that you are not available for training.

Event Format

Preparing for a tournament involves knowing as much as you can about the round, location, and schedule of activities. These and other matters should be factored into your preparations.

What Round Is Being Shot?

A round is defined as a set number of arrows shot in a defined number of ends at prescribed distances. A tournament can comprise multiple rounds: individual, team, and novelty.

How Many Arrows Will You Need to Be Prepared to Shoot Every Day?

Remember to count any unofficial practice *and* official practice arrows you might have the opportunity to shoot, plus the official round, and then train for one and a half to two times that amount. The stress of competition takes a toll on you mentally and physically. Being conditioned to shoot more than the minimum number of arrows can help mitigate the effects of stress. If you're not currently shooting enough arrows, go back to the calendar, working forward this time, starting with the current day, and increase arrow counts in your training sessions at a regular pace.

Figure 12.1 provides an example in calendar form of arrow count buildup using a three-week cycle. Please note that the three-week cycle incorporates a taper period in the week prior to the event. This cycle is repeatable for longer training periods.

Does the Event Format Include a Team Round?

Have you shot in a team round? If not, you might want to recruit some local archery friends to train with you in a team round format. Be sure to practice every distance

Figure 12.1 Three-Week Arrow Count Buildup Calendar

Monday	Tuesday	Wednesday	Thursday	Friday	Saturday	Sunday
14 Low 96-108	15 Off	16 High 132-156	17 Medium 120-144	18 Low 108-132	19 High 168-216 (84-108 × 2)	20 High 168-216 (84-108 × 2)
21 Low 108-120	22 Off	23 High 144-168	24 Medium 132-156	25 Low 120-144	26 High 216-240 (108-120 × 2)	27 High 216-240 (108-120 × 2)
28 Low 96-108	29 Off	30 High 132-156	1 Medium 120-144	2 Low 108-132	3 Tournament 72 competitive plus ~120 practice	4 Tournament 72 competitive plus ~120 practice
Current high session = 120			Goal: 180-240			

that you will shoot in the tournament. Practice at the event is *not* the time to shoot a distance for the first time.

What Is the Schedule of Activities?

Knowing the schedule of activities might help to better define how you prepare for the competition. Ask yourself some of the following questions to see whether they will affect how you will train for an upcoming competition: What time of day will you start competing? Does the schedule indicate how much time will be allotted for practice? Will there be a separate practice facility? Will there be a break for lunch? If so, how long? Will it mean leaving the venue to go out for lunch, or having to pack a lunch in the morning or the night before the tournament? Are you a morning person or a night person? Will the process of getting up early throw your system into disorder? If this describes you, go back to the calendar and mark some days when you will practice getting up early and being active. Since most tournaments are on the weekends, make your up-early practice on the weekends as well.

How Long Does It Normally Take to Set Up Your Archery Equipment?

Be sure to add time for finding a parking spot and hauling your archery equipment, plus your chair, perhaps an umbrella, and a cooler for drinks and snacks, and plan on arriving 30 to 60 minutes before practice starts. Moreover, that amount of time does not account for any traffic congestion, stops for gas or coffee, or other unforeseen delays.

Event Location

Make time to visit the site and check out the terrain and surrounding areas before the event. This will give you an idea of how much travel time you need. Being at the site before you compete provides a visual tool to incorporate into practice sessions. If you cannot get to the location before the tournament, the Internet is a great resource, and you might even be able to see an aerial view of the site.

   If you are considering using shoes other than your regular shooting shoes, be sure to practice in them before you get to the event because different shoes might affect your balance and stability. For example, if you normally shoot on a grass field and the event will be shot on a gravel surface, will you consider that difference distinct enough to consider different shoes?

Weather Conditions

Since the tournament is local, you should have a good idea of what to expect weatherwise. Even so, about 10 days before the tournament, start watching local weather forecasts, particularly weather approaching your area. The National Weather Service predictions are generally reliable up to 10 days. If a change in weather is predicted, do you have the right protective gear to accommodate the change? Do you know how the gear will perform in a competition setting? If not, put it on and practice in it!

Equipment

In addition to your usual setup, you need to be sure you have the minimum amount of backup equipment and be confident in how that equipment performs.

Arrows

If you are shooting in a format that calls for six arrows per end, have at least another six arrows in your tackle box. Take the time to practice with any arrows you could potentially shoot in a tournament. Have replacement nocks, points, and fletching in your tackle box and the appropriate glue or tape for a repair. Having an alternate color of nocks could be considered a luxury item if you are a beginning archer, but if you are assigned to a target with three other people, chances are good that at least one will be shooting the same color nocks as you. The ability to change nock color to easily identify your arrows is money well spent. Make sure you practice with both colors.

Strings/Cables

Long gone are the days of fast-flight strings, which broke by the dozens at tournaments. Even with today's string materials, you need to have at least one backup string that you have shot for feel and consistency. Having a second cable setup for a compound bow is not quite the same situation. However, with a portable compound bow press, it is almost as easy to change out a cable as it is to replace a string on a recurve bow. If you shoot a D-loop, have some material cut and the ends burned so all you have to do is tie it on.

Finger Tabs/Releases

You must have a backup finger tab or release. Break it in during practice and know how it performs. Other items such as replacement limbs, stabilizers, and sights or scopes fall lower on the list of must-haves. You will find that the archery community can be very open and often a competitor will loan equipment to another competitor in a pinch. Nevertheless, don't rely on others to help you out of an equipment failure.

Arrow Rest and Cushion Button

If you shoot a recurve bow, it might not be within your budget to have a complete backup set of equipment, but having some of the smaller items, such as an arrow rest or cushion button as a replacement part, can be critical if equipment fails. The same thing is true if you shoot a compound bow: You might not have a complete backup arrow rest, but you should at least have spare parts for the most vulnerable parts.

Accessories

Accessories include things such as rain gear, hats, visors, sunglasses, sunscreen, binoculars, spotting scopes, and bug spray. Most archery events are held outdoors, and many of these accessories help make the experience better.

Wear all clothing accessories such as rain gear, hats, visors, and sunglasses at several practice sessions so you can determine whether your shot routine or technique changes significantly with the addition of an accessory. Sunscreen and bug spray might be accessories you do not usually use in practice, but they could affect your performance if you decide to apply them during the event. Applying sunscreen or bug spray could leave a residue on your hands and change your grip on the bow. Apply these types of accessories before you go out to the range, or take some wipes along to clean your hands after application.

Spotting scopes and binoculars are very helpful accessories. However, if you have not taken the time to practice with them, they could be very distracting to your rhythm.

Keep a small bag with essential accessories permanently packed. When it is time for the next tournament the accessories are ready to go regardless of the location.

Rules

Archery is full of rules. Rules are important because they ensure the competition is held to a set of standards that have been agreed on within the organization. They also ensure the safety of those competing, judging, organizing, and watching the event. Competition rules cover the format, scoring procedures, dress code, tournament etiquette, and settling of disputes and submission of appeals. Tournament officials are responsible for ensuring the rules are upheld and should have current copies of the rulebook in their possession at the event so they can be referred to should a question arise. However, you are responsible for knowing the rules of the event.

Nutrition

Given the usual length of a competition day and the number of shooting repetitions, archery can easily be described as an endurance sport, making nutrition particularly important in the days leading up to and on the day of the event. Waiting until the night before an event to make changes in nutrition is not going to greatly affect your performance. What will make a larger difference is experimenting with different foods and eating times in the weeks leading up to the event. Try out different types of meals the night before shooting practice, and note how you feel and perform the next day. Do you fatigue, or does your score lag in a certain area of the shooting format? If yes, experiment with different snacks you can take with you for munching on during competition. One thing to consider is to avoid large amounts of sugary foods because they could leave you with a blood sugar lower than what you had before you snacked. If a bit of sweet inspiration helps your energy stay up until the lunch break or to finish out the day, start with small amounts of your favorite snack *before* you see that performance dip you noted in practice, and keep up the intake until the lunch break or the end of the day.

Hydration is also an important part of nutrition. On a typical day do you normally drink two or more cups of coffee in the morning? Do you continue to drink coffee during the day? Remember that caffeine is a banned substance when it reaches a certain level in your system. This amount is different for each person because height, weight, and metabolic rate differ. Use general guidelines to estimate the amount of caffeine you can ingest without going over the limit. Know how caffeine affects your system. If you are a two or more cup a day coffee drinker, going cold turkey the morning of an event is not the best way to reduce caffeine in your system. Use your planning calendar to gradually reduce your caffeine intake, and note how your system reacts and whether your performance is affected.

Goals

Goal setting goes hand in hand with pre-event planning. You can even use the same spreadsheet or calendar for both. In setting goals, remember to focus on objectives that are measurable and reasonably obtainable. For example, a worthwhile goal for your first few tournaments might be to simply learn how to shoot a tournament and to become familiar with the rules and procedures, and the same goes for your first national indoor event, your first outdoor tournament, your first time traveling with an international team, and so on.

PREPARING FOR OUT-OF-TOWN EVENTS

Planning for out-of-town competitions is more complex, perhaps because of different food choices available or being out of your usual environment.

Tournament Dates

Planning for an out-of-town event means a longer prep period because you must consider more logistical elements. You not only need to plan how to get your shooting ready, you also need to plan how to get yourself to the event. If you can start preparations a year in advance, you have a better chance of success. If a year out is not possible, I would suggest at least three months. Get out a calendar or spreadsheet, and mark the event dates and today's date, similar to how you started preparing for a local event. Decide how you will travel to the event. Are you flying, driving, or taking the train or bus? What will your budget allow for? Flying is sure to be faster than taking the bus, yet also more expensive. Now, mark any days just prior to the tournament for travel and days in the preparation period that are not available for training. Note these dates because you might not be able to train for several days just prior to the event. Do you know how nonshooting days affect your shot technique? If there is a marked difference, then you might need to build in an extra day or two at the event location to acclimate not only to changes in time zones or weather but also to travel days that do not allow for training.

Event Format

You will discover that unlike most local events, most out-of-town events are generally multiple-day events. How do you respond to shooting under stress four or five days in a row? Continue building out the training calendar, keeping in mind arrow count and intensity. If you start planning enough in advance you could have multiple opportunities to experiment with the load and length of a training cycle so that you can determine what will best prepare you for this upcoming event. You might even have an opportunity to incorporate a local event into a cycle. Remember to build in at least one rest day each week.

Event Location

The terrain, toilets, parking, and shelter are all things to consider when you plan to attend an out-of-town event. The Internet is a valuable resource for an aerial view of the venue that shows the terrain and surrounding landscape but most likely does not indicate shelter or toilets that might be temporarily staged for the tournament. Be prepared to tote your equipment and essential tournament gear at least a couple of hundred yards. Luggage wheels and multiple trips to and from the car will become part of your setup routine.

Weather Conditions

Another useful Internet tool is the almanac or historical data on a weather site. It can give you a summary of average precipitation, humidity, and sunshine for the dates of the event. Start checking the weather at the event location 10 days to two weeks prior. In addition, the radar map can tell you what weather systems might be headed in the direction of the event. If weather looks like it will affect the event, try to practice in as many different types of weather as you can. Obviously, if you live where it is cold and the event is in a warm place, that is not something you can easily simulate unless you can shoot inside a facility and turn the heat up—a lot! On the other hand, if you live in a dry climate, you might have to turn on the sprinklers to simulate rain. Simulating weather conditions not only lets you see how you and your archery equipment function, it also provides an opportunity to be sure rain gear will not interfere with your shot or to see what happens to your binoculars or scope if it gets wet. Do you have a system in place to handle foggy optics?

Equipment

Essential and backup equipment needs are pretty much the same for out-of-town events as for local events with some exceptions. Much of the time, traveling to out-of-town events means the event is important. Regional, national, and world championship events require extensive preparation regarding your equipment. Upper-level events such as these require that you have a complete backup bow, as well as backup risers, limbs, sights, stabilizers, weights, cushion buttons, arrow rests, finger tabs, releases, string, cable, D-loops, nocks, and fletchings, and the proper tools to work on your equipment. Set up a second bow and shoot it at all the distances, at different times of the day and in different weather conditions. Get to know your backup bow as well as you do your primary bow. You don't have to like your backup bow, you just need to have confidence in how it will perform.

Nutrition

Preparing for and shooting in local events hopefully will have helped you formulate a good nutrition plan. When you are traveling to an out-of-town event or possibly an out-of-country event, you need to consider whether pre-event meals will be available to you on the road. Can you buy your snacks when you are traveling, or do you need to bring an ample supply with you? For more general information on nutrition, please refer to chapter 9.

Medication and Competing Clean

Another concern in the nutrition arena, particularly when attending higher level events, is medications and supplements. Archers at national and international events are subject to drug testing, which is regulated by the United States Anti-Doping Agency (USADA). If you take prescription or over-the-counter (OTC) medications, be sure that you or your doctor ensures that you can take the medication during competition, before you start a medicine regime. Oftentimes popular medications have alternatives that will alleviate your symptoms that are not on the banned substance list. If no alternatives are available you could file a TUE (therapeutic use exemption) and carry it with you. Some herbal supplements have the same properties as pharmaceutical drugs and will test positive. Whenever you attend an event where you think antidoping control tests might be administered, take the prescription bottle or the original packaging for the OTC medications with you. If you are selected for drug testing, you will need to list every medication you have taken, including pain relievers and supplements, during the preceding 48 hours. Do not take medications offered to you from others. For more information on antidoping practices and competing clean, visit http://www.usada.org.

Travel

How you are going to get to the event, where you are going to stay, and how you will get around once you are there are all things to consider when you attend an out-of-town event. Logistical issues are one of the reasons planning for an out-of-town event requires more time than planning for a local event. Taking advantage of better travel deals requires that you start searching for airfares, hotels, and rental cars sometimes as much as three months prior to an event.

The decision to travel to an event also requires a fair assessment of where you are in your training. If you are not physically ready to handle the number of arrows or mentally prepared for the challenge of stress that a higher level tournament brings, attending it might not be the best use of your hard-earned money.

The theme of this chapter is to plan ahead and practice for contingencies. Until you get used to the tournament circuit, making a list is one way to be sure you are prepared.

PEAKING FOR COMPETITION

The best athletic performances are a timely blending of the physical, technical, tactical, and mental domains, best realized by the appropriate training in each of the three cycles: preseason, in-season, and postseason.

Physical Domain

The physical domain includes general conditioning, strength, and power, all typically developed in the weight room or at a fitness center. The heaviest part of conditioning is usually implemented in the preseason phase of your training. Preseason is that time of the year after you have taken a break, with little or no archery training or competition in your calendar. Preseason conditioning lays the foundation for being able to handle the repeated stresses of training and competition. Figure 12.2 shows what the physical training intensity over the course of a year might look like.

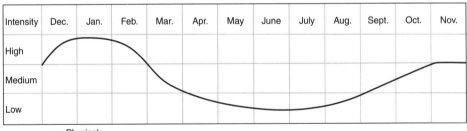

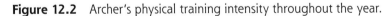

Figure 12.2 Archer's physical training intensity throughout the year.

Technical Domain

The technical domain deals with the specifics of how to move in the sport. In archery, this is the meat and potatoes of the sport—actually shooting the shot, and learning what makes a good shot and what happens when the shot is not as good as you would like it.

In this book, training cycles are discussed. On a very elemental level, cycles are in place in everything you do, right down to your sleep/wake cycles or your circadian rhythm. Do you know what your shot cycle is—how long it usually takes from anchor to release? Do you start an end with higher scoring arrows and finish with lower scoring arrows or vice versa? Perhaps you start out with modest-scoring arrows, have a couple of high-scoring arrows in the middle of the end, and finish modestly. The same cycle applies to ends. Figure 12.3 shows what the technical training intensity over the course of a year might look like.

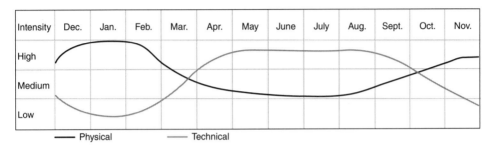

Figure 12.3 Archer's technical training intensity throughout the year.

Tactical Domain

The tactical domain deals with decision making and reacting to situations: shooting in wind, under timing restraints, in cold and hot weather, and during other stressful situations to understand how you and your equipment respond.

If wind is an element, make a wind flag, carry it in your tackle box, and put it up every time you practice, but know that a single wind flag is not going to tell you the whole story. Look at the trees or other vegetation around the edges of the range. Check the horizon for businesses flying national or state flags. Notice how the wind feels as it goes around you. When do you actually check the wind flag in your shot routine?

Shoot in hot weather so you know whether your sunscreen is going to run into your eyes when you sweat. In cold weather, experience the sharp sting in your release fingers when you let go of the string or how painfully cold a bow handle can get when you leave it in the trunk of a car overnight. The time requirements, which are part of every competition, can create stress just knowing time is limited. How do your physical and mental systems respond to your having 30 seconds left and three arrows to shoot? Have you tried this in practice?

Rules are part of the tactical domain. If another archer challenges you on a call or a judge notifies you that you are not in compliance with a rule, will it disrupt your mental state? How you deal with these things is what makes a difference. Figure 12.4 shows what the tactical training intensity over the course of a year might look like.

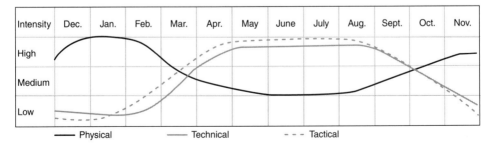

Figure 12.4 Archer's tactical training intensity throughout the year.

Mental Domain

The mental domain has to do with how you perform in mentally challenging situations: level of arousal, self-talk, mental rehearsal, recovery from a poor shot, and so on. A mental game plan incorporates both an off-the-field approach involving mental rehearsals and self-talk, and building mental elements into regular training, although many situations cannot be simulated and must be learned from actual experience.

What happens to your mental state when you shoot a 10? What happens to your mental state when you shoot a two? The answer to either question can be telling. After shooting a two, do you try harder on the next arrow to shoot a 10? Do you feel like the game is over when you shoot a two? The best response is that you learn from each experience and prepare for the next shot with a confident outlook.

Mental rehearsal is more than just seeing yourself shoot a shot. It is seeing yourself shoot well in every imagined situation. You could be the only person on the archery range practicing, yet in your mind you are at the World Championships or the Olympic Games. The crowd is cheering, the announcer is speaking, and the coach is giving you advice. How do you see yourself performing? Can you picture yourself on the field of play? Can you see the spectators? Are you confident? Actually being in a situation such as the one described is truly the best way to learn how you perform. Nonetheless, if you can imagine the steps you will take, the breath you will take, how you will load your bow and execute your shot, you will go a long way toward being prepared for that level of competition when you finally do step onto the field. In the first part of this chapter, I mentioned using the visual of the competition field in training. If you are not able to physically travel to the venue, at least try for an aerial view on the Internet; then when you practice see yourself on the tournament field. Figure 12.5 shows what the mental training intensity over the course of a year might look like.

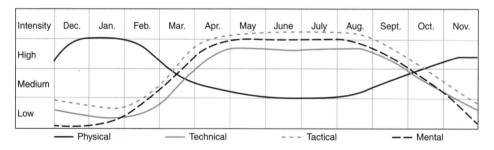

Figure 12.5 Archer's mental training intensity throughout the year.

The purpose of this chapter is to give you a sense of what it means to begin competing and to give you a road map to help you along the way. Ultimately, there is no substitute for experience, and parents and coaches must accept that the only way for you to learn how to win is to go to tournaments for the sake of learning how to compete. You must know that the only way to gain confidence during competition is to train well, maintain a positive attitude, and prepare carefully for every tournament you attend. When you are prepared and well trained, and you approach the event with a positive attitude and an open mind, you will be able to get the most out of your tournament experience.

13

Developing Young Archers

Diane Watson

The world of youth athletics has become unbelievably competitive, and this includes archery. Archery has become an extremely competitive sport from the younger stages of an archer's life through her adult years. The *Wall Street Journal* reported that more than four billion dollars a year are spent on training and coaching for young athletes in the United States alone. This number doesn't directly correlate to young archers, but it gives you an idea of how important it is to many parents such as yourself, coaches, and athletes in the world. The demand for training and coaching for young athletes leads to the question, are world-class athletes born champions, or are champions developed?

Study after study shows that champions are developed. The studies also show the most influential coach in the young athlete's career is his first coach. In some cases that first instructor might be you, or your young athlete's first contact with archery might be at the most basic level through summer camp, the Boy Scouts, the Girl Scouts, or 4H. These programs are wonderful for introducing the sport of archery to young people, but they tend to be short term. From the instructors in such programs, your young archer learns the basic skill set needed to shoot an arrow into the target and enough to be safe while on the archery range. Such programs provide a great foundation, and your child will hopefully have a positive experience with the sport of archery from the very beginning. Your young archer might stay at this stage for a couple of years, or he might come home wanting to progress the skills he has just learned while participating in a short-term program. At this stage your young athlete decides whether archery is his sport of choice. The next step is the critical one in developing your young beginner into a lifelong competitive archer.

FIRST STEPS FOR YOUTH

Generally your young archer's first instructor is the person who lays the foundation on which she learns to build. Finding a more structured program can be the next step in the development of your young archer. She will probably still come into contact with an instructor versus a coach, but at this early stage, that is fine. You might find that the most practical and affordable option is a beginner group program, which allows your archer to progress as her skills improve. Let your child have fun with shooting, meeting friends, and developing her joy for the sport. While this is happening your young archer is developing the necessary skill sets to improve her success as an athlete. Those skill sets might include the skills necessary for setting a strong, basic technique as well as personal skills, such as self-reliance, confidence, focus, and patience. Specifically in archery, and life in general, those skills become very important.

Your young archer is now beginning to grow, and it is up to him to decide what he would like to do: enter the sport as a more structured activity or continue to just have fun. If he chooses to enter a more structured program, he is now beginning to move into the competitive world. The instructor whom he has been accustomed to now becomes his coach. His first coach lays a solid foundation to begin developing his talent. A word of caution: The next step in archery should be a group discussion including you, the coach, and your athlete regarding which path your young athlete will follow. His first coach has the power to start the greatness in him by inspiring him to challenge himself beyond the ordinary, making the first structured program very influential in the foundation of your young archer.

STRUCTURED PROGRAM FOR YOUTH

The Junior Olympic Archery Development (JOAD) program offered by USA Archery is an excellent structured program that has developed many young archers across the country. The JOAD program is designed to teach archery to young athletes over a series of classes taught by a certified USA Archery instructor or coach. The JOAD program offers both recurve and compound archers the opportunity to learn range safety and proper shooting techniques in an environment that fosters focus, increased self-confidence, and team-building skills. The JOAD program grows with your young archer. Even though

Figure 13.1 JOAD Star Pin Score Levels

	OUTDOORS (36-ARROW ROUND/122M FACE)				
	Green Star	Purple Star	Gray Star	White Star	Black Star
Distance	15 m	20 m	25 m	30 m	40 m
Novice	130	155	180	205	
Olympic Outer 10 Ring	155	180	205	230	240
Compound Outer 10 Ring	180	205	230	245	265
	INDOORS (30-ARROW ROUND)				
Distance and face	Green Star	Purple Star	Gray Star	White Star	Black Star
9 m Olympic and novice—60 cm compound—40 cm	50	100	150	200	
18 m Olympic and novice—60 cm compound—40 cm		30	50	100	150
18 m Olympic—outer 10 compound—inner 10					

your young archer might have had basic instruction in archery from the Boy Scouts, Girl Scouts, 4H, and other such organizations, introductory JOAD classes teach the fundamentals of proper shooting form. As your young archer develops her archery and personal skills, she will learn more advanced techniques. USA Archery's JOAD program can be purely recreational, or it can aid in the development of a competitive archer in hopes of becoming an Olympic, Paralympic, or World Championship archer.

You might ask when you will know whether your child has the potential to become competitive on a national or international level? One of the best things about the sport of archery is that there is no specific time frame. Some young archers learn to develop the necessary skills to achieve higher levels at a very young age, and some learn at an older age. Archery is one of those sports that can be learned at any age, and an individual can become an elite-level archer at most any age. The JOAD program addresses these age and developmental issues by offering an official achievement award system during its class scoring sessions. The JOAD program starts archers at age eight and runs through age 20. The achievement system is geared to enhance your young archer's learned skill sets necessary for her to develop into an experienced, skilled athlete.

"Junior Olympic Archery Development (JOAD) is fun and rewarding and gives kids the tools they need to succeed. It helps to build self-confidence, focus, patience and self-reliance," says Denise Parker, three-time U.S. Olympic team member and Olympic bronze medalist, who started her archery career in JOAD.

The JOAD program encourages the use of the USA Archery Coach Certification network, which ensures that archers across the country receive consistent instruction in USA Archery's National Training System. Introductory JOAD classes teach the fundamentals of proper shooting form. As your young archer develops he will learn more advanced techniques. Figure 13.1 demonstrates the score that needs to be achieved at each level. The first scoring goals are set so beginners can easily attain them. As the skill level increases the awards become more challenging to achieve, requiring your archer's skill sets to improve in order to achieve the higher levels.

Blue Star	Red Star	Yellow Star	Bronze Olympian	Silver Olympian	Gold Olympian
50 m	50 m	60 m/70 m	60 m/70 m	60 m/70 m	60 m/70 m
240	275	290/270	310/295	325/305	335/320
265	300	310/300	335/325	350/335	355/340

Blue Star	Red Star	Yellow Star	Bronze Olympian	Silver Olympian	Gold Olympian
200	250	270	290	295	300
	240	260	280	285	290

The National Training System (NTS) was developed by National Head Coach KiSik Lee to help build a better, stronger archery technique that is unique to the world of competitive archery. NTS, taught exclusively in the United States and explored further in other chapters in this book, is designed to provide your archer with a repeatable shooting technique that helps to prevent injury and is based on biomechanical science. Instructors from the most basic level are taught versions of NTS that are suited to their specific audiences, for archers as young as six years old. In other words, chances are good that the beginning techniques your child learned at summer camp were taught by a USA Archery Certified Instructor, who in turn taught your child those basic foundation steps that will translate well to later learning of the complete NTS technique.

Coach–Archer Relationship

How do I know whether I have the right coach for my child? No one individual other than yourself and your archer will be able to determine that. Communication and confidence will help you determine the answer to that question. Listen to your archer; see whether she understands what the coach is telling her. Listen to the coach to see whether he is explaining the techniques in a manner that can be understood. Is your child feeling confident with what she is learning? Does the coach teach in a positive manner, or does he focus on the negative? If confidence and/or communication are missing from the coach–archer relationship, it is time to explore other options. From the very beginning, remember that excellent coaching is just as important in archery as it is in any other sport. For example, if your child were showing significant talent at golf, tennis, or any other major sport, you'd seek out the best coach possible based on your family's financial circumstances.

Because archery is a smaller (though growing) sport, you might need to travel farther away to find the right coach for your child's personality and skill level. If you're not sure what your options are, contact USA Archery, and ask how you can find a coach for your child. The important thing to remember is that every archery coach is different, and communication styles, coaching techniques, and even the form that is taught will change from coach to coach. Many coaches will teach NTS, but some will focus on other types of shooting technique. One coach is not necessarily better than another by virtue of her communication style or the technique she teaches, just different.

LONG-TERM DEVELOPMENT

While your archer wants to get an edge and you want to provide every opportunity for her to excel, the question of how to provide for your competitive archer's long-term development is key. It can take years of systematic training and frequent high-quality coaching to develop your young archer athlete. Many sports and national Olympic committees have spent decades of research and millions of dollars trying to learn how to identify future champions. They have all confirmed that success at an early age does not predict elite-level success within the sport later on. In many studies, young athletes who were considered superior at ages 12 to 14 dropped out of the sport later in life. The same principle can be applied specifically to the sport of archery. Although your young archer might have success at an early age, that doesn't necessarily mean she will go on to become a World, Olympic, or Paralympic champion.

During the early years of archery development, a key goal should be to help your young archer develop a solid base of fundamental skills. You should encourage participation in multiple sports in the early years of growth, which will encourage physical fitness, athletic awareness, skill building, and confidence that will carry over into archery.

For most athletes, success equates to fun, but fun doesn't always equate to success. Taking a systematic approach to long-term development might help to achieve the success that your young athlete seeks, as outlined below:

1. FUNdamental development
2. Learning to train
3. Training to train
4. Training to compete

Stage 1: FUNdamental Development

FUNdamental development can happen in archery from a very early age, starting as young as six to seven years old, but generally age eight is when your young archer has the patience, strength, and self-discipline to begin shooting. The objective for the early years is to learn the basic skills of the NTS. Your young archer might quickly develop the skills necessary to shoot longer distances than the beginner distance at which she started shooting. For example, your young archer in a beginning class might start shooting at targets four and a half meters away. When he becomes consistent at that distance, the instructor will opt to move the target to a distance of nine meters, which is also the distance at which young archers can begin earning JOAD achievement awards.

Once your archer has succeeded in achieving her first four achievement pins for consistency at the nine-meter target, the instructor will gradually move the target back until she is able to shoot targets at 18 meters—the legal distance for competition. As your archer becomes confident and consistent at 18 meters, she might be ready to try the fun and excitement of shooting a "fun" or youth tournament—not for the sake of winning but to gain experience and experience the fun and camaraderie of tournament shooting. The goal of the first tournament outing—and most competitions in general—should always be "form and fun." There should never be a score-based goal or a placement goal in mind, just the idea that tournaments are a time to have fun and an opportunity to challenge herself to shoot good form while under positive pressure.

Stage 2: Learning to Train

At this stage your young athlete has begun to realize that he enjoys archery and is beginning to understand the need to become more proficient at his skill sets. It is important at this stage of development that the window of opportunity be seized for refined development of your archer's skill sets. If your archer or his coach does not seize the opportunity, then archery tends to become frustrating to your young archer, and his development becomes stagnant. The objective for this stage is to begin to introduce intermediate skill sets and continue to refine the NTS fundamentals. If your archer has opportunities to continue trying tournaments, it's a great idea to keep him engaged on that front as well. Time and again, our country's strongest youth archery programs have had success with introducing tournaments as something to be tried for the sake of fun and experience, and keeping your young archer feeling connected to friends and having the fun of trying to beat his own personal best game.

At this stage, it's important to introduce the concept that improvement in skill comes only from practice and that improvement in scores comes only from the increased strength and confidence that practice brings. You might note at this stage that you do not want to be the "practice police," or you might become overly invested in your child's practice regimen. It's a great opportunity to have an honest talk with your child and her coach about what the expectations are for an archer who wants to be competitive; then it is up to your child to self-motivate when it comes to practice.

Stage 3: Training to Train

In this stage the objectives for your young archer are to continue to build his physical base, further refine his skill sets, and begin to develop a strong mental game. This stage can also be considered as a window of opportunity for accelerated adaptation. Things start to click, and your young athlete makes strides in both her personal growth and her growth as a competitor. Her true foundation is set in this stage, and her mindset of wanting to become a champion is forming. The foundation for future success is laid in this stage. The platform for this stage is typically that your archer might be seeing some competitive success at the local, stage, regional, or even national level, and becomes inspired to focus on bigger objectives. For many archers, competing in a national event such as USA Archery's National Indoor Championships or JOAD's National Indoor Championships is the catalyst for that moment of inspiration. For others, it's trying their first season of outdoor competition and realizing some success on that level. Interestingly, it's not always winning that helps your archer to focus on the next step. Sometimes it's meeting an Olympian, watching a national or world champion compete, or even failing to win and understanding that serious training could help him realize his potential.

Stage 4: Training to Compete

The objectives in this stage are to optimize preparation, and set and meet measurable goals. At this point, your young archer should be building on the lessons he has already learned, applying them in increasingly competitive situations. By now, your archer will have established a relationship with a coach who is guiding him, as well as be in a practice and training routine of his own designed to help him reach his goals. Throughout this and all phases of development, it is critical for you to realize the importance of your role in your archer's development: to provide positive emotional and financial support as your archer works toward his goals. Some of the saddest stories in any sport involve bright, young athletes with amazing potential whose early careers are cut short by difficulty in the athlete–parent relationship. It is vital that you realize that archery is your child's game and her wins and losses are hers alone. This mindset should become a habit from the very beginning of your child's involvement in the sport. The coach's job is to coach, and yours is to parent.

The best models for archer–parent relationships that involve the archer's successfully competing at the national and international level show relationships that are supportive and encouraging but that allow the archer to "call the shots" in terms of parent involvement. Your involvement can mean whether you watch your athlete's tournaments, how involved you become in training, whether you try to coach, or whether you provide positive reinforcement or create negative pressure in the form of expectations. In most cases, if you provide positive support and assistance that is athlete driven, you will see your child enjoy a positive experience in archery. At the highest levels of competition, supportive parents see their archer develop the kind of confidence and positive mental game that are integral to the archer's "owning" her training regimen, games, and wins and losses.

YOUR ROLE AND YOUR YOUNG ARCHER

Now that I have talked about developing young archers in some detail and the role of parents in general, the next issue is where you fit in and what concrete steps you can take in helping to develop your athlete. The reality is that your young archer will need your support for several practical matters such as transportation and funding lessons, training, and tournaments. You will support your young athlete in many ways, but one of the most important ways is through building self-esteem. One of the greatest components in your athlete's progress can be directly related to how she feels about herself. You do not want to deny your child a chance at fully achieving her goals, but sometimes the parent–coach role can become clouded. That athletes learn faster, perform better, and have fewer bad performances when they feel good about themselves has been proven. Following are a few specific suggestions for you to support the athlete–coach relationship and help your young athlete develop in a positive way:

Treat Your Athlete With Respect

Speak to your young athlete the way you would like to be spoken to. Respect him in what he is trying to accomplish; as respect is modeled for your young athlete, he will learn to give respect in turn. His learning curve will be shorter, and as a rule training can become more productive. Be careful never to humiliate or demean your young archer; this can cause him to lose confidence inside and outside of competition, and can eventually lead to a breakdown of your relationship with him.

Avoid Comparisons

Too often parents make the mistake of comparing their child to siblings or to her teammates or competitors. Comparisons almost always make the young athlete feel bad and generate unhealthy attitudes toward competition. Finally, feeling as though the athlete has to "beat" her competitors can lead to negative attitudes, unsportsmanlike conduct, and issues with ethics in sports. Remember that your child's goal is always to earn your approval. By teaching your child athlete that she can earn your approval through being a good person first and a good athlete second, you have set a solid foundation for positive growth and development.

Remember the Whole Person

Taking an interest in your athlete beyond his archery abilities will take you a long way toward making him feel special. If your athlete knows that you care about him as a person and not just for what he can do for you while competing, he will "reward" you with trust and a positive attitude in general and on the field, with high intensity and increased motivation.

Give Your Archer What She Needs Most

When your child has a bad performance or "lets you down," she is not less of a person. Remember that the game is your child's and not yours. At the end of the day, she needs to take credit for her own wins and evaluate her own struggles in competition. If you feel that your child is letting you down or you feel disappointed in her because of her performance, you have become too invested in her athletic activities and need to step back. Continuing along that path can cause irreparable damage to your archer as an athlete and as your child. What your child athlete needs most from you after a difficult loss or frustration in training is reassurance, an ear to listen, and help in reminding her of all of the good she is accomplishing in her training.

Challenge Your Archer

When you really want your young athlete to practice or perform, challenge him. Encourage him to think and work his way through the situation and reinforce that he can do what he is trying to achieve. A challenge is a positive way to interact with him. Challenges raise self-esteem when you can work together to accomplish the goal for the moment or for the day. Remember that threats generally diminish self-esteem and will set up the wrong kind of message because they are perceived as punishment. Rather, the goals and challenges that you discuss with your child should be measurable goals that are easily attainable and not necessarily score based. For example, if your archer expresses frustration with a problem during practice, you could challenge her to work with her coach on a solution and reward her for meeting the challenge. This is a great example of positive reinforcement that then creates increased drive and positive motivation. Remember, when planning in the broader sense with your child, both short- and long-term goals are necessary to create a road map for success, and the coach should always be involved in helping to set these goals.

Work Through Frustration

View your athlete's sport difficulties as challenges that you can work through as a team, and make that an opportunity to develop your relationship with her. Many parents become frustrated if their archers become upset, angry, or depressed during practice or competitions, but the reality is that every archer will have bad days, some worse than others. Instead of viewing bad days as a problem, see them as opportunities to help your archer work through his issues and develop tools for evaluating and solving challenges. Remember that your archer, if she remains serious about competition, will encounter challenges and difficulties throughout her archery career. A can-do attitude from an archer who has faced challenges before and overcome them can help that same archer tremendously when she faces increased pressure later in her shooting career.

Communicate

Be open, direct, and honest in your communication with your young athlete. Let him know how you feel. Remember that the heart of communication is listening. The way to make your athlete feel better about himself is to listen to him and accept his feelings, because he is entitled to them. Listening communicates caring on your part and helps him feel better about himself and his performances. If you feel that you can't directly help your athlete, enlist the help of others. Remind your child that the most important thing is that he talks about how he feels, even if it isn't with you. Facilitate open communication between your archer and his coach, and know when it's time to ask for help.

Be Empathetic

There is nothing else that makes us feel as good about ourselves as knowing that someone we respect understands us. Step into your child's shoes when she comes to you with her problems. View the world from her perspective rather than from your own. Remember how you would have felt at their age in her situation, participating in a competitive sport. If you let her know that you understand what it's like to be in her shoes, you'll make her feel cared about and valued. Communication with empathy is a key tool to meeting the challenges of being the parent of an archer athlete.

Use Recognition

Recognition is one of the most powerful motivators there is and another important way you can help your archer feel better and believe in himself. Simple comments such as "great job," "good effort," and "way to focus" will go a long way in the development of his confidence and self-esteem. Remember that although your child may have made some mistakes during his tournament or practice (and who doesn't make mistakes?), he did many more things correctly. Help your archer to focus on the positive in his training and competition, remembering that the proverbial glass is always half full in competitive sports. Sometimes it takes only a simple pat on the back to change how your archer feels about the way he competed that day and to help him leave practice or a tournament on a positive note.

Be Positive

Nothing good comes from negative thinking, particularly in competitive sports. Positive feedback is much more effective than negative feedback. Consistently getting down on your archer will not make her feel good about what she is trying to accomplish, and it certainly won't inspire her. On the other hand, praise and positive encouragement help your archer to build self-esteem and the confidence that is so critical to her performance in competition. Without confidence, your archer will experience difficulty and frustration in any sport and will eventually lose her love of the game, whereas good self-esteem and confidence in your archer will give her the tools she needs to be mentally strong when she trains and competes. Be positive, no matter what. You'll be amazed at how that positive attitude translates to other parts of your child's life, such as in academics and family relationships.

Handle Failures, Setbacks, and Mistakes Constructively

Teach your archer that mistakes and failures are a necessary part of the learning process. Remind him that it is always OK to make a mistake and even to finish in last place. Archery is a great sport in that competitors get the opportunity to try again and again. If your archer learns from the beginning that the sport is played one arrow at a time, he will also learn that he needs to concentrate on making only one good shot at a time and that a bad shot is gone and not worth agonizing over. The more your archer learns to concentrate on only the arrow that's on the string, the better he will perform overall.

Set the Right Example

Do not allow your archer to put herself or anyone else down. Allowing demeaning or hurtful behavior to go unchecked can lead to problems within your child's team and coaching relationships, and especially in her athletic development. In archery circles, archers are often heard quietly berating themselves for making a poor shot. If you hear this negative behavior from your archer, help her change her thoughts by encouraging her to say, "That shot was not as good as I wanted it to be, and here's how I can work on it." Changing her thoughts allows her to focus on the positive aspects of her game and teaches her the very important habit of building self-confidence even when the pressure is on.

Remember that all of the efforts toward developing your young athlete should be focused on helping him develop in a positive way that encourages a can-do attitude and self-confidence, and that provides a sense of achievement through training and reaching measurable goals. Being the parent and the coach simultaneously can be very difficult; separating these roles between two individuals is almost always better so that the expectations of a coach are completely separate from the relationship between you and your child. Developing your young athlete is a conscious effort on your part, and that of the coach and others who put the needs of your athlete first. Whether your archer is in the very beginning weeks of her first archery class or has competed on a World Championship team, know that the basics are the same and that the game always needs to be a fun, positive experience to keep your archer interested and growing.

14

Building Your Support Team

Robby K. Beyer

Your support team can comprise any number of individuals dedicated to advocating for your success. Support team members provide you with assistance, guidance, and recommendations in multiple areas of an athletic competition, theoretically providing you a well-rounded, fundamental approach to reaching your full athletic potential. The assistance, guidance, and recommendations of your support team members reach into the logistical, emotional, financial, and technical arenas, encompassing every facet of your competitive and social life.

The role of your support team should always be anchored in what is in your best interests. Your best interests are served by enabling and promoting a positive, winning attitude and culture. As with any team, each member of your support team plays an important role at crucial times in your development. In short, your support team members are advocates for you, championing and endorsing a winning attitude, individually and within a team environment.

WHO IS YOUR SUPPORT TEAM?

After having defined the role of your support team, I need to define the members of your support team. Your support team members can be composed of any number of individuals with whom you come into contact over the span of your career. Over the course of your career you will interact with numerous individuals who might become trusted members of your support team. The challenge lies with you and those closest to you to determine which prospective team members will work for your best interests. The prioritization of your best interests above all else is a critical determining factor in who should become a part of your support team.

The most logical members of your core support team are those individuals who have been with you throughout your career. If your core support team is your inner circle, then the members of that team might include your parents, guardians, siblings, extended family, coaches, and teammates. Build your core support team with those individuals you trust the most, and they will become your confidants who help to guide your development. The individuals within your core support team assist you in managing the details surrounding preparations for or during training and competitions.

Many other people will be outside of your core group, surrounding you, but who are still in positions to help and support you and who also can play critical roles in your development and success. These individuals have an impact on supplemental areas surrounding your training and competition. The following list outlines some of the individuals who can become part of your support team, including but not limited to the following:

- Coach
- Family (immediate and extended)
- Friends
- Medical staff
- Sport psyche/mental training experts
- Nutritionist
- Strength and conditioning coach
- Administrative and management personnel
- Sponsors
- Industry insiders
- Tournament organizers
- School officials
- Travel agents

BUILDING YOUR SUPPORT TEAM

The growth of your support team is natural to you as you learn the sport of archery. The growth will be dependent on coaches and clubs in your community and how quickly you learn a sport. One of the most common ways for you to begin a sport is through your family members. Teaching family members the sport of archery is a great way for you to begin shooting. In this particular instance, in which you are introduced to the sport by family, your family members comprise your core support team. More on developing young archers can be found in chapter 13.

What if your family is not involved in the sport? How do you build your support team? You need to utilize social collateral to open opportunities to learn the sport of archery. Particularly for archery this can include any number of clubs or organizations directly or indirectly connected to the sport of archery. Members of your support team in this case might be teachers, members of the community, camp counselors, and others who volunteer to help teach an introductory archery program.

Chapter 13 discusses the many routes available to athlete development for young archers. One of the best ways for you to get started in the Olympic sport of archery is to join a local Junior Olympic Archery Development (JOAD) club. A local JOAD club can provide you with the necessary resources to begin training and access to an instructor or coach who teaches the National Training System. Upon entering the JOAD club environment you will begin to build your core support team.

The constant to your core support team, regardless of your stage of development, is your finding the appropriate balance of encouragement and assistance. As you develop and mature in the sport, you will need encouragement from your core support team. You need your core support team to serve as your trusted group of confidants. In your core support team, *trust* must key; for you to concentrate on training and developing the skills you need for competition, you must be able to rely on your core support team without question.

WHEN TO GROW YOUR SUPPORT TEAM

If you decide to take your training and competition to the next level, your support team will need to grow and develop along with you. As you develop your skills and find competitive success regionally and nationally, you will incur new training and competitive experiences. Your support team plays an important role in helping you to process all of these experiences and can help you to see a failure as a learning experience. As a support team member—for example, as a parent—you might be the first person with whom the athlete interacts as she leaves the shooting line at a competition. As a good friend or coach, you might be the person the athlete turns to when she has had a great success. The primary role of your support team in this case is to help you to process the experience in a way that will help you grow and develop as a competitive archer.

At times, you and your support team might need to seek advice from professionals within or outside of the sport, including the assistance of more knowledgeable coaches, equipment manufacturers, sports psychologists, physical therapists, nutritionists, and others, all of whom become members of your extended support team. By reaching out to professionals, you will continue the growth and development of your support team.

The growth and development of your support team is dependent on you and your stage of development. If you are in the beginning stages of development you will have needs different from those of an Olympic team member. Both types of archers need a support team; however, each archer requires different assistance from her support team because her needs are different. Remember also that all athletes, even those who are seemingly at the same level of competitive experience, develop at different levels and therefore have different expectations of their support teams.

Open communication within your support team is critical to your success and your team as a whole. The members of your team must be focused on what is in your best interests and be willing to put aside personality and other differences to do what is best for you. For example, if your support team enlists the help of your parents, siblings, coach, archery range and pro shop personnel, close friends, and JOAD club teammates, you have a big team behind you. All of those teammates, however, need to find a way to interact and work together in a way that supports your development. Your coach directs your training. You will practice at the local archery range, and the pro shop personnel will help you work on your equipment and order replacements when necessary. Your parents will provide access to practice and transportation to competitions, and support the cost of weekly lessons, equipment, and tournaments. Your parents, siblings, and friends will provide emotional support and encouragement in your personal life, and your parents will assist you with balancing a busy school and archery schedule. Your friends and siblings might come to archery competitions to provide encouragement at a critical time, but only if you want them there. Your JOAD club teammates also play a critical role in encouraging you and providing a healthy environment in which to practice competitive skills without the pressure of a tournament.

Although their roles are different, all of these teammates are equally important to your success, whether you are at the very beginning stages of development or training for Olympic team placement. During the entire training process, you are responsible for absorbing your coach's instruction, keeping an open mind to new competitive experiences, maintaining a positive mental attitude, and above all else, training as much as is necessary to reach your goals. As you develop your skills, potentially several years from beginning archery, open dialogue between you and your coach, you and your parents, and you and the other members of your support team is a must. Your support team must foster an environment in which you are not afraid to speak up for fear of hurting feelings; rather you must be able to express your needs in a way that will help you meet your goals.

All of the members of your support team must also be able to work together cooperatively, using open communication, to provide the best help for you. Open communication during training and competition, and even during downtime, is an absolute requirement for you to be productive and continue to develop during competition and training. This open communication between you and your support team leads to a planned calendar of training and competition. The planning of a season is termed periodization, which helps you set up your annual calendar (see chapter 8).

PERIODIZATION OF YOUR SUPPORT TEAM

Athletic training cycles can be broken into periods of training depending on the timing of development and/or competition calendar. The general concept is called *periodization*, simply defined as *a division of time periods*. You and your support team must go through periodization stages, which will include development, training, and competition cycles. The support team detail listed in the growth section reflects periodization over the course of a career.

Along with career periodizations of your support team, you will have smaller changes, called *microcycles*, during a season. The microcycles of your support team will be dependent on the time of the season. During preseason (preparation) training cycles, you might need more support from medical personnel, strength and conditioning coaches, sponsors, and industry insiders. These individuals on your support team enable you to keep training through heavy training loads and changes with equipment.

As the beginning of the competition season approaches, the individuals of your support team shift from supporting preparations to supporting competitions. Support in-season includes the organization of logistical and operational details for each event. During the competitive season it is best for you to continue building on your foundation set in the preparation phases. During the competitive season you should be more focused on fine-tuning equipment compared to making major equipment changes, and the same philosophy applies to your support team. There might be certain exceptions to this rule, but in general, the competition season is not the time to be making major changes to equipment or your support team.

Role of Your Support Team During Training Versus Competition

During the course of your career you will undergo changes and adjustments to your equipment and/or training cycles. You and your support team members might ask about the correct timing in making major changes to your equipment, training schedules, or even to the members of your support team. Ideally, you and your support team members will make changes and adjustments during training situations. Competitions are the time to display what has occurred during training sessions. As a general rule, except in cases of equipment failure or other dire circumstances, you should *not* make major changes in the middle of a competition.

Training sessions and competitions are two different venues for you and your support team. You will develop separate routines for training and for competition. You and your support team are responsible for understanding the routines that work best for you. Communication between you and your support team is a necessity for planning routines for training and competitions.

You and your support team members need to understand that training sessions are the time to develop your technique and to fine-tune equipment. Major technique adjustments and equipment changes should take place during off-season training sessions, when you still have sufficient time to commit the changes to muscle memory, thus making the changes a permanent part of your shot cycle. Changes, whether to equipment or shooting form, can require significant time for you to become comfortable with them during the pressure of competition. You need to develop your technical skills during training sessions if you intend to have successful competitions. A good training philosophy is for you to work on increasing your average arrow scores during training sessions. Improving training scores provides a confidence that should translate into greater competitive success.

Competitive success depends on your technical skill and ability, and the success of your support team translates to your success in terms of making training and competition a productive and positive experience. If you and your support team have trained appropriately, you need only to compete as you have trained, and your support team need only to provide logistical support and big-picture guidance. Your support team assists you in staying focused, relaxed, and physically present for the competitive season.

LANGUAGE AND COMMUNICATION WITHIN YOUR SUPPORT TEAM

The single most important component of your support team is open communication between you and your support team members. A consistent support team should be able to build open, honest communication with you. You and your support team must learn how to communicate with each other and to build trust, which takes time to develop.

How should you and your support team communicate with each other? The broad stroke answer is that it depends on the individuals involved. Your support team members and you will develop your own style of talking to one another as communication between your support team members and you takes on various roles. The communication between you and your support team members consists of three components: nonverbal (body language), verbal (verbal cues), and paraverbal (vocal fluctuations).

Multiple studies have attributed various percentages of communication to the three types of communication. The largest portion of communication is nonverbal, with 55 percent of communication attributed to body language. The next largest percentage is vocal fluctuations at 38 percent. Amazingly, verbal cues make up just 7 percent of all communication (Mehrabian 1971). With this in mind, the development of a communication system between you and your support team is best accomplished by working together in person on a regular basis.

Communication between you and your support team will be built either on positive or negative words. What effects do positive and negative words have on human beings? A Japanese doctor, Masaru Emoto (2004), studied water and how positive or negative words affect water's crystallized structure. Through his research Dr. Emoto found that frozen water exposed to positive words such as *thank you* creates beautiful crystal structures. He also found that frozen water exposed to negative words such as *you fool* created unattractive crystallized structures.

Dr. Emoto's studies have been questioned for their scientific validity based on whether he used appropriate scientific processes to conduct his research. Regardless of whether Dr. Emoto's work has complete scientific validity, his experiments raise some intriguing insights into how words can affect the structure of water within our bodies and thus, our bodies.

Based on scientific merit, one concept of communication integral in a support team is positive reinforcement. By providing positive verbal reinforcement to you, a support team member is likely to see the action repeated. Positive reinforcement can be used in *all* phases of your development and needs to be structured based on your training age and the desired response. For positive reinforcement to work properly your support team members need to understand your likes and dislikes. By knowing your motivating factors, a support team member will have a greater likelihood of seeing reproducible positive actions from you. Using positive language and reinforcement to highlight positive actions develops your self-image and goes a long way in building long-lasting, successful partnership relationships. Your support team is responsible for helping to structure positive communication to develop an honest and open relationship with you.

ADVANTAGES AND DISADVANTAGES OF YOUR SUPPORT TEAM

Your support team can make the difference between your reaching the podium stand or being defeated in the first round of competition. You have the responsibility to compete at the top of your abilities, and your support team has the responsibility to prepare you for competition. In preparation for the competition your support team creates an environment that fosters your independence and a can-do attitude. Once a competition has begun your support team is responsible for letting you perform.

Major distractions while preparing for a tournament create unnecessary stress on you. By focusing on your individual needs, a well-organized support team minimizes distractions, thus enabling you to compete at your highest level of competition and being the difference between receiving a gold or a silver medal. Your support team must fully understand you and your individual needs by being familiar with your reactions when you are placed under stressful situations, and knowing and respecting the boundaries you have set while under the pressure of competition.

A mismanaged support team, on the other hand, will create more headaches and stress over a season or career and can be detrimental to your performance. In a worst-case scenario, for example, an overzealous parent or coach who uses negative criticism or is self-focused rather than focused on helping you can cause you to become resentful of the competition experience and unwilling to participate in the sport any longer. You already face pressure in preparing for competition and during the tournament itself, and mismanaged situations will only complicate your preparations and performance.

Support team members with ulterior motives can also create distractions. This disadvantage can be difficult to identify because every individual of your support team talks about what is best for you. The individuals of your support team might be looking to gain fame or fortune by claiming they were a part of your development or simply be living out their own competitive dreams through your success.

Support team members with selfish ambitions eventually show their true intentions to you and your other support team members. Generally, a support team member who uses negative criticism, places unfair expectations on you, or is focused on how your performance affects him personally probably does not place your interests first. Rely on your own intuition along with feedback and input from your core support team members about whom you allow into your support team.

YOU AND YOUR SUPPORT TEAM

Your support team members play many vital roles in your development. They assist with the logistical details surrounding competition, communicate with positive words, and help to periodize training and minimize distractions. Your support team members' assistance reaches beyond the archery range into all phases of your life, and they will continue to offer you support, whether as parents, spouses, coaches, or trusted confidants, when you transition away from competitive archery. A solid support team provides assistance with finding the next steps in your life journey and help with emotional support.

An effective support team provides the following:

- Advice
- Empathy
- Structure
- Camaraderie
- Leadership
- Guidance
- Enthusiasm
- Encouragement
- Belief

The support provided by a team member has a positive influence on you for life. Each member of your support team leaves an indelible imprint on you, and your team members must make a conscious decision to make their contributions positive. Being a member of a support team is a privilege regardless of your athlete's level of competitive success. You must be aware of how you are influencing the athlete for her future success in life. Through positive interaction with the archer, you will be able to help her accomplish goals she once thought unattainable.

Your support team is a necessary and valuable component to your development and success in your chosen sport, in this case archery. Your support team might develop naturally, or your team members might need to be carefully chosen to provide the most effective team for you. Team members who play to your strengths are able to step back and watch you soar to your athletic potential!

Appendix

Working With Para-Archers
By Randi Smith

When an archer shows up for your program in a wheelchair or with another disability, there is really no need to panic! Many people who have disabilities can shoot with very few adaptations—one of the reasons that archery can be such a positive experience. For some, especially at the beginning, the changes can just be very simple ones: shorter distances, bigger targets, more time. Also, remember that with a beginning para-archer, you don't need to worry about rules. Figure out what works and use it. If and when the para-archer decides to be competitive, then you can worry about rules. Therefore, assume that a para-archer is actually there to learn archery and isn't participating in just a one-time clinic or activity.

TYPES OF DISABILITIES

People with almost any type of disability can participate in archery. Amputations are probably the most common disability and occur in both children and adults. Cerebral palsy, ADHD, and birth defects all begin at birth but never go away, so you may have individuals of all ages who have those disabilities and want to try archery. Traumatic brain injury, stroke, and spinal cord injury are more common in teens and adults, mostly as the result of accidents.

Amputation and Missing Limbs
These conditions can be caused by traumatic injuries, illnesses, or birth defects. Some people choose to use prosthetics; others do not. With lower-limb amputations, lack of stability is usually a concern, especially on uneven ground. Pain and irritation from the prosthetic can be problems especially in hot, sticky weather.

Spinal Cord Injury
This condition generally occurs from traumatic injuries or birth defects. There is usually a loss of function and sensation below the injury; it may be partial or complete. People with lower-body disabilities are often considered paraplegic; people with both upper- and lower-body disabilities are considered quadriplegic or tetraplegic. They may use assistive devices such as wheelchairs or crutches. Concerns can include bowel and bladder issues, problems with controlling body temperature, and injuries due to lack of movement and lack of sensation. It is important that both the instructor and the athlete watch for potential injuries and situations that can cause injury. (For example, lack of sensation may keep an athlete from realizing he is getting sunburned.)

Stroke and Traumatic Brain Injury
Both result in damage to the brain. The location of the injury causes different types of injuries. The person may lose function on just one side of the body, or there may be a more general loss. TBI often occurs with other injuries (such as spinal cord injury). Both stroke and TBI can cause both expressive and receptive language issues. Emotions and the ability to control them and memory are often affected as well.

Cerebral Palsy

This refers to several neurological disorders caused by abnormalities in the brain that appear during infancy or childhood. Body movement and coordination are permanently affected, but CP does not get worse. The effects of cerebral palsy are very individualized. It may be mild or severe. Muscles may be stiff and spastic or floppy and weak; one limb may be affected, or the whole body may be affected. Many people with CP also have trouble talking.

Orthopedic and Neuromuscular Impairment

People who have disabilities such as multiple sclerosis, scoliosis, or arthritis are often placed in this category. The condition may be degenerative, meaning it gets worse as time goes by. It's important to keep the communication lines open and to watch for changes. A standing archer may need to eventually sit; an archer who uses a cane may eventually need a wheelchair.

ADHD and Learning Disability

There are usually not any adaptations necessary in the basic archery form. However, there are ways to help the archer be more successful. Following a definite routine (getting equipment, warming up, scoring, and cleaning up) can make things easier. Marks on the floor for feet, smaller groups, minimizing distractions, and repetition can all help as well. Patience from the instructor and the realization that the archer is not intentionally misbehaving are the two things that often make the biggest difference.

Visual Impairment

Like the other disabilities, visual impairments vary from person to person. It's important to ensure the range is free of obstructions and that things are not placed where someone could trip over them. When outdoors, make sure there are no holes or other hazards between the shooting line and the target.

INSTRUCTION FOR PARA-ARCHERS

When working with para-archers, start your instruction as you would with any new archer. Find out the abilities of the archer and if they have ever done archery before and what they want to do with their skills. Are they going to compete, or do they want to go hunting? Will archery be an occasional activity, or will it be something they do regularly?

Once you've established these things, start instruction beginning with the stance. Look at stability and balance. Determine how the archer will be most stable; be sure to think about the whole shot—setup, execution, and follow-through.

Stance, Stability, and Balance

Stance, stability, and balance are important for all archers. Stance is the foundation of the shot, the part that everything else is built on. However, if the archer has a good stance but no stability and no balance, he will not be able to consistently shoot a good shot. For the archer in the wheelchair, that stability includes a solid place for the chair as well as the body in the chair. The archer in the wheelchair may be unable to use the leg or trunk muscles to help stabilize the body, so getting the body to where it has the best balance is especially critical. The archer who is standing most likely has better trunk and leg muscles but may have other issues (such as legs that are different lengths) that you need to consider.

When Off-the-Shelf Equipment Doesn't Work

Although most adaptations are fairly easy, sometimes things need to be more complicated and coaches need to be a bit more creative. Following are a few examples of the adaptations you may see in archery.

Mechanical Releases

There are several types of mechanical releases. Sometimes just trying out the various types and finding one that works are all that you need to do. Some are held in the hand and some have wrist straps, and some hook on to the elbow. If releasing the arrow is the issue, there are several ways to release it. It can be pushed against the chin or cheek or the chin or cheek can push against it. For shooters with just one arm who wish to use a mechanical release, a harness or shell can be developed and the release can be attached to it.

Mouth Tabs

Some shooters with just one arm prefer to use mouth tabs. A mouth tab is a tab that is tied to the string. The archer bites on the tab and uses it to pull back the bowstring. The string is released when the archer opens the mouth. Archers hold the mouth tab in the teeth and push out with the arm. When using a mouth tab, it is important for the archer to use the back teeth and to start with lightweight bows. Mouth tabs are not commercially available but are not difficult to make.

Gloves

Some archers will need assistance holding on to the bow and the release. Quad gloves are easy to make and use, but they can be bulky. A quad glove looks like a mitten but has Velcro around the wrist to hold it on and has a strap at the fingers. The bow is placed in the hand, and the fingers are placed around the bow. The strap at the fingers is then wrapped around the wrist. Archery gloves or other sporting gloves can be used to make less bulky gloves.

Visual Adaptations

This depends a lot on the degree of impairment and the type of shooting the archer wants to do. For an archer who just wants to shoot for fun and has some sight, the only adaptation may be moving the target closer. Other things that can be done include putting a guide rope from the shooting line to the target (tie a knot a few feet from each end) and gluing string to the target on the lines dividing the scoring areas (so the archer can feel where the arrows scored). For national and international competition, archers use "blackout" blindfolds or glasses so they all have no sight. Sighting is done by mounting the sight on a tripod and then touching the sight with a part of the hand. A guide for the feet is usually built and the tripod is often connected to it. A spotter stands behind the archer and tells the archer where the arrows have landed.

Wheelchair

For the archer in a wheelchair, stance, stability, and balance can affect the shot in several ways. Front-to-back balance is important so the archer can sit up as straight as possible. Side-to-side balance keeps the archer from falling out of the chair when pulling back the string or releasing it. The archer needs to be stable in all directions and able to maintain balance; sometimes this results in form that is not technically perfect.

Look at the person in the wheelchair as well as the wheelchair, and then ask yourself these questions:

- *Does the wheelchair fit the person*? If not, it may be easier to use another chair. You can also use some sort of cushioning or padding on the draw side of the chair.
- *Does the wheelchair have a solid seat*? A saggy seat doesn't help posture while shooting. You can temporarily place a board in the seat, usually under the cushion.
- *Are feet on something solid (floor or footrest)*? If not, find something to put the feet on. If they can't be on the floor or the footrest of the wheelchair, some kind of solid block can also work. For some people, you may have to strap the legs or the feet so they don't react with the shot.
- *How is the archer's balance in the wheelchair*? If the person has poor balance, they may fall out of the chair or tip over during the draw or when the arrow is released. This is a good time to use a strap, usually around the chest. If balance is good, and the archer won't fall out, it's generally a good idea to take the armrest off the bow-arm side of the chair.
- *What happens during the shot*? Make sure the string clears the wheel as well as all body parts. If not, a shorter bow (or occasionally a longer bow) may be necessary. If only the tip of the bow hits the wheel during the follow-through, you can cover the wheel so the bow is not damaged.
- *What will happen during the follow-through*? Make sure the release hand won't hit anything. Also check the feet and the torso and make sure the follow-through won't cause a loss of balance.

Standing

Archers can have several types of disabilities that allow them to stand or use a stool. One of the first things to think about for a standing archer is stability. The archer needs to be stable in all conditions—wind, mud, uneven ground. Archers with upper-body disabilities and some below-knee amputations may need no adaptations to stance. With other disabilities, you may have to be a little more creative. Sometimes a stand can be developed for the archer to lean against; sometimes a block under one foot can help. If an archer is shooting on a slippery surface, you can find something less slippery for the archer to stand on. Indoors, it could be a nonslip rug; outdoors, it might be a piece of plywood.

If the archer is able to stand but has poor balance or stability, it is possible to use a chair or stool to shoot from. You can try several types of chairs, but stools without backs generally work the best. Sometimes something to lean against, rather than to sit on, works better. Feet should be able to reach the floor.

Shooting the Shot

If the archer has good function in both hands and both arms, you can use the regular method of eye dominance to determine which hand should be used for the bow and for the release. If not, you will probably have to use some trial and error to see which way works best. Some people prefer to use the better hand to hold the bow; others prefer to use the better hand to release the string. It will also make a difference if one arm extends better than the other arm. It's not common, but some archers have chosen to shoot with the bow out in front rather than to the side. Stands have also been developed to hold the bow so the archer is able to concentrate on pulling and aiming.

To help hold the bow or a mechanical release in the hand, an archer can use quad gloves, an adapted glove, or elastic bandages. Sometimes a release with a wrist strap can also be used. If a release is used, it will be necessary to determine how the release will be released. If the finger won't work, it may be possible to use a cheekbone or the tongue against the cheek. To start with, an assistant may have to set off the release while the archer does the aiming. Pay attention to the follow-through of the release!

The string is usually pulled using the fingers or a release just as in able-bodied archery; however, there are some exceptions. Sometimes the release needs to be tied or fastened into the hand. This can be done using an adapted glove, or sometimes a wrist strap can work. If the archer is missing an arm or for some reason does not have another way to hold the string, a mouth tab can be used. A simple mouth tab is quick and easy to make and can be used to give archery a try. It's important when trying a mouth tab that the archer start with a very lightweight bow and use the back molars to hold the tab. After trying it out, the archer may want to try some different materials for the mouth tab and try different lengths to find a length that works.

Releasing the string can be done in the conventional manner; for archers using a mechanical release, it can be done by pushing the release against the cheekbone, using the tongue, or hooking up a clothespin or camera-release mechanism. These items are not available commercially but can be fairly easy to put together.

COMPETITION

Most archers get their first competition experiences at local tournaments. It is important to check with the tournament organizers and see what is required. Many local tournaments are more interested in participation than sticking to the rules and will allow anyone to shoot with any type of equipment. Some tournaments will allow anyone to shoot, but they will have a separate category for archers who need exceptions to the rules. A local tournament is a good place to go to find out the rules and to get experience.

If an archer decides to be competitive, you need to consider some things. First is equipment. Currently in the United States, the JOAD program does not worry about the IPC (International Paralympic Committee) rules as far as wheelchairs and shooting aids are concerned. If a JOAD archer shoots a compound bow, she shoots in the compound class; if the archer shoots a recurve bow, she shoots in the recurve class. Archers can use any type of wheelchair or chair and any release as long as they do not interfere with the other archers. An assistant can also load arrows. However, it is important for the JOAD archer and the coach (and usually parents) to understand that they can't interfere with other archers. They can't take up extra space, they can't take extra time, they don't get extra shots, and they have to shoot the same distances as everyone else. (Of course, on a local level, tournament directors can make their own decisions, but the local tournaments are also a great chance to practice for state and national tournaments.) Usually, the parent or coach pulls and scores the arrows, but often the other archers on the target are willing to do it.

For adults, things are a bit different. Again, at local and club tournaments, the rules may be a little different, and things are often easier to adapt. By the time an archer is ready to go to a state or national tournament, he should know and be able to follow the rules. The following information applies to Paralympic or FITA competitions. Other organizations have different rules.

There are three classifications in para-archery. They are referred to as ST, W2, and W1:

- ST archers are archers who have physical disabilities but shoot from a standing position or with a chair or stool. They have both feet on the ground and they shoot recurve bows following FITA rules.

- W2 archers shoot from wheelchairs and use wheelchairs for daily mobility. They also use recurve bows and follow FITA equipment rules.

- W1 archers use wheelchairs, but they also have a disability in their hands or arms. They can use compound bows, but there are restrictions. Men have a maximum weight of 45 pounds; the maximum for women is 35 pounds. The bow can have the same equipment as that used on a recurve bow according to the FITA rules—basically, no magnification, no level, and no peep sight.

There is a fourth shooting division; archers who are classified as any of the previously mentioned can choose to shoot in the Open Compound division. Usually, it is fairly easy to tell which class a person will fit into, but all archers are eventually officially classified by a team of classifiers and therapists. The classifying committee can clarify exceptions for individual archers, allowing things such as mouth tabs, mechanical releases, or assistants to load arrows. When shooting in the Open Compound division, it uses FITA compound bow rules, and archers can stay on the line instead of coming off and on. If this is the case, it's very important for the tournament director to know ahead of time that this is the plan. The archer should not take up more than her own designated space. As with all archers, the archer with a disability can designate an agent to pull and score her own arrows. However, only the agent or the archer can go to the target, not both. If the archer cannot or does not put the bow down between ends, it is important that the judge know how to tell when the archer is finished.

Remember, adapting for archers with disabilities is usually easy but occasionally does require some creativity. Physical and occupational therapists can be great resources (especially if they know archery or are willing to come to wherever you are shooting). Information and photos of archers with disabilities are available at USA Archery's website at www.usarchery.org or World Archery's website at www.archery.org.

References

Chapter 3

Lee, KiSik, and Robert de Bondt. 2009. *Total archery*. GamJeong-Dong, GimPo-City, Korea: Samick Sports.

Chapter 10

Nierenberg, Cari. 2011. How much protein do you need? www.webmd.com/diet/healthy-kitchen-11/how-much-protein.

Chapter 15

Emoto, Masaru. 2004. *The hidden messages in water*. Translated by David A. Thayne. Hillsboro, OR: Beyond Words.

Mehrabian, Albert. 1971. *Silent messages*. 1st ed. Belmont, CA: Wadsworth.

Index

PLEASE NOTE: Page numbers followed by an italicized *f* or *t* indicate that there is a figure or table on that page, respectively.

A

ADHD. *See* attention deficit hyperactivity disorder
After School Archery Program (ASAP) 2
age divisions 3*t*
aiming 41
    drill 108
    in recurve archery 82-84, 84*f*
aim-off training 130
aluminum bows 13
amputation 201
anchoring 39, 39*f*
    angular 70
    in compound archery 106, 106*f*
    in recurve archery 70-73, 71*f*
    with sternocleidomastoid 71, 72*f*
anchor point 71-72
angular motion
    in drawing 60, 65, 104*f*
    in recurve archery 47, 88
    in recurve archery expansion 77
antidoping practices 179
Archery Shooters Association 2
arm across the chest stretch 138, 138*f*
arm raise drill 99
arrow count buildup
    calendar 174*f*
    before local events 174
arrow rests 14
    fall-away 14*f*
    fixed-blade 14*f*
    for local events 176
arrows 13-14
    for local events 176
    nocking 33-34, 33*f*
    parallel 14
ASAP. *See* After School Archery Program
athlete-parent relationship 188-189
attention deficit hyperactivity disorder (ADHD) 202
attitude 6
awareness 29-30

B

back-to-hand tension ratio 64
balance
    for para-archer instruction 202-204
    training 154
bare-shaft tuning 26-27
barrel of the gun position 35
    length of 82
    in recurve archery 46, 59*f*, 60*f*
    in recurve archery transfer 75
Bassham, Lanny 162

belief statements 162-163
binoculars 176
biomechanics 30
    barrel of the gun length and 82
blank bale shooting 122, 122*f*
bone alignment, during holding 40*f*
bow-arm position, in compound archery 99-100, 99*f*
bow release drill 124, 124*f*
bows. *See also* compound bows; recurve bows
    lightweight 120
    materials 13
    types of 11-13
Boys and Girls Clubs 3
Boy Scouts 185
breathing cycle 82
burnout 171

C

cables 176
carbohydrates 134
carbon fiber
    bows 13
    sights 14
cardiorespiratory conditioning 140-141
casting 13
center shot
    for compound bows 19
    paper tuning for 24
    for recurve bows 22, 22*f*
cerebral palsy 202
clickers 41-42
    position during holding 77*f*
    in recurve archery expansion 77-79
CNC. *See* Computer Numerical Control
coaches
    background checks of 5
    certification of 185-186
    choosing 4-5
    levels of 4-5
    style 4-5
    youth 186
comfort zone 166
communication
    with support team 195-198
    types of 198
    with youths 190
comparisons 189
competition
    analysis 170
    handling pressure in 167-168
    mental domain and 182

competition *(continued)*
    para-archers in 205-206
    peaking for 180-182
    physical domain and 180
    preparation for 169
    support team during 197
    tactical domain and 181
    technical domain and 180-181
    training 129, 188-189
    weight training in 142, 146*f*
compound archery
    aiming drill 108
    anchoring in 106, 106*f*
    bow-arm position in 99-100, 99*f*
    drawing in 104-105, 104*f*, 105*f*
    expansion in 108
    follow-through in 109, 109*f*
    grip in 101
    head position in 96, 96*f*
    holding in 107, 107*f*
    hook in 100-101
    mindset in 93
    posture in 95-100, 95*f*
    reaffirmation in 110
    release in 108, 108*f*
    setup position in 102-103, 102*f*, 103*f*
    stance in 94-95, 94*f*
    transfer in 107
compound bows 12
    bare-shaft tuning for 26-27
    cam-and-a-half 12
    center shot setting for 19
    characteristics of 4*t*
    draw length 17
    draw weight 18-19
    grip drill 102
    high-speed camera turning for 27
    line tuning for 25-26, 26*f*
    nocking point 18
    paper tuning 23-24, 24*f*, 25*f*
    recurve bows compared to 93
    releases 100-101, 100*f*
    setup 17-19
    solo-cam 12
    tiller adjustment of 19, 19*f*
    tiller tuning for 25
    tuning 23-27
    two-cam 12
Computer Numerical Control (CNC) 13
consistency, in recurve shot cycle 90
C-spot 78, 78*f*
    during recurve archery release 86
cushion button 176

D
dampeners 16*f*
de Bondt, Robert 30
determination 1
disabilities 201-202
distance shooting 129

distractions
    pressure and 9-10
    training 8, 159
D-loop 176
drawing 37, 37*f*
    angular motion in 60, 65, 104*f*
    in compound archery 104-105, 104*f*, 105*f*
    length 17
    linear 104
    in recurve archery 63-66, 64*f*, 66*f*
    velocity 68
    weight 18-19

E
elbow over the head stretch 139, 139*f*
elbow rotation, in recurve archery 56*f*
Emoto, Masuro 198
empathy 191
endorphins 141
endurance training 142
equipment 13-17
    accessories 176
    analysis 169-170
    for local events 175-176
    for out-of-town events 179
    quality of 166-167
    set up time 175
    style 4
events
    format 174-175, 178
    local 173-177
    location 175, 178
    out-of-town 177-180
Evernote 169
examples 191-192
execution drill 123, 123*f*
execution improvement activities 123-130
expansion 41
    in compound archery 108
    in recurve archery 77-79
experience 166
external rotation exercise 147, 147*f*
external shoulder rotation exercise
    at 90-degree abduction 153, 153*f*
    synchronized 152, 152*f*
eye dominance 84

F
failures 191
fat 134
FDA. *See* Food and Drug Administration
feedback 42-43
finger sling 101, 101*f*
finger spacer 51*f*, 52*f*
finger tabs 176
fishtailing 26-27
FITA. *See* World Archery
fletching 167
flexibility
    recurve shot cycle and 90
    SPT drill 78, 126, 126*f*

fluids 134-135
focus 2
    mental training 158-159
    mindset and 35
    under pressure 168-169
follow-through 41-42, 42*f*
    in compound archery 109, 109*f*
    in recurve archery 86-87, 87*f*, 88*f*
Food and Drug Administration (FDA) 135
Formaster 114, 123
foundation, in recurve archery 63
4-H 185
four-minute drill 129
frustration 190
FUNdamental development 187

G
Girl Scouts 185
gloves 203
goals
    for local events 177
    long-term 160
    outcome-based 7
    performance-based 7
    practice 8-9
    process-based 5
    setting 5-9, 160-161
    short-term 161
Gold Game 129, 159
grip 34, 34*f*
    during anchoring 39
    in compound archery 101
    drill 102
    pitch, yaw, and roll of 56-57, 57*f*
    in recurve archery 54-57, 54*f*, 55*f*

H
Haberl, Peter 158
hamstring stretch 137, 137*f*
head movement drill 97, 97*f*
head position
    in compound archery 96, 96*f*
    posture drill and 125
    in recurve archery 73, 73*f*, 74*f*
heart rate
    activities 130-132
    conditioning 140-141
    pressure and 156
herbal supplements 179
high-speed camera tuning 27
holding 30, 40, 40*f*
    clicker position during 77*f*
    in compound archery 107, 107*f*
    connection 76*f*
    in recurve archery 46, 46*f*, 76-77
    SPT drill 77, 126
    squeeze drill and 41
hook 34, 34*f*
    during anchoring 39
    in compound archery 100-101
    drill 52, 53*f*
    in recurve archery 50-52, 50*f*, 51*f*, 52*f*
hydration 133-136

I
indoor archery 13
intensity practice 132
internal rotation exercise 148, 148*f*
internal shoulder rotation exercise 154, 154*f*
International Paralympic Committee (IPC) 205

J
JDT. *See* Junior Dream Team
JOAD. *See* Junior Olympic Archery Development
journals 161
Junior Dream Team (JDT) 3
Junior Olympic Archery Development (JOAD) 3,
    184-185
    para-archer competition and 205-206
    Star Pin Score Levels 184*f*-185*f*

L
LAN 2 32, 32*f*, 37
    in recurve archery 47, 47*f*, 65*f*
    in recurve archery transfer 75
    during transfer 39
language 197-198
learning disabilities 202
Lee, KiSik 30, 186
lightweight bow training drill 120
limb alignment 21
limb bolts 19*f*
linear motion
    in recurve archery 47
    in recurve archery follow-through 86-87
line tuning 25-28, 26*f*
loading
    incorrect 69, 69*f*
    phase 38
    position 38, 38*f*
    in recurve archery 67-69, 68*f*, 69*f*
    shoulder alignment during 70*f*
log books 161-162, 169-170
low-intensity activity 136

M
macrocycles 112
macronutrients 134-135
medications 179
meditation
    breathing-centered 157-158
    mindfulness 158
    thought-centered 158
mental domain 182
mental game 6
mental imagery 156-157
Mental Management Systems 162
mental training
    belief statements in 162-163
    distraction training and 159
    focus 158-159

mental training (*continued*)
goal setting in 160-161
intensity 182*f*
log books for 161-162
meditation in 157-158
mental imagery in 156-157
Olympic Round Set Play and 156
pressure and 10
reasons for 155-156
weight training and 141
mesocycles 112, 112*f*
weight training in 142
microcycles 112, 113*f*, 196
mimetics 86
mindset 35
in compound archery 93
in recurve archery 58
mistakes 191
mouth tabs 203
muscle contraction 32
MyPlate 135, 135*f*

N

National Field Archery Association 2
National Indoor Championship 2, 188
National Target Championships 9, 168
National Training System (NTS) 5, 30
JOAD and 185-186
neck stretch 139, 139*f*
nerves 167-168
neuromuscular impairment 202
Newton's laws of motion 31
nocking 33-34, 33*f*
nocking point
compound bow 18
recurve bow 20
release loop and 18*f*
NTS. *See* National Training System
nutrition 133-136
for local events 177
for out-of-town events 179
plans 135-136
supplements 135

O

Olympic Round Set Play
drills 131
mental training and 156
Olympic Training Center 3
Olympic Trials 167
1,000-Arrow Challenge 130
orthopedic impairment 202

P

Pan Am Games 167
paper tuning 23-24, 23*f*, 24*f*
para-archers
classification of 206
in competition 205-206
instruction for 202-205
types of disabilities of 201-202

parents
athlete-parent relationship and 188-189
role of 189-192
Parker, Denise 185
pelvis tilt drill 97
periodization
of support team 196
of training 112
personal trainers 140
physical domain 180, 180*f*
physical form 10
pitch, of recurve archery grip 56-57, 57*f*
pivot points, in recurve archery grip 54-56, 54*f*, 55*f*
porpoising 26
positivity 191, 198
posture 36
in compound archery 95-100, 95*f*
drill 66, 125, 125*f*
in recurve archery 58, 67*f*
in recurve archery stance 49
practice goals 8-9
precompetition phase 142, 144*f*-145*f*
preshooting warm-up 136-140
pressure 9-10
focus under 168-169
handling 167-168
heart rate and 156
pressure points, in recurve archery grip 54-56, 54*f*, 55*f*
programs 2-3
protein 134

Q

quad stretch 138, 138*f*

R

reaffirmation, in compound archery 110
recognition 191
recurve archery
aiming in 82-84, 84*f*
anchoring in 70-73, 71*f*
anchor point in 71-72
angular motion in 47, 88
back-to-hand tension ratio in 64
barrel of the gun position in 46, 59*f*, 60*f*
breathing cycle in 82
drawing in 63-66, 64*f*, 66*f*
elbow rotation in 56*f*
expansion in 77-79
follow-through in 86-87, 87*f*, 88*f*
foundation in 63
grip in 54-57, 54*f*, 55*f*
head position in 73, 73*f*, 74*f*
holding in 46, 46*f*, 76-77
hook in 50-52, 50*f*, 51*f*, 52*f*
LAN 2 in 47, 47*f*, 65*f*
linear motion in 47
loading in 67-69, 68*f*, 69*f*
mindset in 58
posture in 58, 67*f*
release in 85-86, 85*f*

set position in 58, 58*f*
setting up for 45-48
setup position in 59-61, 60*f*, 65*f*
shot completion in 81-82
shot cycle 89-92, 90*t*
shoulder alignment in 59*f*
stance in 48-49, 48*f*
string alignment in 83-84, 83*f*
transfer in 75, 75*f*
trapezius muscles in 47
recurve bows 11-12
bare-shaft tuning for 27
center shot setting for 22, 22*f*
characteristics of 4*t*
compound bows compared to 93
length 20
limb alignment 21
line tuning for 27-28
nocking point 20
Olympic competition and 3
setup 20-22
stabilizer alignment 21, 21*f*
stabilizer setup for 22
tuning 27-28
releases 41-42
in compound archery 108, 108*f*
compound bow 100-101, 100*f*
drill 124, 124*f*
linear 87*f*
for local events 176
loops 18*f*
mechanical 203
in recurve archery 85-86, 85*f*
repetitive motion injury 37
Resident Athlete Program 3
respect, for youths 189
rhythm strategies 90-91
risers 13
roll, of recurve archery grip 56-57, 57*f*
rules
for local events 177
for para-archer competition 206

S
sacrifice 10
scapular protraction exercise 149, 149*f*
scapular retraction exercise 150, 150*f*
schedule of activities, for local events 175
scopes 15
spotting 176
self-confidence 9
self-discipline 1
set position 35, 35*f*
in recurve archery 58, 58*f*
setup position 35-36, 36*f*
in compound archery 102-103, 102*f*, 103*f*
in recurve archery 59-61, 60*f*, 65*f*
shooting
analysis 169-170
blank bale 122, 122*f*

distance 129
individualized 168-169
para-archer instruction and 205
stretch-band 114, 120, 120*f*
wind 90-91
shot completion, in recurve archery 81-82
shot cycle 30-43
recurve archery 89-92, 90*t*
rhythm of 89-91
steps of 30*f*, 31
shot sequence 29-30
evaluation of 42-43
Shot Trainer 114
shoulder alignment
in compound archery 98, 98*f*
during loading 70*f*
in recurve archery 59*f*
shoulder extension exercise 151, 151*f*
shoulder strength training 147-154
side bend with straight arms 137, 137*f*
sights
aperture 84*f*
movable 14-15, 16*f*
pin 14-15, 16*f*
Specific Physical Training (SPT) drills 114, 126-128
flexibility 78, 126, 126*f*
holding 77, 126
power 128, 128*f*
structure 77, 127, 127*f*
spinal cord injury 201
spotting scopes 176
SPT drills. *See* Specific Physical Training drills
squeeze drill 41, 46, 77
stability 202-204
stabilizers 16-17
alignment 21, 21*f*
with dampener 16*f*
setup 22
side bar 16*f*, 17
V-bar 16*f*, 17
stance 33
in compound archery 94-95, 94*f*
for para-archer instruction 202-204
in recurve archery 48-49, 48*f*
standing 204
static strap training drill 121, 121*f*
step times, in recurve shot cycle 90*t*
sternocleidomastoid 71, 72*f*
stretch-band shooting 114
drill 120, 120*f*
strings
alignment 83-84, 83*f*
for local events 176
stroke 201
supercompensation 112
support team 6, 166
building 194-195
communication with 195-198
growing of 195-196
influence of 199-200

support team (continued)
    members of 193-194
    periodization of 196
    responsibility of 198-199
    during training versus competition 197

T
tactical domain 181
target archery 13
target line 48
team rounds 174-175
technical domain 180-181
therapeutic use exemption (TUE) 179
3D archery 14
tillers
    adjustment 19, 19f
    tuning 25
time management 5-9
timing 29
Total Archery (Lee & de Bondt) 30
tournament dates
    for local events 173
    for out-of-town events 177
training. See also mental training; weight training
    aim-off 130
    analysis 170
    balance 154
    breaks from 170-172
    cardiorespiratory 140-141
    competition 129, 188-189
    distraction 8, 159
    drills 119
    endurance 142
    environment 9-10
    increased heart rate 130-132
    individualized 114
    learning to 187-188
    before local events 173
    periodized 112
    physical 180f
    program development 111-114
    schedule 115f, 116f, 117f, 118f
    shoulder strength 147-154
    support team during 197
    tactical 181f
    technical 181f
    time management and 7-8
    training to 188
transfer 39
    in compound archery 107
    drill 76
    in recurve archery 75, 75f
trapezius muscles 32, 32f
    in recurve archery 47
    in recurve archery loading 68f
traumatic brain injury 201
travel 180
trials event format practice 131
triceps muscles 32, 32f
TUE. See therapeutic use exemption

tuning
    bare-shaft 26-27
    compound bows 23-27
    high-speed camera 27
    line 25-26, 26f
    paper 23-24, 23f, 24f
    recurve bows 27-28
    tiller 25

U
United States Anti-Doping Agency (USADA) 179
USA Archery 2-3
    age divisions 3t
    Coach Certification 185-186
USADA. See United States Anti-Doping Agency

V
visual adaptations 203
visual impairment 202
volume practice 131

W
waist twist drill 97
warm-up
    activities 119-122
    preshooting 136-140
weather
    accessories 176
    for local events 175
    for out-of-town events 178-179
    recurve shot cycle and 90
    variations 181
weight training 141-146
    competition and 146f
    off-season 143f-144f
    precompetition phase 144f-145f
wheelchairs 204
windage adjustment 15
wind shooting 90-91
winning
    meaning of 165-167
    planning for 172
With Winning in Mind (Bassham) 162
World Archery (FITA)
    arrows 14
    Championships 3
    para-archery competition and 206
wrist position, in hook drill 53f
wrist stretch 140, 140f

Y
yardage adjustments 15
yaw, of recurve archery grip 56-57
youths
    coaches for 186
    communication with 190
    first steps for 183-184
    frustration and 190
    long-term development of 186-189
    respect for 189
    support for 190

About USA Archery

USA Archery (USAA) is the national governing body for the sport of archery in the United States. It is also a member association of World Archery, the international governing body for archery as recognized by the International Olympic Committee. The mission of USA Archery is to provide the necessary resources for fostering athletes' participation, competition, and training in the sport.

USAA facilitates target archery competition in the United States, sanctioning hundreds of local, state, regional, and national events each year. The organization also facilitates the growth of archery through instructor and coach certification and grassroots archery programs, such as Junior Olympic Archery Development, Adult Archery Achievement, and JOAD Xperience. USA Archery oversees the selection and training of archers for international events such as the Archery World Cup; World Archery Championships; World Archery Para Championships; and the Pan Am, Parapan Am, Paralympic, and Olympic Games.

USA Archery is headquartered in Colorado Springs, Colorado.

Teresa Iaconi, the project coordinator for this book, specializes in public relations and social media, and combines her love of archery with her passion for communications in her daily work, most recently serving as the press attache for the U.S. Olympic Team for Archery at the 2012 Olympic Games. A Level 4 NTS certified archery coach, Teresa was also a compound and recurve competitor for nearly ten years before turning to coaching. She is the recipient of USA Archery's 2010 Coach of the Year Award, and coaches Olympic hopefuls from her home in Woodstock, Connecticut.

About the Contributors

Butch Johnson is a five-time U.S. Olympic team member, Olympic team gold and bronze medalist, multitime Pan Am Games team gold medalist, and European Grand Prix champion. Johnson, who has held as many as seven world records at one time, is also a World Cup team silver medalist and a World Archery Indoor Championships team gold and individual silver medalist. An accomplished compound archer before he turned to recurve, Johnson has amassed an incredible 47 national championship titles between the two disciplines across multiple event formats. Johnson, who coaches while helping to manage Hall's Arrow Indoor Archery Range, continues to compete in national and international events.

Mel Nichols is a level 5 NTS coach and has been an archery coach for over 20 years. As a member of USA Archery's international teams staff, Nichols has accompanied multiple medal-winning teams to key international events, including the 2012 Olympic Games, World Cups, Indoor and Outdoor World Archery Championships, Pan Am Games, and London Archery Classic. A staff coach for the Junior Dream Team, USA Archery's elite youth development program, Nichols is also active with Junior Olympic Archery Development programs and youth archery camps in Arizona. Nichols, who was USA Archery's National Coach of the Year in 2010, started his own career as an archer, competing with a compound bow for many years in the 3D and target archery disciplines.

Guy Krueger is the current assistant head coach for USA Archery at the Olympic Training Center in Chula Vista, California, and a level 5 NTS coach. Krueger has worked closely with the Resident Athlete Program at the Olympic Training Center since 2008. An experienced competitor himself, Krueger was the World University Games champion in 2000 in Madrid, Spain, and the 2002 World University bronze medalist. He also won an individual silver medal and team gold medal in the 2003 Pan Am Games and has competed at several world championships and other international events. Krueger also won the 2005 U.S. Open and several junior and collegiate national championships. He has been involved in archery for over 24 years and was a junior and senior national team member from 1996 to 2008.

KiSik Lee was hired as USA Archery's national head coach in 2006 and is credited with helping to transform the organization's athlete and coach development programs. Lee has one of the most accomplished coaching records in archery history: The 2012 U.S. archery team was the seventh team he led to the Olympic Games. Under Lee's guidance, his students have won nine Olympic gold medals. During his years of coaching, Lee developed the world's only biomechanically based step-by-step method for shooting a bow. He has authored two books on the subject, both translated into several languages and referenced as top coaching texts worldwide. In introducing this system in the United States, now called the national training system, Lee revolutionized the way archery is taught to students and changed the way coaches are trained to work with archers. Lee was awarded the U.S. Olympic Committee's Order of Ikkos by the silver medal–winning men's U.S. Olympic archery team in 2012.

Sheri Rhodes is the coach development manager for USA Archery. Rhodes began her career in 1976 as head coach for Arizona State University; during her time there, her students accumulated 45 individual and collegiate championship titles and over 100 All-American titles. Rhodes served as a U.S. Olympic archery team coach in 1988 and 2004; under her direction, athletes took individual gold, team silver, and team bronze. Rhodes was the technical delegate at the 2012 Paralympic Games in London. She resides in Arizona.

Diane Watson has over 30 years of experience as a competitor and coach. Watson has competed in both recurve and compound divisions and at target, field, and 3D events. Watson began shooting archery in the Junior Olympic Archery Development Program in the early 1970s and has several national and international podium finishes to her credit, including World Cup and World Championships team and individual medals. Watson continues to coach and compete today.

Robby K. Beyer, MS, is the former high-performance manager and former national teams manager for USA Archery. After completing his master's degree in sport and recreational management, Beyer worked with USA Archery for three years, during which time the teams he helped to support tripled their medal counts from previous seasons. Beyer is responsible for helping to construct USA Archery's national ranking system, restructuring the organization's team selection procedures, and supporting athletes through many international events in the lead-up to the 2012 Olympic Games. Using his experiences in coaching Division I and III track and field athletes, Beyer has a guiding philosophy focused on improving the complete individual and athlete. Currently Beyer is coaching athletes in central Iowa.

Randi Smith, USA Archery's Paralympic national head coach, has been an archery coach since 1984, working with youth and adult archers as well as training other instructors. Smith has focused on outreach to disabled archers for many years, working with military athletes and events such as the Endeavor Games. She has served as coach and team leader for many international events, including the World Archery Para Championships and Paralympic Games. She most recently coached two archers to medal wins at the 2012 Paralympic Games and was awarded the U.S. Olympic Committee's Order of Ikkos for her athletes' medal-winning performances at the 2008 and 2012 Paralympic Games.